EDUCATION AND DEVELOPMENT IN AFRICA

A Contemporary Survey

Jonathan Nwomonoh

EDUCATION AND DEVELOPMENT IN AFRICA

A Contemporary Survey

Jonathan Nwomonoh

International Scholars Publications
San Francisco - London - Bethesda
1998

Library of Congress Cataloging-in-Publication Data

Nwomonoh, Jonathan, 1937-
Education and development in Africa : a contemporary survey /
Jonathan Nwomonoh.
p. cm.
Includes bibliographical references and index.
ISBN 1-57309- 011-5 (hardcover : alk. paper). -- ISBN 1-57309-010-7
(pbk. : alk. paper)
1. Education--Social aspects--Africa. 2. Economic development-
-Effect of education on--Africa. 3. Education and state--Africa.
I. Title.
LC191.8.A4N86 1998
306.43'2'096--dc21 98-13510
CIP

Editorial Inquiries:
International Scholars Publications
7831 Woodmont Avenue, #345
Bethesda, MD 20814

To order: (800) 55-PUBLISH

ACKNOWLEDGMENTS

A work of this scope obviously involves the help of literally many publishers and authors whose generosity and expertise I acknowledge with thanks.The author gratefully acknowledges permission to reprint from the following sources:

Apollo Rwomire, *"Education and Development: African Perspectives,"* first published in *Prospects*, Vol. XX11, No. 2, 1992: 227-239 Reproduced by permission of UNESCO. Reference UPO/D/A/ 95-013 CLT

Mark Bray, Peter Clarke and David Stephens. 1986 *Education and Society in Africa*, London:Edward Arnold Publishers Ltd. Reproduced by permission of Hodder and Stoughton Limited: 23-35,79-100,101-113.

Dorothy L. Njeuma, "An Overview of Women's Education in Africa," in Jill Conway and Susan Bourke, *The Politics of Women's Education*, Ann Arbor: The University of Michigan Press, 1995. Reproduced by permission of University of Michigan Press.

J.R. Minnis, "Adult Education and the African State in the Post Cold War Era," *Convergence*, Volume XXVI, No 2, 1993: 11-18. Included with permission of Convergence and the International Council for Adult Education.

Eva M. Rathgeber, "Integrating Gender into Environmental Education in Africa,"*Canadian Journal of Development Studies*, Special Issue, 1995: 89-103. Included with permission of Canadian Journal of Development Studies.

David Baine and Tuntufye Mwamwenda, "Education in Southern Africa: Current Conditions and Future Directions", *International Review of Education*, Vol.40, No 2, 1994: 113-134. Reprinted by permission of Kluwer Academic Publishers.

My greatest debt, of course, is to the contributors, leading scholars on African affairs from all the regions of Sub-Saharan Africa. Susan Peabody took over from the former typist and guided this volume to its completion, and I am heavily in debt. Pamela Porter gave me many helpful comments along with her moral support. I am very grateful to her also for painstakingly editing most of the chapters. I am equally grateful to Nofoao Leau who provided superb secretarial support. I am indepted to Robert West for his warm encouragement, patience, moral and financial support. My two daughters, Dorita and Jane also deserve the highest praise along with special thanks and appreciation to my wife, Ray. They were very helpful in typing the preliminaries. Finally, others who contributed to individual chapters are acknowledged separately by chapter authors.

CONTENTS

TABLES

PREFACE

Traditional African societies have a remarkable history of educational tradition. All indigenous ethnic groups used education to transmit cultural identity, develop skills for men and women, and prepare youth to respond to the pressing problems found in local communities. Before the introduction of Western style of schooling the only formal schooling received by millions of people in Africa was the Islamic system, and it has much older roots in the continent than does the Western system. Arab culture and language were adopted in much of North Africa. The Islamic faith won converts in West Africa, East African states such as Uganda and Kenya and in much of the Horn of Africa.

The missionaries who had started to penetrate Africa in the nineteenth century introduced the Western style of education. Education was seen by the missionaries as an essential part of evalgelism and they established schools soon after they arrived. The colonial administrators saw the need for trained help and skilled labor. Throughout the colonial era, curricular were based for the most part on overseas models and reflected little in the way of the African continent.

The decade of the 1960's brought independence to many African nations, and soon it became evident that the educational systems inherited by the African nations were quite inadequate. The need to move away from the educational system inherited from the former colonial governments also became clear. The decades of the 1960's and 1970's chronicled the fast pace of educational expansion on the continent.

The 1980's saw African governments begin to realize there were limits to the amount of resources available to expand education. They could not be expected to continue to increase substantially public allocation to education. As a result of the financial crisis of this decade, only a lower proportion of the young could be admitted to educational institutions, leading, therefore, to stagnation of enrollment and a decline in overall quality of education. The educational crisis has continued in the 1990's. Increased investment without careful plannig was risky; to support the planning, the first chapter on Education and Development forms the foundation for this volume. The analysis and the various recommendations in this book should contribute tremendously to the renewal of progress in Africa's education. Realising that there is much to learn from developments in other parts of Africa, comparisons of educational issues and concerns across the continent will enable students and policymakers to understand that problems are shared by other African nations.

The impetus for this book came as a result of many years of teaching a course in Education and Development in Africa, without the advantage of a single text book that covers most of the topics on the subject. I hope that this single comprehensive overview will be augmented with only a few case studies. I do, however, urge readers, to use other literature in the field. It is my hope that scholars, researchers, policy makers and students of African education will find this volume very useful in the endeavor to find ways to revitalize Africa's education.

Jonathan Nkem Nwomonoh
California State University, Los Angeles
March 1998

INTRODUCTION: AN OVERVIEW OF EDUCATION IN AFRICA

Jonathan Nwomonoh

Since independance the progress achieved in African education has been remarkable, the most spectacular educational feature being the rapid rate of expansion. Enrollments at the primary, secondary, vocational and higher level institutions have been impressive. Education was made available to millions who were denied access to educational opportunities previously.

African governments have invested heavily in education, some as much as 20% of their national budget to education, a third of the $1.2 billion of Namibia's national budget goes to education, one of the highest in Africa[1] . Country after country built more secondary schools and opened, at least, one national university. The construction of schools and training of teachers to house students were all outstanding achievements.

Many nations have introduced programs such as universal and compulsory primary education. Some have also introduced a quota system into admission policy as a means of correcting educational imbalance.

In some countries, the development of higher education has been particularly rapid since the last 30years. For example, at independence Nigeria had only one university, the University of Ibadan. Within two years of independence, four more universities had been established-Universities of Ife, Lagos, Nsukka, and Zaira. By 1979, the number of universities had risen to 13 and by the end of 1983, the country had about 24 federal universities, excluding the state-owned universities. By 1997 the country has 40 state and federal universities.

Apart from the former disciplines of arts, natural and social sciences, agriculture and forestry, medicine and engineering, new disciplines like administration, education, law, environmental design and pharmacy were introduced. This massive expansion has been made possible through the infusion of large sums of money by new governments who saw the expansion of educational opportunity as a political necessity. The record of this period is a tribute to the determination of African leaders and the sacrifices of African parents in their quest to provide a better standard of living for their children's generation.[2]

However, the exponential expansion of the education industry, Rwomire argues in chapter 1, has been accompanied by manifold challenges and dilemmas. During the last two decades, the education enterprise has generated a number of severe predicaments, so that the initial euphoric confidence in education has to a considerable extent been replaced by a mood of dissilusionment.

Bigala and Moorad added to this dissilusionment by commenting that inspite of the great enthusiasm and faith placed in education and the heavy public expenditure devoted to formal schooling, most African countries have not made any spectacular advances either in educational development itself or in the expected economic growth and public welfare or in achieving such desirable social and political unity, the unification of Africa and the promotion of human rights and respect for law and order. The World Bank went further in categorizing the main educational issues in Africa as stagnation of enrollments and the erosion of educational quality.[3]

In many countries, the State educational systems are in a state of disarray and heading for total disintegration. Mounting economic and social problems have caused the reversals in educational development on the continent. It is for these reasons that the chapters in this book have been contributed by scholars renowned in the field of education, each primarily concerned with, at least, a factor that contributes to educational problems in the continent and also with suggestions on how to renew progress in the continent's education. In addition chapters range widely across Sub-Saharan Africa.

Similarily an attempt has been made to see the African concept of education as a whole by examining its indigenous, Islamic and Western forms and how each form complements the other. The result is a pioneer work, exploring more comprehensively than any other single study the major issues with which this book is concerned and which in the opinion of its authors merit examination.

The book is divided into four parts: (1) Local, National and Global Education, (2) Adult/Women and Environmental Education, (3) Current Trends in Educational Reforms, (4) Education and the State.

In Chapter 1, Rwomire attempts to investigate the role of formal education in the development process, and examines the functions, dynamics and challenges of the education enterprise in Sub-Saharan Africa. Chapter 2 permits Bray, Clarke and Stephens to examine indigenous education systems in their own right and to discuss the influence of the

Western, Islamic and indigenous education systems on each other. In Chapter 3, Bray, Clarke and Stephens survey the history of Islamic education in Sub-Saharan Africa, and analyze the structure and goals of Islamic education. They discuss Islamic education theory and school organization, the interaction between the Islamic and Western systems of education, and the role of Islamic education, as Muslims themselves understand it, in the process of development and nation building. Ekechi in Chapter 4 focuses on the African initiative in education, a theme that is often neglected in the study of education in Africa. More specifically, his article concerns the pioneering work of Rev M.D. Opara of Nigeria, who in 1942 founded the Zion Mission. By 1965, the mission had over thirty elementary and two postprimary institutions. In Chapter 5, Njeuma discusses the many problems that still hinder the education of women and girls in Africa and certain lines of action that need to be followed. Minnis in Chapter 6 explores the tentative and emerging relationship between adult education and the African state in light of development of powerful pro-democracy movements from 1989 to the present.

James in Chapter 7 discusses the importance of environmental education in the sustainable development of Africa. He argues that the primary, secondary , and university curricular must reflect serious inclusion of environmental training. He further argues that conservation and preservation innovations must be integral parts of development and appropriate education has a role to play in sustainable development. In Chapter 8, Rathberger argues that the integration of a gender dimension into environmental education curricula will promote both environmental conscientization and environmental responsibility among African school children.

In Chapter 9, Fobih and Koomson argue that the history of education reform in Ghana is impregnated with vital lessons for developing countries which continually experience political instability, weak economic base, low living standards and low rate of development. In as much as education remains the main conduit for national development, it stands to reason that devising an appropriate educational package that is both cost-effective and qualitatively affordable, as well as, relevant to the needs and aspirations of the people must be the over-arching goal of developing countries. Though the education reform of Ghana is in the infantile stage, its structure, which is consistent with the systems of most of the world powers, has significantly decentralized the delivery of education services and reduced the net expenditure of the Government on education. In what I would consider to be one of the most important documents on the renewed programs of education in Southern Africa, Baine and Mwamwenda in Chaper 10 provide a concise summary of selected topics of contemporary, primary and secondary education of black students in Southern Africa. Both argue that in spite of the enormous achievements in the field of education in Africa, despite vast limitations of resources: economic, personnel, technological and material, and given the magnitude and complexity of educational development, a number of problems continue to exist. These problems are reviewed as are various recommendations for change.

In Chapter 11, Bigala and Moorad attempt to show that the goal of universal education is unlikely to be achieved by educational policy alone. Education liberation, like all other movements in the extension of freedom, can only follow a broader struggle for economic, social and political liberation. Most achievenments of the ambitious educational expansion in most Sub-Saharan African countries were quantitative. While they argue that quantity and quality are difficult to reconcile, they accept that universal educational balance cannot be achieved without some quantitative expansion. But in the short run it may still not be achieved because of the quantitative expansion, which involves some deterioration of quality. The two authors show that Botswana's case study presents a remarkable growth from going beyond universalizing primary education to include three more years of junior secondary schooling for all.

In the light of current comprehensive policy inititiatives which are aimed at creating a non-discriminatory unitary system of education and training acceptable to all South Africans, Lemmer in Chapter 12 gives an overview of current educational developments in South Africa in the new democratic era, starting from 1994. This is done against the background of a brief history of education and educational legacies of the apartheid era. Lemmer argues that the demise of apartheid and the new democratic era in South Africa is considered a modern day miracle. The country now has a unique opportunity to redress the inequality of the past and to build a better and fairer society which will benefit all. In this endeavor, particularly high expectations are cherished of education. However, a new political dispensation does not automatically ensure improved education. In terms of policy intitiatives, considerable progress towards a new system has been made. The implemenattion of this policy, the evaluation of innovative strategies and its continuous improvement Lemmer maintains, are the challenge of the immediate future.

Bray, Clarke, and Stephens in Chapter 13 argue that the fostering of a national identity has become one of the most important tasks of African governments and education is seen as a major instrument for doing this. Both the formal school system and adult education campaigns are often explicitly geared to this end, while informal education plays, at least, as significant a part. The authors discuss the ways education can promote unity.

By assuming that civil society as a sphere of activity is separate from both the state and the economy, Minnis in Chapter 14, examines how a vibrant system of education can emerge in Malawi if the relationship between state and civil society is fundamentally altered. Against the background of the change from a single to a multi-party system, Minnis argues that education needs to be re-cast in the form of a contested terrain stressing diversity and pluralism in terms of provision and power sharing between state and non-state interests. The author outlines six areas of contestation which can contribute to revitalizing education in an atmosphere of democratic change.

Msiska in Chapter 15 argues that the basic human needs approach to understanding the role of education in rural development suggests that at best the school could be an accelerator and not the cause of development. As such, the link between formal schooling and rural devlopment is neither myth nor practical reality. It is not just myth because formal schooling makes one adept, hence, more articulate in a dynamic context, given that everything else is provided. The second point is that in so far as schooling contributes to development and improvement of communication skills, including an awareness of the modern sector economy, it can make an important contribution to modernization of agriculture. Rural people need not understand development in order to develop their areas. All they need, using Malawi as a case study, Msiska argues, is assistance to improve their living standards, and later appreciate living a better life.

Chapter 16 ends the textbook on Education and Development in Africa on a practical note. Lemmer explores issues in Language in education policy and practice in the education systems of Namibia and Zimbabwe against the background of a set of assumptions about language influencing language planners, in general and in Africa, in particular. Lemmer argues that the use of English as the language of world-wide communication and agent of nation-building in linguistically diverse communities appears to have been solidly entrenched. In this regard, Zimbabwe building on its colonial past, has been established as an English second language country. Namibia, however, is endeavoring to move towards English second language status through the implementation of a radically interventionist language policy. In order to provide effective education in lingusitically diverse countries of Africa, Lemmer maintains, it is essential that the goals of language in education policies are carefully established and the means of implementation meticulously selected.

I am quite sure that these articles are insightful enough to stimulate meaningful discourse. It is critical that we start this discourse to help us chart a course for the future. Our major task here is toward finding ways to renew progress in education in Africa.

The book is mainly intended as a basic text for students in universities and teachers' colleges. I hope that the book will be found of value to all who are concerned with studying and promoting development in Africa and all those who are interested in African affairs. And may the book help stimulate more intensive research and discussion of fundamental issues involved in Education and Development in Africa.

Notes

1. Donald McNeil "Free Namibia Stumps the Naysayers". *The New York Times*, Sunday, November 16, 1997, p.4.
2. The World Bank, *Education in Sub-Saharan Africa: Policies for Adjustment, Revitilization, and Expansion*, Washington, D.C. The World Bank, 1993, p.11.
3. The World Bank, *Education in Sub-Saharan Africa: Policies for Adjustment, Revitilization, and Expansion*, Washington D.C. The World Bank, 1993 p.2.

PART I
LOCAL, NATIONAL, AND GLOBAL PERSPECTIVES

— 1 —
EDUCATION AND DEVELOPMENT: AFRICAN PERSPECTIVES

Apollo Rwomire

If you give a man a fish, he will eat, once. If you teach a man to fish, he will eat for the rest of his life. If you are thinking a year ahead, sow seed. If you are thinking ten years ahead, plant a tree. If you are thinking a hundred years ahead, educate the people. By planting a tree, you will harvest tenfold. By educating the people, you will harvest one hundredfold. (Kuan-tsu)

The above epigram underlines, at least potentially, the role of education in personal and national development. Indeed, the widespread preoccupation with education is not difficult to demonstrate, given the rapidly growing commitment to individual and mass education throughout the world. But why has education become such big business?

During the past three decades, a number of renowned scholars have spearheaded the campaign for investment in human capital. The Nobel Laureate Theodore Schultz has perhaps done more than anybody else to fuel interest in the contribution of education to development. In his voluminous printed works, Schultz has argued that population quality and knowledge constitute the principal determinants of the future welfare of mankind (Schultz, 1981). Harbison, another influential advocate of investment in human capital, has posited that the wealth of nations depends on the development of human resources—not so much on physical capital or material resources. In this connection, he has been widely quoted as saying that: `A country which is unable to develop the skills and knowledge of its people and to utilize them effectively in the national economy will be unable to develop anything else' (Harbison, 1973, p. 3). For his part, Drucker (1961) has contended that an abundance of highly educated people is a precondition of national survival, an indispensable instrument of economic and social development, and a source of military strength. According to Psacharopoulos (1988, p. 5), education is widely regarded as the route to economic prosperity, the key to scientific and technological advancement, the means to combat unemployment, the foundation of social equality, and the spearhead of political socialization and cultural vitality.

In light of these claims on behalf of education, this study investigates the relationship between education and development. We focus on formal education which is largely obtained through study or instruction in schools and colleges.

Education and Development: a Conceptual Framework

Many writers dealing with the topics of education and development tend to omit definitions of these concepts, seemingly taking it for granted that everyone understands their meaning. However, education and development come in various forms. There are different types of education taking place in different institutions. Thus the education provided in a university may be different from that given at a polytechnic or college of technology. Development is a multi-faceted concept which still generates much debate about its true meaning, let alone its significance. In fact, there are different types and degrees of development.

By and large, education refers to any process by which individuals gain knowledge or develop attitudes or skills. The purpose of education is to convey to individuals the collective knowledge and experience of the past and present so as to enable them to become more productive and effective members of society. Accordingly, Julius Nyerere (1974, p. 47) observes that the purpose of education is to transmit knowledge and wisdom from one generation to the next. Nyerere points out that education is supposed to liberate man, both physically and mentally. He distinguishes between a system of education which turns men and women into tools and one which makes them liberated and skilled users of tools.

Likewise, Sicinski (1985) has identified three main objectives of education: education of the worker, education of the citizen, and education of the human being.

The education of the worker puts emphasis on the inculcation of vocation-relevant skills, and treats the individual principally as an object of production. In the education of the citizen, the nature of a person's training tends to be determined by the needs of the community or society, but the individual's interests only receive limited attention. Finally, in the education of the human being, the individual is viewed as a unique and multi-functional member of the society. In this type of education, the individual is exposed to a diversity of cultural values as well as to problem-solving and decision making techniques.

Development is `one of the most depreciated terms in social science literature, having been used vastly more than it has been understood' (Uphoff and Ilchman, 1972, p. ix). We are essentially dealing with a large, highly elastic and value-loaded concept with historical, philosophical, ideological and economic dimensions.

It is extremely difficult to provide a precise and self-contained definition of development. This is largely because there are various conceptions of, means towards, and goals of development. Hence the perpetual controversy over the so-called universal determinants and correlates of development.

The term development is influenced by ideology in that, for instance, a Marxist definition will differ from a capitalist one. Since the 1950s, the United Nations and other international bodies such as the World Bank, which are largely dominated by capitalist countries, have tended to define development with reference to certain economic indicators. Needless to say, GNP per capita, which is basically an economic index, has been the major criterion used for dividing the world into developed and underdeveloped countries. Thus, countries which have high GNP per capita are seen as more developed, while those with low per capita incomes as less developed. Despite the emergence of the so-called newly industrializing countries, virtually all nations in Africa, Latin America and most of Asia are still classified as less developed countries (LDCs).

According to some development economists, LDCs were poor because they lacked substantial savings and investment, the necessary ingredients for economic `take-off', in Rostowian terms. What was required was an infusion of capital to lift these ailing economies, and heavy industrialization was the means. Although many LDCs achieved the stipulated target of a 5 per cent GNP growth rate, there was still no take-off. In other words, despite the fact that many LDCs have attained impressive levels of economic growth during the last three decades, evidence shows that the majority population have not benefited from the increase in GNP. The reality of the situations is that only a minority élite are enjoying the benefits, while nothing or very little is reaching the poor (Magagula, 1987, pp. 2-5).

With respect to Africa, reports indicate that creditable rates of economic growth in many countries have not been accompanied by any significant reduction in the level of poverty, inequality and unemployment. Messages concerning economic and political decay or disaster continue to pour in. For example, it has been ominously predicted that `The continent is on the brink of an economic crisis so vast that many countries...could eventually disappear' (*Newsweek*, 9 June 1986). The economic crisis is simply one of the problems confronting Africa that have prompted some scholars to write about what they call a process of decay in Africa (Mazrui, 1980).

Be that as it may, controversy typifies discussions about the presumed correlation between economic growth and development. The illogicalities and limitations of GNP as an indicator of national well-being have been so well documented that they hardly require reiteration. Although GNP per capita can be easily computed and conveniently used to provide an overall picture of economic measures such as GNP per capita, several attempts have been made to construct more comprehensive and composite measures of human welfare, taking into account a number of quantitative and qualitative variables (Ram, 1982; United Nations Research Institute, 1972). In this connection, the Physical Quality of Life Index (PQLI) constitutes one of the most ambitious endeavors (Morris, 1979). Another possible alternative measure to GNP per capita is a New Index of Development Status proposed by Tata and Schultz (1988). This New Index represents a robust and versatile measure, based on what these authors call variables of systems outputs: for example, physical = total value of primary industry output per capita, persons per square kilometer of arable land; economic= GNP per capita, and manufacturing value-added per capita; social = infant deaths per 1,000 live births, percentage of age-group in higher education, and percentage of rural population; political = government expenditures per capita, political rights index, and number of radios per 1,000 inhabitants (Tata and Schultz, 1988, p. 580).

Given the above, we can say that development means the improvement of the economic and social conditions of the masses. It entails a substantial reduction of poverty, ignorance, disease, hunger, unemployment, oppression, injustice, corruption and the like.

Educations's Role in Development: Ideals Versus Realities

The era of Great Expectations and Optimism

More than forty years have elapsed sine the United Nations declared education to be a basic human right. Since then, especially following the attainment of political independence by most former colonies, educational ambitions have assumed infectious and explosive dimensions (Coombs, 1985, p. 211; Watson, 1988, p. 137). There was a widespread belief that educational development would bring about, *inter alia*, accelerated economic growth, more wealth and income distribution, greater equality of opportunity, availability of skilled/productive human power, a decline in population growth, replacement of expatriate staff by indigenous personnel, national unity and political stability. In other words, education was seen as a short-cut to development, a panacea for virtually all the socio-economic ills confronting the newly independent nations. Thus, during the period 1950-80 there were more students enrolled in formal education than there were at any time in all previous history combined (Watson, 1988, pp. 137-9).

Quantitative Expansion Versus Qualitative Outcomes

Owing to the burgeoning faith in education as a panacea for all sorts of social and economic problems, virtually every country has invested heavily in the educational enterprise. In most countries, apart from defence, education is the largest single item in the national budget, sometimes the biggest single sector of the economy.

To a great extent, the above-mentioned aspirations of the post-independence leaders were largely responsible for the phenomenal growth of education systems as indicated below. Moreover, educational expansion can be attributed to the scrapping of racial discrimination and the incorporation of groups that previously lacked access to formal education, as well as the increased public spending and community development efforts (Court and Kinyanjui, 1986, p. 362).

According to UNESCO (1985, p. 14), school enrolment on a world scale increased from 436.1 million in 1960 to 845.3 million in 1980. With reference to LDCs, there are indications that investment in education has simply been unprecedented. In developing countries between 1960 and 1985—enrollments at the primary, secondary and tertiary levels rose from 163 million to 455 million (Todaro, 1985, p. 328). Between 1960 and 1980 these countries recorded increases of 142, 358 and 528 per cent in primary, secondary and higher education respectively. In the same order, Africa itself recorded increases of 218, 636 and 709 per cent in the three levels of education (Watson, 1988, p. 141).

If these statistics are anything to go by, we are truly witnessing an `educational explosion', which basically refers to the unprecedented demand for and supply of education. This is the phenomenon that has been described as a `revolution of rising expectations' and an `educational revolution'.

Notwithstanding the foregoing, LDCs had no time to examine critically the type of education most appropriate to their development needs; they simply carried on using an expanded version of the system left by the former colonial rulers. Thus, most LDCs started with an imported colonial education system which was so inappropriate that in the 1980s they resembled an international trade fair displaying assorted models and ideologies from Europe and North America. To be sure, Africa has become what one scholar has called a graveyard of educational experiments (Ki-Zerbo, 1974, p. 53). In an effort to compensate for decades of educational malnutrition almost overnight, African countries `have been devouring Western education with a speed and gusto that makes no allowance for its healthful digestion in relation to society's social and economic well-being' (Ayandele, 1982, p. 165).

Despite the massive quantitative expansion in institutions of formal education worldwide, controversy and cautious optimism seem to characterize informed discussions about the educational enterprise—in all its intentional, process-related and consequential attributes.

For instance, it would seem that in many LDCs there has been a mismatch between educational outputs and educational outcomes. In the opinion of one observer, head count alone is not enough. What is in the heads—the educational outcomes—must be evaluated, especially with respect to individual competence and effectiveness in the work-place and also in terms of equality of opportunity (Husen, 1979, p. xiii).

The exponential expansion of the education industry has been accompanied by manifold challenges and dilemmas, especially in developing countries. During the last two decades, the education enterprise has generated a number of severe predicaments, so that the initial euphoric confidence in education has to a considerable extent been replaced by a mood of disillusionment.

The education system has been denounced for inculcating egocentric and materialistic values at the cost of collective effort and responsibility; for adopting irrelevant and rigid curricula; for embracing antiquated teaching and learning techniques; for spreading sexual and older forms of immorality; for dampening initiative and curiosity; for producing docile and dependent-minded graduates; and for widening the gap between the rich and poor. As if these charges were not enough, the following problems and issues are commonly associated with educational institutions, especially in less developed countries: wastage in the form of high drop-out and repetition rates; high rates of unemployment and the related issue of `over-education', i.e. the surplus production of graduates; acute shortage of teaching staff; inadequate funding; allocation of funds to trivial and grandiose projects; explosive pupil/student enrolment leading to overcrowded and overstretched physical and social facilities; lack of accurate statistics and information needed for planning and evaluation; and over-concentration of educational facilities in urban centres at the expense of rural areas where the majority of children live. The above catalogue of problems is not exhaustive, but it is sufficiently indicative of the nature and magnitude of the difficulties confronting the educational system.

Movement Towards Universal Primary Education

The quest for universal primary education (UPE) derives from the belief that education will emancipate LDCs from such problems as ignorance, disease and hunger (Lee, 1988, p. 1481). Advocates of UPE contend that mass education will result in an increased supply of educated human power, accelerated economic growth, more social justice, reduced regional disparities, and improved social welfare. At any rate, all children will have an equal start in life regardless of sex, socio-economic background, or geographical location (Coombs, 1985, p. 70). Accordingly, African, Asian and Latin American governments expressed their intentions in the early 1960s to achieve UPE within two decades.

Despite impressive accomplishments in UPE, only a handful of these countries managed to beat the deadline, that is, 1980. In sub-Saharan Africa, efforts to promote UPE have only been partially successful. In fact, if UPE were defined as the education of all children who start primary education at the specified minimum age and complete the full cycle, then only the Congo, Madagascar and Togo might be said to have achieved UPE by the year 1980 (Lee,1988, p. 1482). Thus, for several reasons, the gap between ambition and achievement remains quite wide. Excessive population growth, fiscal austerity, disagreement among policymakers over the methods and means of promoting mass education, persistent socio-economic inequalities and cultural factors have impeded the full realization of UPE in developing countries.

By the 1970s a number of issues had arisen which forced theorists to question the direction of educational development. There was concern about irregular school attendance, wastage and increasing drop-out rates as well as regional and sexual inequalities, where there was access to better schools for urban children rather than rural children and more for boys than girls. There existed four fundamental dilemmas facing governments committed to educational development (Watson, 1988, p. 137).

The first dilemma was the attempt to reconcile the apparently conflicting role of education in society—whether it should be the one emanating from the West, emphasizing individual fulfillment, or the Soviet bloc type of education, concerned with the wider social and political needs of the society. Secondly, there was the problem of, on the one hand, preserving the cultural and religious traditions of the past while, on the other hand, preparing children for a new and changing society. Thirdly, while the government tried to use education to prepare for national concerns, it also wished to serve local community needs and interests. The fourth dilemma lay in the extent to which government should expand secondary and higher education at the expense of basic, rural primary education.

In trying to deal with these dilemmas, theorists, aid agencies and governments turned to developing and improving education in the rural areas. Education was seen as the key to rural transformation, which itself was the key to the whole process of development. Hence, the emphasis on non-formal education.

The Role of the University in Development

At the top of the educational pyramidal structure is university education. The functions of a university are as multifaceted as those of universal primary education (Jenkins, 1988; Porter, 1972; Watson, 1988; Yesufu,1973). A useful summary of the functions of universities, especially in developing countries, would include the following components:

- Pursuit, promotion and dissemination of useful knowledge, including provision of intellectual leadership.

- Conducting research, both pure and applied; but special attention must be given to research designed to meet certain vocational and utilitarian needs: the eradication of poverty, rural development, food production, health care, etc.

- Development and adaptation of technologies, especially appropriate technologies, e.g. developing new energy sources.

- Promotion of regional and international understanding and co-operation in order to eliminate ignorance, ethnocentrism, xenophobia, linguistic and cultural barriers.

- Production of high-level human power, particularly that which is critically required for development.

- Stimulation of economic and industrial growth. Participation in non-formal education and public service, including adult education, literacy campaigns, community health, extension services, etc.

- Development and preservation of the cultural heritage and tradition.

Many nations aspired to have at least one national university after independence. In Africa, by 1960 there were 185,000 students enrolled at the tertiary level. This grew to 1,366,000 by 1980, an increase of 709 per cent (Watson, 1988, p. 144). These are no doubt remarkable statistics. Interest in the role of the university has increased because of the great concern that they are supposed to resolve such socio-economic problems as poverty, low production, unemployment, hunger, disease and so forth (Mosha, 1986, p. 93).

Universities have provided manpower for strategic positions in government and industry. Also, they have attempted to bring together men and women with differing social, economic, tribal and religious backgrounds under one roof and provided some education for them. They have attempted to create research and consultancy skills of international standard among local staff. Furthermore, they have devised examinations of a local nature and have started issuing degrees and diplomas in their own names (Mosha, 1986, p. 105). Besides, in an attempt to reverse the academic bias of the system, the Zimbabwean government, for example, has embarked upon a new programme of vocational and technical training for both the formal and informal educational sectors. Students in both the technical and academic stream will have to take at least one practical subject (McIvor, 1987, p. 24).

Notwithstanding these achievements there are several key problems that face most African universities today.

By and large, cost is the main problem, for the expense involved in producing a university graduate may range from 80 to 400 times as much as producing a primary-school leaver (Watson, 1988, p. 145). Thus, if a country lends more weight to university education, this may lead to the devaluation of UPE or reduce funds for teacher training and improvement. Indeed, as one scholar has observed, the African university is a very expensive enterprise, with its demand for European-type physical facilities, subsidized European-type living quarters, and a salary structure that bears no relationship whatsoever to social justice in the country (Ayandele, 1982, p. 167).

Owing to shortage of financial resources, African universities lack the required numbers of quality lecturers and researchers. Those recruited make up a mixed bag whom it may be difficult to mesh together in meaningful work. The ones who are qualified seek posts in other universities or join international organizations, looking for greener pastures. Left behind them are the newly graduated who lack experience or old professors whose effectiveness has declined. The few good scholars are weighed down by heavy teaching loads and rely on `yellow notes' as they do not have time to upgrade their materials (Mosha, 1986, p. 107). This problem is then made worse by the shortage of foreign exchange, making it difficult to buy up-to-date texts, journals, materials and equipment.

Secondly, there are fears that Western education serves as a major instrument of cultural domination and intellectual servitude. For instance, Carnoy (1974) contends that there is a strong link between Western formal education and imperialist domination, designed to maintain inequality between and within countries. According to Mazrui (1980), the university is like a cultural multinational corporation, essentially because of the intellectual penetration and dependency with which it is usually associated. For his part, Nyerere (1974, p. 46) suspects that a major purpose of education in Africa is to transform Africans into black Europeans or black Americans. This view is corroborated by Ayandele (1982, p. 172), who points out that African universities remain centers for the diffusion of Western culture: `Culturally, they are amorphous, a class of Africans with English, French or American veneer.'

Given the foregoing, the third problem revolves around the controversial issue of educational curricula. Most African universities use a structure and curricula based on European or North American models. They make up Euro-American enclaves within their countries yet they lack such necessary accompaniments as adequate buildings, facilities and maintenance and funds (Goldschmidt, 1987, p. 21). Furthermore, unlike their counterparts they do not enjoy a natural reciprocal relationship with their social, cultural and economic environment. This makes for additional societal pressure on them to make a contribution to the problems in the way of development. Few universities have tried to change their curricula radically in an attempt to develop programmes more relevant to local conditions. This is partly due to the fact that it is very expensive to restructure a syllabus from the past, since this needs the production of new books, classroom facilities, teacher training colleges, etc. This is the kind of expense that few countries can afford. In addition to that, students and parents still believe in the present curricula, which emphasize academic subjects, as the key to prosperity and wealth. Pupils are reluctant to pursue subjects like metalwork and rural science as they are seen as reserved for the less intelligent and uneducated. Also, because postgraduate study is still largely done overseas, dependence persists, coupled with the internationalization of norms and attitudes at odds with what most African nations aspire to develop. Moreover, in Africa, most of the books and other materials used originate in Western Europe or North America.

The fourth problem concerns the universities' seeming lack of direction, in that priorities have not been clearly stated, or if they are, the necessary resources to implement them are directed elsewhere. Worse still is the tendency to talk about problems without doing anything about them. African academics and politicians `claim that agriculture is the backbone of our economy without finding out whether effort has been or is being directed towards realization of this goal' (Mosha, 1986, p. 107). Although African leaders often blame the colonialists for having drawn a sharp distinction between formal and non-formal education, between education and training, and between urban and rural development, they have not done enough to rectify this legacy of the colonial education system. Furthermore, in African and other LDCs, `talent for original and creative research is scarce and does not increase proportionately with the supply of academic institutions and faculty appointments' (Streeten, 1988, p. 639).

Education, Employment, Income and Inequalities

The economics of education only emerged as a separate field of study in the late 1950s. This was as a result of the realization that not all increases in national output could be accounted for by increasing inputs like physical capital, land and labour. In other words, education is a form of investment.

Education has two main effects, particularly on economic development. The first is that of resource utilization leading to higher income. There is widespread evidence that one's income increases with each extra year of schooling (Psacharopoulos, 1988, p. 100). The argument is that education makes the individual more productive in the market-place.

The rates of return on education tend to be higher in primary education, followed by secondary and then university levels. The reason for this is that the unit costs in primary education are small compared with the extra lifetime income of productivity derived from literacy. For university education the opposite is true. Owing to public subsidization of education in most countries, private returns are higher than social returns. The social return for Africa as a whole towards the late 1970s in the primary, secondary and higher levels was 26, 17 and 13 per cent respectively. The same figures for private return were 45, 26 and 32 per cent (Psacharopoulos, 1988, p. 101).

The field of study and the sex of the individual may also influence the rate of return. Technical education and agronomy tend to be associated with lower returns than the more general academic subjects like law, social sciences and so on. Even though the absolute earnings of men are higher than women's, the opportunity cost of study for women is often lower (Psacharopoulos, 1988, pp. 101-2). In light of the above, if expenditure on education produces a higher rate of social return, then there is a positive link between the expansion of education and economic growth. Furthermore, education has been seen as having a positive impact on productivity and growth. Easterlin's study (cited by Psacharopoulos) of twenty-five of the world's largest countries led him to conclude that the spread of technology was dependent on the learning potential and motivation linked to the development of formal schooling (Psacharopoulos, 1988, p. 103).

Upon closer observation, however, backed by more recent data, it would seem that the human capital theory suffers some weakness. The labour force in an increasing number of developing countries is characterized by unemployment among the educated. In Sudan, Peru and Pakistan, for example, unemployment increases until reaching its highest point at the secondary completed level. Similar patterns have been reported in Argentina, India, Malaysia, etc. (Simmons,1980, p. 32). Unemployment among those who have graduated from secondary school is higher than that among illiterates. Kenya has an opposite experience in that unemployment is highest among people who have graduated from higher-level institutions.

The high unemployment in this latter group may be due to rising expectations in job-seeking as well as financial security provided by middle—to high-income parents. In traditional societies like those found in Africa and other developing areas, private networks allocate jobs, and therefore a college graduate may simply bide his time until his entry into a `suitable' position is secured by friends or relatives. Underdevelopment is also exacerbated where secondary-school leavers take jobs once only done by primary-school graduates. Moreover, there are students seeking entry into fields that are experiencing great unemployment. Thus people still want to pursue engineering or business studies, even though there may be high unemployment among them. The explanation for this is that even though getting a job as a teacher may be easier, the lifetime earnings of an engineer are higher, and so people opt for the gamble of waiting longer for a better job.

This evidence suggests that education may not make a major contribution to the creation of employment, except where nationals replaced expatriates and jobs were created in the education sector. It is large wage differentials between occupations, according to incrementalists, that cause high unemployment among the educated. This is made even more acute in developing countries, where a doctor may earn 100 times as much as a mechanic. In Uganda a secondary-school graduate's average income may be twenty times the per capita income (Simmons, 1980, p. 35). In developed countries the ratios of average annual earnings for those with higher education to those with primary range from 2.13 to 2.63, whereas in developing countries they range from 2.24 to 12.07 (Simmons, 1980). Thus the incentive of getting a certificate here is more. This results in an oversupply of higher-level graduates, who end up unemployed.

The obvious thing to do would be to try to reduce wage differentials. The problem in developing societies is the market mechanism, for labour allocation is subordinated to a social network that often considers political and familial credentials as criteria for job allocation.

The second effect of education on economic development is that of income distribution. Since education has such a great impact on individual earnings, it follows that it also affects the way income is distributed. The net effect of the expansion of schooling has been a reduction in the dispersion of earnings and hence a more equal income distribution (Psacharopoulos, 1988, p. 103).

The equity of income depends on which level of education is expanded. The equity impact is greatest at the basic level of education, as the low earnings of illiterates are raised closer to the overall mean. The expansion of university education, however, has the opposite effect in that the income of workers who earn above the mean may be pushed even further above. As most university students come from middle-to upper-income families, state subsidies for their education will increase their income at the expense of the general taxpayers, who are less likely to be able to afford to send their children for higher education (Psacharopoulos, 1988, pp. 1034).

Despite the fact that for some people education enhances social mobility and redistributes income, the hard reality is that it also serves to widen the gap between rich and poor. Evidence suggests that children of upper-income groups are more likely to receive more years of education than children of the poor. Research conducted in Brazil, India and Colombia all points to the fact that the educational process acts as a disequalizer of income. Not only have governments failed to adjust these disequalizing forces but they have reinforced them. Furthermore, the poor pay a higher percentage of their income in taxes than the rich. It is this tax that pays the cost of expensive education (Simmons, 1980, p. 40).

While it is not the only factor, education is an essential part of the increasing social inequality, for it serves to legitimize the achievement of high-status occupations and also increases the human capital of the rich. Children from upper-income families have an advantage over their peers right from the beginning. They are better fed and cared for and are more exposed to those things conducive to the development and advancement of cognitive skills useful in schools and in white-collar work. In many developing countries, a second language is used in primary school, and those children coming from homes where this language is understood, usually middle-to upper-class families, are at an obvious advantage for educational advancement. In all, the educational system does not reduce inequality from one generation to the next because `the richer students have more opportunities to get a good elementary and high-school education, to get into college, to remain in college, and therefore to get a high-income job after college—and then to send their children to college' (Hunt and Sherman, 1975, p. 317).

From a social viewpoint one can appreciate the social frustration and political dangers of unemployment of the educated. A more highly educated society is supposed to be a more politically democratic society (Carnoy, 1974, p. 7). Such a notion is derived from the suggestion that countries with more education per capita are more likely to have Western-style democracies characterized by regular, free and fair elections and representative governments. This level of political maturity is a necessary feature for any government or country to claim to be developed. The situation, however, has been that more education has simply resulted in the replacement of less educated labour by the more highly educated. The number of jobs has not been growing as rapidly as the number of graduates being put out so that the increase in average schooling has not been used by the economy. There is still a high demand for high-level education and this takes a large part of government budgets. These resources could instead be used to create jobs for the impoverished, but, as the political clout of this group is less than that of the middle-to higher-class groups, this is not done. `The primary school has become not the place where one is educated for a useful life, but the place where one competes for an exit visa from rural society' (Dore, 1980, p. 71). It is no wonder, then, that disadvantaged children choose to opt out of primary if they have little chance of getting into secondary, for they know there is no job for them after primary.

The modern sector has grown too slowly to accommodate the whole of the labour force. Development was seen as a matter of creating an outpost of modernity in an otherwise traditional society; through natural economic forces (initiated by certain inputs) the former would engulf the latter, creating a modern society. The flaws in this strategy are now being experienced. The salaries of modern sector workers are out of proportion to traditional sector incomes, and, as inequalities grow, so too do social tensions. In this situation, it is in the interest of the state, especially the capitalist state, to try to keep the lid on the problem.

According to Bowles (1980, p. 207), the educational system as a significant influence on political life, ideology and development of labour power is one of the indispensable instruments of the state. The features of educational inequality and inequality of income discussed earlier are reflections of the class structure of capitalist societies. These class relations circumscribe the contribution educational policies could make to either growth or equality. In capitalist countries the school system contributes to the expansion of capitalism by serving both as a recruiter and gatekeeper for the capitalist sector. As a recruiter the system turns out a labour force able and resigned to working productively within the capitalist firm. Productivity is increased through education firstly by transmitting and reinforcing values necessary for adequate job performance and smooth functioning of the labour market and secondly by developing the technical and scientific skills needed for efficient production (Bowles, 1980, p. 215).

Young people are integrated in the capitalist mode when the education system is beyond their or their parents' control; when success is measured by external examinations; and when this structure suppresses any personal interest in knowledge or learning. Features of class, sex and race are reflected in differential access to school, drop-out rates and promotion prospects. These are, according to Bowles, the capitalist social relations of production reflected in the schools. Thus, it is in the capitalists' interests to pattern the structure of education after the social relations found in this societal formation.

Analogously, it is in their interest to regulate the growth of the education system to the expansion of the actual mode of production. This is the gatekeeper function of the educational system. Sometimes, owing to the ideological emphasis on education as the route to success, popular demand outstrips the rate appropriate to the employment needs of the economy at that point in time. An important point to consider in the expansion of education, particularly for the ruling class, is the amount of ideological or political benefit that expansion will produce. However, the overexpansion of education has risks for the capitalist class. First, it may bring about productivity increases and technological progress in the traditional mode, thereby diminishing the pool of cheap labour found in the traditional sector. Second, the costs of expansion constitute a tax burden on capitalists and a diversion of state resources that might otherwise have been used for more profit-generating projects. Third, if the entire population of a specific age-group received a fairly high level of education, they might all expect employment in the capitalist mode—an expectation which, in reality, might not be met, therefore leading to great social frustration and tension.

This serves to demonstrate that the particular social formation has a bearing on the educational system found. We must not be too hasty in condemning the educational system as an instrument for bringing about growth and income distribution; instead, we must take a closer look at the wider society within which the system functions. These issues must be seriously addressed before any true performance evaluation of the critical role education plays in national development can be undertaken.

Conclusion

This study has attempted to investigate the role of formal education in the development process. It has examined the functions, dynamics and challenges of the education enterprise in sub-Saharan Africa.

In general, the manifest functions of the education enterprise include the socialization of the young; cultural transmission and social integration; the creation of new knowledge; the development of personal skills; training for work; and the promotion of social and economic mobility over time. However, education also has latent or hidden functions. For instance, it has been argued that educational institutions sometimes operate as deadly instruments of oppression and exploitation. As Rodney (1972) put it: `colonial schooling was education for subordination, exploitation and the development of underdevelopment.' To a very great extent, Rodney's argument is applicable to post-independence Africa, even if what is happening now is not necessarily a consequence of deliberate policy-making, but of the inherited colonial legacy. The principal indictments against colonial (and, to a certain degree, neo-colonial) education include the following:

- Colonial education was an instrument of imperialist domination and economic exploitation. This brand of education was partly responsible for the prevailing economic and political crises in Africa.

- Colonial education was a major source of economic inequalities and social stratification. For instance, a handful of Africans had access to education, which they used to exploit and dominate other Africans. As a result, those tribal, ethnic or regional groupings which were denied this type of education increasingly became economically and socially disadvantaged.

- For Africa, colonial education served as an instrument of intellectual and cultural servitude. Western culture was promoted at the expense of the indigenous culture. Some of the consequences of colonial education include acquisitive egocentricity, religious fanaticism, and political alienation. The curricula and models of colonial education were largely inadequate and irrelevant to the development of Africa.

These were some of the characteristics and problems of the education system that was bequeathed to the newly independent countries. Colonial education was different from pre-colonial education, which laid emphasis on `social responsibility, job orientation, political participation and spiritual and moral values' (Fafunwa and Aisiku, 1982, p. 9).

Following the achievement of political independence in the 1950s and 1960s, the new nations set out to modify the colonial education legacies, for instance, by trying to establish systems of education corresponding to their social, economic and political aspirations and circumstances. There was general agreement that education was a panacea for miscellaneous socio-economic ills; it was seen as a key to economic growth and a weapon against deep-seated inequalities and injustices. In short, it was rightly believed that there was a link between education and modernization.

In connection with the quantitative expansion of educational services, it goes without saying that impressive progress has been made. Since the early 1960s student enrolment at primary, secondary and tertiary levels has doubled or even tripled. To be sure, post-independence education systems of LDCs are far different from what they were during the colonial era. The importance of education has been recognized and measures to rectify the limitations of colonial education taken. The building of institutions, development plans, curriculum changes, increased allocation of funds to education, accelerated educational development in rural areas and non-formal education are all bold attempts to universalize and democratize education systems.

Unfortunately, these measures are set against the backdrop of colonial legacies that make development plans and strategies all the harder to realize. Despite the phenomenal expansion of educational systems, there is a widespread feeling that the qualitative aspects of education have not received enough attention.

With reference to Africa, it is felt that educational institutions are producing academic robots—or, to use Leopold Senghor's famous terminology, `photographic negatives'—of the British, French, Portuguese and Belgian colonial rulers.

Many of the educational and development strategies initiated by LDCs over the past twenty or thirty years have not been as successful as previously anticipated owing to certain problems and dilemmas, including, *inter alia*, the following: rapid population growth; the maladjustment between modernity and tradition; the misfit between economic development and social development; the imbalances between education and development needs; the wide gap between education and lucrative employment; the disparities in educational provision rooted in geography, social grouping or gender; untimely localization and institutional overload and mismanagement.

We are convinced that education and development are strongly correlated. However, the successful synthesis of the two will depend on our ability to resolve effectively the above-mentioned predicaments. The struggle for total liberation continues.

References

Ayandele, E. A. 1982. Africa: The Challenge of Higher Education. *Daedalus*, Vol. 111, No. 2.

Bowles, S. 1980. Education, Class Conflict and Uneven Development. In: J. Simmons (ed.), *The Education Dilemma: Policy Issues for Developing Counties in the 1980s*. Washington, D.C., World Bank.

Carnoy, M. 1974. *Education as Cultural Imperialism*. New York, McKay.

Coombs, P. 1985. *The World Crisis in Education*. New York, Oxford University Press.

Court, D.; KINYANJUI, A. 1986. African Education: Problems in a High-growth Sector. In: R. J. Berg and J. S. Whitaker (eds.), *Strategies for African Development*. Berkeley, Calif., University of California Press.

Dore, R. 1980. The Future of Education. In: J. Simmons (ed.), *The Education Dilemma*. Oxford, Pergamon Press.

Drucker, P. 1961. The Educational Revolution. In: A. H. Halsey et al., *Education, Economy and Society*. New York, The Free Press.

Fafunwa, B.; AISIKU, J. U. 1982. *Education in Africa: A Comparative Survey*. London, George Allen & Unwin.

Goldschmidt, D. 1987. The Role of Universities in Development. *Development and Cooperation*, No. 6.

Harbison, F. H. 1973. *Human Resources as the Wealth of Nations*. New York, Oxford University Press.

Hawes, H.; COOMBE, T. 1986. *Education Priorities and Aid Response in Sub-Saharan Africa*. London, Overseas Development Administration.

Hummel, Charles. 1977. *Education Today for the World of Tomorrow*. Paris, UNESCO.

Hunt, E. K.; SHERMAN, H. J. 1975. *Economics: An Introduction to Traditional and Radical Views*. New York, Harper & Row.

Husen, T. 1979. *The School in Question*. Oxford, Oxford University Press.

Jenkins, D. 1988. What is the Purpose of a University, and what Light does Christian Faith Shed on this Question? *Studies in Higher Education*, Vol. 13, No. 3.

Ki-Zerbo, J. 1974. Historical Aspects of Education in French-speaking Africa and the Question of Development. *Development Dialogue*, No.

2.

Lee, K. H. 1988. Universal Primary Education: An African Dilemma. *World Development*, Vol. 16, No. 12.

Magagula, M. C. M. 1987. Education for Development. (Paper presented at the Professors World Peace Academy Conference, Johannesburg.)

Mazrui, A. 1980. *The Africa Condition: The Reith Lectures*. London, Heinemann.

Mc Ivor, C. 1987. Zimbabwe Tackles Education Problem. *Development and Cooperation*, No. 6.

Morris, D. M. 1979. *Measuring the Condition of the World's Poor: The Physical Quality of Life Index*. London, Frank Cass.

Mosha, H. J. 1986. The Role of African Universities in National development: A Critical Analysis. *Comparative Education*, Vol. 22, No. 2.

Nyerere, J. 1974. Education and Liberation. *Development Dialogue*. (Opening address.)

Porter, A. T. 1972. University Development in English-speaking Africa: Problems and Opportunities. *Journal of the Royal African Society*, Vol. 71, No. 282.

Psacharopoulos, G. 1988. *Education and Development: A Review*. Washington, D.C., World Bank.

Ram, R. 1982. Composite Indices of Physical Quality of Life, Basic Needs Fulfillment and Income: A Principal Component Representation. *Journal of Development Economics*, No. 11, pp. 227-48.

Rodney, W. 1972. *How Europe Underdeveloped Africa*. Dar es Salaam, Tanzania Publishing House.

Schultz, T. W. 1981. *Investing in People*. Berkeley, Calif., University of California Press.

Sicinski, A. 1985. Educational Objectives and Cultural Values. *Reflections on the Future Development of Education*. Paris, UNESCO.

Simmons, J. (ed.). 1980. *The Educational Dilemma: Policy Issues for Developing Countries in the 1980s*. New York, Pergamon Press.

Streeten, P. 1988. Reflections on the Role of the University and the Developing Countries. *World Development*, Vol. 16, No. 5, pp. 639-40.

Tata, R. J.; SCHULTZ, R. R. 1988. World Variation in Human Welfare: A New Index of Development Status. *Annals of the Association of American Geographers*, Vol. 78, No. 4, pp. 580-93.

Todaro, M. 1985. *Economic Development in the Third World*. London,

Longman.

Unesco. 1985. *Reflections on the Future Development of Education*. Paris, UNESCO.

——— 1988. *Goals of Development*. Paris, UNESCO.

United Nations Research Institute For Social Development. 1972. *Contents and Measurement of Socio-economic Development*. New York.

Uphoff, N. T.; ILCHMAN, W F. 1972. *The Political Economy of Development. Theoretical and Empirical Contributions*. Berkeley, Calif., University of California Press.

Watson, K. 1988. Forty Years of Education and Development: From Optimism to Uncertainty. *Educational Review*, Vol. 40, No. 2.

Yesufu, T. M. 1973. The Role and Priorities of the University in Development. In: T. M. Yesufu (ed.), *Creating the African University*. Ibadan (Nigeria), Oxford University Press.

*Apollo Rwomire is a Senior lecturer in sociology and social work at the University of Swaziland. He previously taught sociology at the Universities of Nairobi (Kenya) and Jos (Nigeria). He has authored several monographs and articles on family planning, urban development, education, development and underdevelopment.

— 2 —
INDIGENOUS FORMS OF EDUCATION: THE INDIVIDUAL AND SOCIETY

Mark Bray, Peter Clarke and David Stephens

There is no one, single indigenous form of education in Africa. Societies, differing from each other as they do, have developed education to transmit their own particular knowledge and skills. The differences are not necessarily great, but it is quite clear that, for example, the indigenous system of education among the Yoruba of South-Western Nigeria and that of the Akan in Ghana, differ in method and content.[1] Again, practices such as child weaning which form part of the `curriculum' in the indigenous education systems of many African societies vary widely in method and perspective.[2]

On the other hand indigenous forms of education are sometimes remarkably similar, and one form can be seen to have influenced another. Part of the reason for this is that certain educational specialists, as is the case in the Western-type and Islamic systems, are extremely mobile. The impression has often been given of pre-colonial Africa as consisting of static cultural units dwelling in isolation. However, cultural and economic interaction between different societies has at times been very fluid and intense. An example of this is the way the peoples of different ethnic origin in parts of what are now Ghana and the Ivory Coast came to share some of the same artistic traditions. The mobility of specialists such as the Dyula dyers and Numu blacksmiths in the Ivory Coast and Ghana was in large measure responsible for this.[3]

African Perspectives on Freedom and the Individual

Although there has always been and still is exchange of ideas between societies, one cannot examine indigenous education in just one society and then draw sweeping and unqualified general conclusions about it in Africa as a whole. There is, for example, a considerable difference between the indigenous educational systems of the urbanized Yoruba and those of the pastoral Fulani. One can, however, generalize about the philosophical and sociological foundations of indigenous forms of education in Africa. For instance, African philosophy tends to define people in terms of the social context to which they belong, and this has important implications for the nature and goals of indigenous forms of education. African thought also recognizes the uniqueness of the individual with his or her own personality, talents and `destiny'. Thus in a sense individuals are thought of as transcending the socio-cultural context. There is, however, a strong tendency to situate a person's individuality and freedom within the overall social, cultural and historical context of the community or society.

Among the Dogon of Mali, for example, an individual's actions are regarded as being closely interlinked with the way society in general and the world operate. The individual is not thought of as a being having one `self' or '`soul', but rather as a multiple entity made up of several `selves' or `souls', each one of which reflects a concrete relationship between that individual and the wider world. Among the Dogon a person at birth is only potentially a human being and it is the society into which that person is born that provides the individual with a spiritual, sexual, social and intellectual identity. This process happens only gradually. The community, for instance, during one of numerous naming ceremonies which the newborn person must undergo, confers upon the child both an `intelligent' soul, which provides the individual with the capacity for acquiring knowledge, and the `grains' which connect the person with the laws of the universe.[4]

One finds a similar set of ideas among the Yoruba for whom, though an individual has freedom and responsibility, life is divinely pre-ordained and sociologically conditioned.[5] The Tallensi of Ghana, like the Dogon and the Yoruba, recognize that each individual is unique and free but also see the thoughts and actions of that individual as being inextricably related to his external, social world.[6] To some, these views may appear to imply conflict between individual freedom and dependence upon society. However, the Tallensi definition of freedom requires social responsibility and maturity, so that the individual adapts his thoughts and actions to the needs and requirements of the world within which he lives. This idea of freedom is compatible with the notion these peoples have of the ideal social and moral order.

Among the Dinka of the southern Sudan the concept *cieng* means both `morality' and `living in harmony', and the product of *cieng* is well being. As one authority expresses it, `a Dinka strives to maintain unity and harmony between himself and the world outside', and this is best achieved by adapting the individual's desires and requests to those of the rest of society.[7] Some knowledge of indigenous ideas concerning the relationship between individual freedom and society, and of how people acquire social identities is essential for an understanding of the goals of indigenous education.

The Goals of Indigenous Education

Although indigenous education can vary from one society to another, the goals of these systems are often strikingly similar. The emphasis, it seems to us, is placed on what we have described in Chapter 5 as normative and expressive goals. To recapitulate, normative goals are concerned with instilling the accepted standards and beliefs governing correct behaviour, and expressive goals with creating unity and consensus. In singling out normative and expressive goals as the principal objectives of indigenous education we do not mean to suggest that there is no competitive element within the system, giving rise to what are termed instrumental goals. Indigenous education does encourage competitiveness in intellectual and practical matter, but this competitiveness is controlled and subordinated to normative and expressive aims.

There is, or ought to be, a direct link between the goals and content of education. A great deal of the content of indigenous education consists of what sociologists like Durkheim refer to moral education. According to Durkheim, morality is `a system of rules and actions that predetermine conduct'.[8] An essential element of morality, Durkheim maintained, was a spirit of discipline, which assumed the existence of organization and authority. With regard to the content of morality in general he stated that: `To act morally is to act in the light of a collective interest'; and he added: `the domain of the moral begins where the domain of the social begins'.[9] According to Durkheim, it was society in the sense of a supra-individual element in social life consisting of collective sentiments and beliefs, which gave moral rules and ideals their authority. In Durkheim's view a child needed to be taught morality, and this meant among other things teaching him or her about the nature of family life and in general `about the nature of the social contexts in which he will be called to live'.[10]

Durkheim's ideas on moral education help us to understand the content and goals of indigenous forms of education. Though indigenous education in its various forms has a many-sided character, it is intimately intertwined with social life. What is taught is related to the social context in which people are called to live. Among the Chagga of Tanzania, for example, there is a `course' for children in what is called `imitative play'. It consists of representations of scenes from adult life by means of which the young are made familiar with the norms and ideals expected from full, responsible members of society.[11]

Indigenous education, however, is not only concerned with the systematic socialization of the younger generation into the norms, religious and moral beliefs, and collective opinions of the wider society. It also lays a very strong emphasis on learning practical skills. It is not that the idea of art for art's sake, or the notion that the acquisition of knowledge and wisdom and the improvement of an individual's intellectual capacities, have no place in indigenous education. They do, as we shall see; but there is greater emphasis on the acquisition of knowledge which is useful to the individual and society as a whole.

The Educators and the Curriculum in the Indigenous Education Process

As we mentioned at the beginning of this chapter, what people learn varies from one African society to another. It depends greatly on the level of stratification and the mode of political and economic organization of the society itself and in many African countries the whole community is the principal educative and socializing agent. However, some specific organizations and individuals have the task of educating the young. Some people specialise in teaching particular disciplines.

On the question of the whole community as the educative agent, one scholar has described how among the Akan of Ghana education is a joint enterprise of both the old and the young. Children have complete freedom to attend many adult activities. At birth they are given a symbolic introduction to adult language, a few weeks later they begin to eat adult food, and from the age of six they commence adult work. The main purpose of this early introduction to adult life is `to free the infant as quickly as possible from dependence upon the parent'.[12] Akan indigenous education is then adult rather than child centred. It is based on the assumption that an individual can participate in community life and benefit from the education the community has to offer at what is, relatively speaking, a very early age.

Among the Chamba of north-eastern Nigeria, the situation is some what different. Educating the individual to be independent is a much longer process, and in one sense the Chamba do not regard the child or even the adolescent as a person or individual. As one informant expressed it: `the child is not a person; he is his father's property . . . a young man, moreover, cannot own what he kills in a hunt without being given it by his father. The father and his brothers have complete control over the children.'[13]

In African societies, including the Akan where there is strong emphasis on the community as educator, parents also play a very important role in the education of their children. There is very often a clearly marked division of labour. The mother educates all children in the early years, but later the father takes over the education of the male children while the mother remains in control of the females. After learning to walk, speak and count, the male child goes to his father and male elders and begins his training for manhood. The female child continues to be taught by her mother, assisted by the other women in the community, and begins to learn how to live and work as a woman in that society. Among the Chamba and in other African societies there exists a conscious model of the ideal man and the ideal woman, and it is with this ideal in mind that the children are educated in the second stage of the educational process. The ideal man preserves and strengthens the cultural, social and moral features of the society. The ideal woman is a wife and mother who, through the bearing of children and in her role as educator, assists her husband in the task of preserving and strengthening the customs and traditions of the group.

This is the ideal that is aspired to; meanwhile both parents attempt to provide their children with a very practical type of education and one based on sound principles of common sense. The nature and content of this practical education, as far as the male child is concerned, is often be determined by his father's occupation. If for example the father is a farmer, then the male children are trained as farmers. Likewise the practical education provided for the female child will be determined by her mother's role as wife and mother and her occupation which might well include cooking, and possibly dyeing or trading. It should be mentioned that though children are instructed and guided by their parents, there is strong emphasis in the learning-process on participant observation.

Apart from the parents, institutions such as age-groups participate in the education process. The age-group is important as a means of moulding the personality of its members and defining their attitude to tasks and problems which they will face in adult life.[14] The age-group encourages and teaches respect for elders, solidarity and cooperation. In many African societies age-groups are also part of a division of labour, for (economic, social, cultural and political functions) are allocated on the basis of age.

In addition to the age-group system there are other institutions such as the craft guilds, the secret societies, of which examples from Sierra Leone are given in the case study at the end of this chapter, and the `convents' where specialists are trained. Many of the crafts are hereditary occupations where the family hands down, usually to the oldest male child, the techniques and secrets of the trade. This seems to have been the case, for example, with beadmaking and blacksmithing. Membership of certain families or clans appear to have been a necessary qualification for entry into the *lantana* beadmaking industry and trade in Ilorin, western Nigeria. One can, however, exaggerate the extent to which certain crafts remained the preserve of certain families and closely knit groups, or the extent to which participation in these crafts was rigidly determined by sex. With regard to the lantana beadmaking craft there is evidence that though the emphasis was on the teaching of family members, anyone could learn the craft. Women also assisted the men in the beadmaking, and even made a special type of bead themselves. Their role, however, was a minor one; but this was not necessarily on account of the fact that they were women, for as one scholar points out it might simply reflect `the difficulty of assigning primary occupations to women who followed a number of activities part-time.'[15]

In other parts of Africa many of the craft guilds were caste based and seem to have been less open than the lantana beadmaking guilds of western Nigeria. This was the case, for example, in parts of Senegal such as Futa Toro where the caste system of Mandinka origin was very rigidly observed. These blacksmiths, jewellers, tanners, tailors and *griots* (praise singers) were all members of different, exclusive castes.

In some parts of Africa, centres also exist for training religions specialists. In the People's Republic of Benin, priests and mediums are taken out of society for a time and trained in `seminaries' and/or `convents'. In these isolated institutions the recruits are transformed into new personalities. This transformation is symbolized in a number of ways. For example, the recruit's hair is shaven off several times during the course of his training, which lasts about nine months. Learning a new language dialect forms part of the training, and the recruit is also given a new name and trained in a new occupation. The whole process aims to create a `new' personality, who will engage in a new kind of life. Recruits learn both about the spirit world and about more practical matters. For instance they are taught how to make the priestly garments and necklaces, and also such things as mats and baskets which are then sold to ordinary people.'[16]

The priests are also the traditional doctors and have to learn a great deal about plants, roots and herbs. Treatment, however, is rarely seen in purely material or physical terms. In his treatment of the patient the doctor must use his knowledge not only of plants, herbs and roots and their healing properties, but also his knowledge of the spiritual universe which enables him, among other things, to release the hidden powers of the medicine.[17] We will return later to the question of the scientific character of medical training and practice in the indigenous education system, while simply mentioning here that the introduction of Western medicine has by no means put an end to traditional medicine. A recent study shows that in many parts of Africa all groups in the population use both traditional and Western medicine constantly.[18]

The training of a diviner can be a long, highly specialized and complicated process. Not all diviners, are trained for the same role in society. Among the Ndembu of north-western Zambia, for example, the diviner is, in addition to being a doctor, concerned with analyzing the past. The Yoruba diviner (*babalawo*) of south-western Nigeria, by contrast, is concerned with forecasting the future. This does not mean, that their functions are essentially dissimilar, however, for both provide their clients with authoritative models for the purpose of decision making. The Ndembu diviner's task is not to reveal the unknown but to give coherence, unity and meaning to all the known facts in a particular case. On this basis he works towards a specific, moral judgement concerning the matter, and having achieved this he prescribes a resolution for the problem. The Yoruba diviner (babalawo) on the other hand seeks to reveal his clients' destiny, and by so doing indicates how the client may improve upon it in this life.

Among both the Ndembu and the Yoruba the diviner is `chosen', though in different ways, for his profession. Among the Ndembu a man becomes a diviner after experiencing the afflictions and sufferings of the spirit Kayongu. A person becomes a babalawo by inheriting the ability from his father or grandfather, or by being specially `chosen' by Orumila, the god of diviners. The training for the babalawo is long and intensive, beginning some time between the ages of seven and twelve. The trainee lives with a master babalawo for about ten years, and must learn a great deal of technical and oral knowledge. By the time he is ready to practice as a diviner for the first time the babalawo will have learnt over one thousand `poems' relating to the problems, anxieties, hopes and aspirations common in Yoruba society. These include illness, bad medicine, evil spirits, money, and family disputes and questions of status, authority and power. An experienced babalawo normally knows twice as many `poems' as the beginner.

We do not intend here to concentrate on how the Yoruba divination system works. There is already plenty of literature available on that subject.[19] What we do want to point to is the feat of memory involved, which is very remarkable. We have indicated that in the indigenous education system one of the main ways of acquiring knowledge and skills is participant observation. This method is also used in the training of the babalawo. However the indigenous education system also places considerable emphasis on the `art of memory', and the training of the babalawo is an excellent example of this. The art of memory was valued by the Greeks and Romans, but it is downplayed and rather despised by Western educationists today.

The trainee babalawo not only learns to memorize a vast amount of poetry, but also a wide range of medical knowledge. As we have seen the diviner is also priest and doctor. The trainee, therefore, has to learn to recognize and to distinguish between various kinds of mental and physical illness. He must know the course a particular illness will take and how to make up the medicine necessary to treat it.

Learning about medicine is a complex process, involving an in-depth study of ritual. For example, the Ndembu doctor treating pregnant women has among other things to cut bark chips from numerous species of the same tree, the Kapwipi tree.[20] This tree is used because its wood is hard, and hardness represents the health and strength desired for the patient. In addition, all these trees share the same ritually important property, namely that bark string cannot be taken from them: `for this would "tie up" the fertility of the patient'. In this sense they may be said to counter Mwengi's medicines. Mwengi is a masked being who wears a costume made of many strings from bark cloth. The bark strings are believed to be deadly to women's procreation.[21]

Indigenous Education and Western Education: Points of Contact

The policy of replacing the indigenous, and we may add the Islamic, education systems in Africa by the Western education system has some times been attacked.[22] Opponents of the full-scale Westernization of education in Africa have advanced numerous criticism against this trend. If it is one of the main purposes of schools to transmit the attitudes, values, skills, social understanding and customs of the society which they serve, then is it not the case, some educationalists point out, that the so-called informal system of education (often referred to as traditional or indigenous education) does precisely this? Indeed perhaps it does it in a more effective way than the Western-type school. It would appear that indigenous forms of education in Africa place far greater emphasis on participant observation, and that they appreciate fully—and this is a point of fundamental importance—the vital link between knowledge and experience. In operating according to the principle that these are inextricably linked, the indigenous system of education can claim the support of Western educationists and philosophers such as Kant, who held that all our knowledge begins with experience.

Of course we are not suggesting that indigenous forms of education in Africa are perfect and therefore in no need of change or improvement. As societies change, education systems also have to change if they are to continue to cater for people's needs. For example, when a country seeks to transform itself from a non-industrial to an industrialized nation the education system has to play a different role from the one designed for a non-industrialized society. Instead of pursuing as one of its main objectives the goals of social stability and continuity, it will increasingly have to assist in the process of advancing controlled change. Further, where a complex, multi-cultural society is attempting to integrate itself and become one nation, the education system will need to be reshaped in order effectively to transmit different attitudes and skills.

Throughout Africa prior to the period of large-scale nationalism and industrialization, the indigenous education systems performed the role of socializing individuals into particular societies where beliefs and values were widely held in common. The education system equipped the same individuals with the skills to perform the tasks assigned by the family and the wider society. In a culturally and religiously diverse society which is undergoing industrialization and in which the extended family system is breaking down, an education system can only be relevant if it provides individuals with the intellectual equipment, moral values and skills needed to cope with the changing situation. It is clear from what we have already said that indigenous forms of education need to undergo major reforms in goals and methods if they are to perform this role effectively.

It is not only relatively recent developments such as nationalism and industrialization which have constituted a challenge to and rendered indigenous forms of education somewhat irrelevant. In West Africa, for example, the eleventh century saw the development of large-scale political entities such as the empire of Ancient Ghana, followed by the Mali and Songhay empires which reached their peaks in the fourteenth and fifteenth century respectively. But indigenous forms of education failed in some respects to meet the requirements of these much larger political units. Consequently the rulers of these empires tended increasingly to look to the Islamic education system for the personnel necessary for the organization, administration, and integration of their empires. The Islamic education system trained people in Arabic, a widely spoken language useful for such purposes as international diplomacy and trade, in which these empires were involved. The Islamic education system also trained accountants, lawyers, historians and clerks, and communicated values and attitudes relevant to the functioning of these larger political organizations. In some respects the Western-type school has been regarded as the most appropriate vehicle for performing the same or similar functions in modern times, and consequently the Islamic and more so the indigenous education systems have come to be regarded, in some African countries at least, as peripheral and irrelevant to the tasks of nation building and industrialization.

It is also worth mentioning a debate which has recently been a live issue among academics, and which is relevant to the whole question of education and the development process. The issue concerns the nature of African traditional thinking. Does it constitute a barrier to the development of a truly scientific approach necessary for modernization? Levy Bruhl advanced the view, which he modified in later writing, that the pre-logical and mystical religious character of `primitive' thought and the rational procedures of modern thought were incompatible. As Evans-Pritchard has pointed out, however, the main theme in Levy Bruhl's treatise cannot be sustained.[23] Horton, though he has his critics, maintains that in substance there is no essential difference between traditional African ways of thinking and Western scientific thinking. Differences do exist, but these are largely differences of idiom, and do not in any way render traditional African thinking any less rational *per se* than Western scientific thinking.[24] Apparent differences in thinking are in fact often differences in language, which is used primarily as a means of representing reality. A people's reality, that is their shared experience, will be represented in the language devised by that people.[25]

Indigenous and Western forms of education therefore should not be seen as opposites; the two approaches can supplement each other in a number of ways. As we have seen indigenous forms of education tend to reflect the values, wisdom and expectations of the community or wider society as a whole. Western forms of education, on the other hand, tend to stress the `intellectual' development of the individual while paying rather less attention to the needs, goals and expectations of the wider society. The solution does not lie in abandoning one form of education for another. A formal education system can play an important role in Africa, but such a system, if it is to meet the cultural, social, moral and intellectual, as well as political and economic needs of Africa needs to be domesticated and indigenized. And it is here that the study of indigenous forms of education becomes crucially important. The philosophy; methodology and content of schooling in Africa needs to be shaped and moulded, not exclusively, but to a far greater extent, by indigenous perspectives. We do not simply mean those that operated before the arrival of the Western and Islamic education systems. We are also referring to the considerations, views, opinions and assessments of past and contemporary African educationists who, through research and experience, have become aware of the needs and goals of African societies. No serious educational planning can be undertaken without identification of the specific needs and goals of particular African societies.

Indigenous, Western, and Islamic forms of education can usefully be integrated. There are, however, pitfalls which need to be avoided, and which can be avoided if needs and goals are formulated and if a sound, African-inspired philosophy of education is developed. One pitfall is that of establishing an education system in which the different forms—the indigenous, Islamic and Western, where they exist in the same society are linked rather than integrated or blended together. Integration, of course, requires a considerable amount of comparative research in the field of the philosophy of education, methodology and curriculum. Indigenous educational theory overlaps to some extent with Western and Islamic educational theory, though there are differences of emphasis and perspective, and even substantive methodological differences. However, having formulated the needs and goals of society, the educationists can develop, on the basis of theoretical perspectives of the different systems, a coherent, integrated education system, and not simply a haphazard mixture which will be of little benefit to the individual or society.

Conclusion

Indigenous forms of education thus tend, more than the Western form, to serve the needs and aspirations of the community as a whole. The emphasis is on normative and expressive goals. Competition between individuals is encouraged, but not to the extent that individualism and introverted élitism are held in higher esteem than education for life in the community. Indigenous educational theory holds that each of the individual's relationships affects and is affected by all the others. Though, as we have pointed out, the notion of art for art's sake exists, indigenous forms of education regard education in terms of its effects upon or consequences for society and in terms of its effects on individuals.

By comparison, Western education tends to be `bookish', and some what divorced from the life and culture of the wider community. It is, therefore, less able in some respects to provide an education that will fit an individual for life in the community. Furthermore it tends to encourage competition at the expense of cooperation. On the other hand it positively seeks to promote originality of thought and outlook which can be valuable assets to any society. There is, therefore, a need to harmonize and integrate the best elements of both indigenous and Western forms of education to create a more viable system of education in Africa.

Case Study: Indigenous Education in Sierra Leone

Although the differences between them have become less pronounced over time, one can distinguish between two types of indigenous education in Sierra Leone. On the one hand there are the education system of the Temnes, Mendes, Limba, Lokkos, Konas and other peoples who mostly live in the interior. On the other hand there is the education system of the Creole population, which comprises descendents of the freed slaves and other settlers who began to arrive in the country in the late eighteenth century and who inhabit what is now called the Western Area.[26]

The clearest examples of indigenous educational institutions, on which this case study will concentrate, are operated by the Poro and Bundu secret societies. These societies exist among several ethnic groups, including the Mendes, Temnes, Konos and Sherbros. The form they take varies from one ethnic group to another, and even within the same group, though one can make some generalizations.[27] The Creoles also have secret societies, which include the Hunting (Ojeh) associations. Like the Poro and Bundu societies, Creole societies have traditional rites and symbols, and members are sworn to secrecy. But while the Poro and Bundu societies play an important role in the all-round education and training of the young, the Creole societies tend to be more ritualistic and ceremonial.

The Poro society among the Temne has a history of at least four and a half centuries.[28] Many Westerners who encountered the Poro society were hostile towards it, and few considered it from an educational viewpoint. They were not alone in this, as we shall see. In the past, the Poro society performed an important political and economic role, serving sometimes as a check on government and as a mutual aid organization for its members. This role has changed, but even in recent times the society has been used to mobilize support for political purposes.[29]

The Poro society initiates and trains boys who are admitted at the onset of puberty may remain in training for one or more years. It operates in the forest or bush on sacred ground. There are different types of sacred ground, but most have entrances resembling arches, and clearings that may contain shelters. Usually the Poro organizer, a man, arranges for the recruiting of boys, the collection of the initiation fees, the provision of food for the sacrifices, and the payment of the priests and diviners. During the period of initiation the boys are cut off from all contact with non-members and sleep alone in separate houses. Most of the day is spent on the farm. Discipline and cooperation are among the main parts of the curriculum. The boys are also taught the signs, symbols, structure and language of the society. In some cases, training is also given in first aid, farming, craftsmanship and construction work. The boys are taught to, endure physical pain and to be self-reliant within their communities.

Some aspects of Poro society organization and work have been strongly criticized. For example, the recruitment methods of some societies have involved seizure of boys for initiation against their own and their parents wishes. Some Poro societies have also administered severe physical punishment to anyone who criticized them or who failed to show respect to the Pora officials. Today, however, Poro recruitment and discipline have been modified under the influence of Christianity, Islam and government legislation. Poro secrecy is no longer as impenetrable as it used to be, partly because of the development of Western education. The Poro society, nevertheless, continues to function, especially in rural areas. Fewer people undergo initiation and many people are only nominal members, but Poro healing and ritual techniques are still actively sought.

The Poro has its female counterpart in the Bundu society, to which girls are admitted from around the age nine.[30] Again, although the disciplinary rules and regulations are not as strict as they used to be, girls still undergo an intensive training which equips them with the skills and techniques deemed necessary in a wife and mother. The Bundu society functions as a pre-marital training institution where girls are taught domestic science, child rearing, basic agricultural skills, craft work, basic medicine, and leisure activities such as music and dance. In addition to being trained for motherhood, they are socialized into the adult female way of life.

These examples indicate the way that education systems in traditional societies train the younger generations. By means of such institutions as we have been describing, the attitudes, beliefs, rituals, work ethics, skills, and communal attitudes are transmitted from one generation to the next. The education system thus serves as a force for social integration and cohesion.

However, it should not be concluded that traditional societies experience no competition, tension or conflict. While considerable common sentiment and group solidarity are characteristic of such societies, inequality, discrimination and violations of the legal and moral are also common. Moreover, education itself has not always served the interests of the whole society, for it may be used by some people to acquire power and authority over others for their own narrow end. Finally, we must observe that societies and their education systems are constantly changing. The Poro and Bundu societies are forced to change and adapt to new circumstances.

Questions and Project Work

1. Assess the similarities and differences of indigenous forms of education in your country or in any African country of your choice.
2. What, in your view, are the most valuable philosophical and sociological insights provided by indigenous forms of education?
3. Are there, in your view, any valuable and relevant philosophical and sociological insights to be gained from a study of the indigenous educational systems of the Dogon, the Yoruba and the Tallensi? (You may widen the scope here to cover other indigenous education systems, for example those found in your own country.)
4. Suggest ways in which indigenous and Western forms of education might complement each other. To answer this question you should, where possible, compare and contrast the two systems of education as they exist in your own area.
5. What are the principal cultural and economic problems of your country and what role, if any, might indigenous education play in solving them?

Notes

1. See Callaway, H. `Indigenous Education in Yoruba Society' and Bartels, F.L. `Akan Indigenous Education' in Brown, G.N. and Hiskett, M. (eds.) *Conflict and Harmony in Education in Tropical Africa.* George Allen and Unwin, London 1975, pp. 26-39 and pp. 39-65 respectively.
2. Hake, C. *Child-Rearing Practices in Northern Nigeria.* Ibadan University Press, Ibadan 1972, and T.O. Pearce, Behavioral Science

and Medicine, unpublished paper.
3. Bravmann, R.A. *Islam and Tribal Art in West Africa.* Cambridge University Press, Cambridge 1974.
4. Griaule, M. `Remarques sur le mécanisme du sacrifice dogon'. *Journal de la Société des Africanistes*, 10, 1940.
5. Horton, R. `Destiny and the Unconscious'. *Africa* Vol. 31, No. 2, 1961; and Bascom, W. `Yoruba Concepts of the Soul' in Wallace, A. (ed.) *Men and Cultures.* University of Pennsylvania Press, Philadelphia 1960.
6. Fortes, M. *Oedipus and Job in West African Religion.* Cambridge University Press, Cambridge 1959.
7. Deng, F.M. *The Dinka of the Sudan.* Holt, Rinehart and Winston, New York 1972, p. 26.
8. Durkheim, E. *Moral Education.* Free Press, New York 1961.
9. Ibid.
10. Ibid.
11. Fafunwa, A. *Babs History of Education in Nigeria.* George Allen and Unwin, London 1974, p. 21.
12. Bartels, op. cit., p. 60.
13. Clarke, P.B. Research notes. Bauchi, Nigeria, 1974.
14. See on this subject Bartels, op. cit.; and Mead, M. *Culture and Commitment: A Study of the Generation Gap.* Panther, St. Albans 1977.
15. O'Hare, Anne `The Lantana Beadmaking Industry and Trade in Ilorin, Western Nigeria'. (Unpublished paper.) Ilorin University, 1981.
16. Parrinder, G. *West African Religion.* Epworth Press, London (third edition) 1969, pp. 86ff.
17. Ibid., p. 158.
18. Pearce, T. `The Sociology of Traditional Medicine'. (Unpublished paper.) 19. See for example Abimbola, W. *Ifa, an Exposition of Ifa Literary Corpus.* Oxford University Press, Ibadan 1976; Bascom, W. *Ifa Divination, Com- munication between Gods and Men in West Africa.* University of Indiana Press, Indiana 1969; and McClelland, E. *The Cult of Ifa Among the Yoruba.* Ethnographica Ltd., London 1982.
20. Turner, V.W. *The Ritual Process.* Penguin, Harmondsworth 1969, p. 24.
21. Ibid., p. 25.
22. Thompson, A.R. *Education and Development in Africa.* Macmillan, London 1981, p. 25.

23. Evans-Pritchard, E.E. `*Theories of Primitive Religion*'. Oxford University Press, Oxford 1965, p. 87.
24. Horton, R. `African Thought and Western Science'. *Africa*, Vol. 37, No. 2, 1967.
25. Cole, M. *et al. The Cultural Context of Learning and Thinking: An Exploration in Experimental Anthropology*. Methuen, London 1971.
26. See Fyfe, C. A *Short History of Sierra Leone*. Longman, London 1979.
27. Dorjahn, V.R. `The Initiation and Training of Temne Poro Members' in Ottenberg, S. (ed.) *African Religious Groups and Beliefs*. Folklore Institute, Berkeley, California n.d., Chap. 2.
28. Ibid., p. 36.
29. Little, K. `The Political Functions of the Poro: Part 1'. *Africa*, Vol. 35, 1965; Little, K. `The Political Functions of the Poro: Part 2'. *Africa*, Vol. 36, 1966.
30. Forde, T.J.L. `Indigenous Education in Sierra Leone'in Brown, G.N. and Hiskett, M. (eds.) *Conflict and Harmony in Education in Tropical Africa*. George, Allen and Unwin, London 1975, pp. 70-1.

— 3 —
ISLAMIC EDUCATION: CONTINUITY AND CHANGE

Mark Bray, Peter Clarke and David Stephens

This chapter surveys the history of Islamic education in sub-Saharan Africa, and analyses the structure and goals of Islamic education. It discusses Islamic educational theory and school organization, the interaction between the Islamic and Western systems of education, and the role of Islamic education, as Muslims themselves understand it, in the processes of development and nation building.

The Growth of Islamic Education in Africa

Islam has a long history in Africa, and its education system has operated much longer than the Western one. A Muslim presence was established in North Africa in the seventh century, and in the eight century Islam began to spread along the trade routes into the western, central and eastern Sudan, and Horn of Africa and East Africa. By the close of the ninth century Arab immigrants had established an Islamic state at Shoe in the Horn of Africa, and by thirteenth century there were several Muslim kingdoms in this region. One of these kingdoms controlled the port of Zayla on the Somali coast, and by the early fourteenth century Muslim students from Zayla were attending the Islamic University of al-Azhar in Cairo. Ibn Battuta (AD 1304—1369) was widely travelled North African Muslim scholar who visited Somalia in AD 1331. Mogadishu, he wrote, was `a town endless in size' which was ruled by a Muslim, Sultan Abu Bakr.[1] Ibn Battuta was given accommodation in a house for students of Islamic religious studies, and he noted the recognition and use of Islamic law.

Likewise, by the tenth and eleventh centuries AD communities of Muslim merchants and scholars had been established in several commercial centres in the Western Sahara and Sahel. By the end of the eleventh century the rulers of kingdoms such as Takrur, Ancient Ghana, Kanem-Borno and Gao had converted to Islam, and had appointed Muslims who were literate in Arabic as advisers.[2] From the fourteenth century the Timbuktu region was also a centre of Islamic learning, exerting an influence far into modern-day Mali and Mauritania.

Centres of higher Islamic education have also existed for many centuries. Even before the world-famous al-Azhar University was founded in Cairo in AD 996, the Qarawiyyin school was established in Morocco. In addition to Timbuktu other towns in West Africa such as Shingit; Jenne, Agades, Kano and N'gazargamu became well known and influential centres of Islamic learning during the period from the thirteenth to the seventeenth centuries.

During the present century the Islamic education system has had to compete with the Western one. In the early years of the century there were many more students in Islamic schools than in Western ones. In Guinea, for example, in 1910 there were about 6,400 Qur'anic schools with 27,000 pupils, but hardly any Western schools.[3] However the statistics for Guinea show a decline in Qur'anic schools and a growth of Western ones. This situation has been paralleled in other countries.

Nevertheless, in parts of Mauritania and Mali there are still more pupils in Qur'anic schools than in Western ones. Efforts have also been made in several countries to modernise and strengthen the Islamic system. Key institutions for this have been the Islamic University in Khartoum (Sudan) the Islamic Institute in Dakar (Senegal), the Islamic Institute of Higher Learning in Boutilimit (Mauritania), the Islamic Education Centre in Kano (Nigeria).

Although aspects of the system have been criticized both by Muslims and non-Muslims, it offers a unique approach to learning and life. It is also held in high esteem both for what it has accomplished in the past and for what it can contribute to African societies today. Particularly notable is the contribution of Islamic education to countries which are attempting to decolonize, to industrialize and to build national unity.

Some Distinctive Features of the Islamic Education System

The Islamic education system has several distinctive features which should be contrasted with those of the Western system. The Islamic system is in many respects far less dependent for its operation on specific administrative, institutional and organizational patterns. It also tends to be much more flexible and, as one scholar comments, has an `Admirable leisureliness'.[4] For example, whereas in the Western system people speak negatively about `perpetual students', in the Islamic system education is seen as an unending process and an individual; can remain a student till old age or death. Some Islamic teachers prefer older and more mature students `who have already shown evidence both of piety and of responsibility'.[5]

The Islamic education system also puts less emphasis on certificates or diplomas than does the Wester one. However, paper qualifications do exist in the Islamic system. The *ijaza*, for example, is a diploma given by a master to his students, and allows a student to teach with authority. Linked to it is the *isnad*. This is a list of names of those who have handed down a tradition or who have taught a given work, which validates the ijaza. A student can find out how prestigious his teacher is by looking at the names of the scholars who appear on the teacher's isnad. If these scholars have a high reputation, then the teacher will also be highly respected.

The theory of Islamic education is found in the Qur'an and in the *hadith* or traditions of the Prophet Mohammed. One hadith states that `the quest for learning is a duty incumbent on every Muslim male and female', another that `wisdom is the goal of the believer and he must seek it irrespective of its source'.[6] Other hadiths describe learning and wisdom as equal to worship, and of men of learning as successors to the prophets. For example, one hadith states that `God eases the way to paradise for him who seeks learning', and another states that `angels spread their wings for the seeker of learning as a mark of God's approval or his purpose'.[7]

Muslims have a long tradition of travel in search of knowledge. The origin of this practice is linked to the geographical spread of Islam. In order to verify whether a hadith was authentic, it was often necessary to travel long distances to question and learn from authorities. Muslims in Africa have been travelling in search of authorities for more than twelve centuries. The Tunisian Muslim scholar Ibn Khaldun (1332-1406) wrote that a scholar's education was greatly improved by travelling in quest of knowledge because `habits acquired through contact with a teacher are more strongly and firmly rooted' than those acquired through other study and lectures.[8] We know that Usuman dan Fodio (1754-1817), the Muslim reformer from northern Nigeria, travelled to Niger in 1774 to study under Shaikh Jibril Umar.[9] The practice of travel continues today, little changed.

Although most Muslim children attend Qur'anic schools, attendance is not usually universal, even at the basic level. Students can attend and leave as they see fit, and registration is not compulsory. Students may leave schools and join others if they want particular subject specialisms.

The time at which classes in Islamic schools begin varies, and is arranged by individual teachers. Two sessions are usually held each day, one in the morning and the other in the afternoon. Sometimes a third evening session is held for pupils unable to attend during a day, often round a bonfire. The existence of evening sessions makes it possible for children to attend both primary and Qur'anic schools. Classes are held from Saturdays to Wednesday, with holidays on Thursdays and Fridays.

Parents can pay for their children's education by giving the teacher a gift or donation. If they cannot afford to do this they can still send their children to Qur'anic schools, and the children pay their way by working on the teacher's farm and by performing a number of other tasks such as collecting firewood. If a student from a very poor background wants to continue his education after Qur'anic school he may simply place himself in bondage to his teacher till he completes his studies and becomes a teacher himself.

Although the system we have just described is more common, some communities do charge a fixed fee for Qur'anic education. One can find a precedent for this far back in Islamic history. In the ninth century AD the Islamic specialist in law, Ibn Sahnun, wrote about the work of teachers. His writing, it has been suggested, shows that the practice of charging fees has already become well established, at least in Tunisia, by the ninth century AD.[10] Al Ghazali, however, who was a Persian (Iranian) authority and lived from AD 1058 to 1111, maintained that a Muslim teacher should not accept payment for teaching religious subjects, but could be paid for teaching such `extra' subjects as mathematics and medicine. The teaching of religious subjects, in Al Ghazali's opinion, was a personal duty of the believer and should be done without charging fees. This does not, of course, prevent the student from working for his Qur'anic teacher or the student's parents from giving the teacher gifts in recognition for what he has done for their child.

The Curriculum

There are basically two types of Islamic schools: the Qur'anic and the Ilm. These schools can be located almost anywhere, for instance under the shade of a tree, in a private house, or in a mosque. The Qur'anic school is equivalent to the Western primary school, and the Ilm school to the Western secondary school.

The age at which children begin Qur'anic school varies. Among the Dyula communities in Mali, Guinea, Burkina Faso and the Ivory Coast, the children usually begin Qur'anic school at the age of six, while among the Jakhanke in Senegal and the Gambia they may begin as early as three.[11] In some cases a formal ceremony takes place on the day a pupil is first admitted to the Qur'anic school. In Jakhanke schools the pupils' heads are shaved, and the words `in the name of Allah' are written on the palms of their hands.[12] The pupils lick the sacred writing while the ink is still fresh. Then they stretch out their hands to receive small balls of pounded grain which are taken home and given to first their fathers and then their mothers. This seems to indicate that the child has in some sense been `bought' by the teacher. At the later passing out ceremony the parents `buy back' their child.

There is some variation in the curriculum of the Qur'anic school, but in most of Islamic Africa it is strikingly uniform. Al Ghazali, the Iranian scholar whom we have just mentioned, had a profound influence on the curriculum of the Islamic schools and universities throughout the world. According to his philosophy, learning contains two elements. There is human reasoning, which involves an effort of mind and body, and there is divine illumination. The latter is more important, but it does not eliminate the need for clear thinking and careful observation. Al Ghazali also insisted on the need for physical exercise. He wrote: `After school the pupil must be allowed to play...To prevent play and to insist on continuous study leads to dullness in the heart, diminution in intelligence and unhappiness'.[13]

Ibn Khaldun had a similar philosophy. He recommended that knowledge should be linked to the capacity of the learner and should be imparted gradually. Ibn Khaldun felt that learning consisted in discovering and understanding the meaning of the spoken and written word, and in building up rules to show the connections between different meanings. This, Ibn Khaldun recognized, is a difficult task even for the advanced student. To the student in difficulty he offered this advice: `Abandon all artificial means of learning and appeal to your rational innate reason...Seek God's guidance which...illuminated the way of learners before you and taught them that which they knew not'.[14]

At the intellectual level, Qur'anic education chiefly consists of memorizing the Qur'an. For this purpose the Qur'an is usually divided into 60 parts. The method employed in memorization may vary slightly, and depends to some extent on the availability of blackboards, chalk, ink, and paper or slates. Of course it also depends on the competence, qualification and dedication of the teacher. In Jahanke (Senegambian) schools, the teacher begins with the letters of the Arabic alphabet, the vowel sounds, and writing.[15] Then, starting with the shortest chapter (*sura*), the pupil goes on to learn the Qu'ran by heart. Some pupils take five years to complete this process, and others take longer. The process of memorizing the Qur'an is divided into five stages, and completion of each stage is marked by a ceremony.

The curriculum of the Qur'anic school has often been strongly criticized. Ibn Khaldun, for example, felt that to restrict students to learning the Qur'an by heart was fruitless. He argued that `a person who [only] knows the Qur'an does not acquire the habit of the Arabic language. It will be his lot to be awkward in expression and to have little fluency in speaking'.[16] He seems to have preferred the method of instruction and the curriculum used in Qur'anic schools in Spain, where the emphasis was on poetry, composition, arithmetic and Arabic grammar, and where the student went on to detailed study of the Qur'an after having studied these subjects.[17] Other observes in more recent times have made similar judgements, suggesting that the instruction of Qur'anic schools has little pedagogical value, and pointing out that in many communities which do not use Arabic in everyday life the students do not even understand the meaning of the words they chant.

Some people, however, evaluate matters differently. For example Wilk's study of Islamic learning in Mali, Guinea, Burkina Faso, Ivory Coast and Ghana suggest that many of the criticisms of the Qur'anic schools are too severe. It points out that the schools do provide at least a grounding in Arabic, which can be built on by those who have the interest and ability, and maintains that `a talented and well taught pupil will rapidly acquire a command of Arabic, and in his early teens may be studying grammar and sytax, and reading basic works of law'.[18] The schools also teach students to respect their elders and the culture of which they are a part.

After Qur'anic school some students go on to an Ilm school of higher learning. In these schools students of all ages learn a wide range of Islamic literary, theological and legal subjects. Many Ilm schools trace their origins back several hundred years. Mauritania, for example, had Ilm schools as far back as the thirteenth century.

In the Ilm schools the formal curriculum consists of tafsir, which is basically the interpretation of the Qur'an, and the study of literature, much of which has been derived from Qur'anic commentary. The study of hadith is also a central part of the Ilm school curriculum. These traditions cover subjects such as marriage, divorce, inheritance, and personal conduct. They give the student a clear idea of the behaviour expected from an orthodox Muslim, and insight into how an Islamic society should be organized, administered and governed.

Ilm students also study *figh*, which is the theory of Islamic sacred law (*Shari'a*). The Qur'an is believed to contain the whole of the Shari'a, and many Muslims feel all that is required from the legal experts is interpretation and advice on how to apply it. For example the Qur'an prescribes the payment of an alms-tax, but since it does not specify how much or on what possessions, legal experts are needed to provide advice. The Shari'a occupies a central position in Islamic society, for upon it depends not only people's status, duties and rights, but also their prospects of eternal reward or punishment. The Shari'a moreover, is believed to apply not only to Muslims but to all mankind.

Ilm students also learn Arabic and about various types of literature. For example, the literature includes (*madih*), which mostly consists of praises addressed to the Prophet Mohammed. There is also *sira* literature in either prose or verse, which contains stories about the life of the Prophet. Wa'z is another type of literature which describes the Islamic notions of paradise and hell. Not every Ilm school teaches all these subjects. Some schools specialize, and gain the reputation as the best ones for the study of particular subjects or for groups of subjects.

In some parts of Africa, students who graduate from the Ilm school are allowed to wear a turban and are henceforth regarded as being the *ulama*, the men of learning. The title given to these people varies. Among the Malinke-speaking people of West Africa they are known as *Karamokos,* while among the Hausa they are called *malamai*. The Swahili word for teacher is *Mwalimu*. It no longer necessarily implies that the teacher is a Muslim, but the word has the same origin as ulama and malam.

When they complete Ilm school, some students go on to further studies in figh or hadith. Others become assistants to an established teacher, while others establish their own schools. Some may acquire positions as *imams* (prayer leaders in the local community) or judges.

The Education of Women in Islam

We have written so far as if learning and teaching were exclusively male activities in Muslim societies. Although in practice some Muslim societies have given this impression, it is certainly not the case in theory. On the right of Muslim women to receive education, Muslim scholars cite verses of the Qur'an such as Chapter 9 verse 39 and refer to several hadiths. They also point out that the Prophet Mohammed's wife Aisha was an Islamic scholar. Usuman dan Fodio, the Muslim reformer from Hausaland, spoke out against the neglect of women's education, and in Egypt in the nine-tenth century there were at least two strong protagonists of women's education. One was Rifa'ah al Tahtawi who called for the provision of the sane education facilities for women as for men, and the other was the lawyer Quasim Amin. In more recent times in Nigeria, Usman Nagogo, Isa Wali and Aminu Kano, among others, have emphasised the right and even the duty of women to be educated.

Women also have the right to teach. Usuman dan Fodio wrote of Muslim widows in Nigeria being employed by the wealthy to teach their families and added that they also had `a collection of children mainly girls to teach in their homes in addition to teaching the grown-ups'.[19] Usumadan dan Fodio's own daughter Khadija gave lessons on Islamic law and the Qur'an, and wrote poetry. His other daughter Asama'u Nana also wrote poetry and taught Islamic religious knowledge. In this century there have been several well-known Muslim women teachers in Nigeria. Among them were Malama Dada in Kano, who taught both men and women, and Malama Atika from Zaria. In 1977 a Women's Arabic Teachers' College was opened in Kano specifically to train female teachers of Islamic religious knowledge.[20] Many Muslims accept, however, that in general there has either been serious neglect or at the very least insufficient attention given to the subject of women's education.[21]

Teacher-Student Relations in the Islamic Education System

Although many Qur'anic teachers are understanding and gentle with their pupils, the majority are commonly said to be harsh taskmasters who punish students severely. Recalling his own education, for example, Sanneh refers to one time he incurred his teacher's displeasure:

> He called me one morning and asked whether I had finished reciting the portion of the Koran he had copied out on my slate the previous day. I said I had memorised it, and when he asked me to recite it in front of him I did so, whereupon he directed me to wash off the old material so that my slate was clean and ready for the new material. During our midday recitations he asked if I had washed my slate. When I answered `Yes', he asked me to bring it to him. I brought the wooden slate to him, but the Arabic characters were still faintly visible on it. That was not really my fault because the ink we used for writing was manufactured by ourselves, and we obtained it by scraping the undersides of cooking pots. There was not always a plentiful supply of the substance, so that we often ended by scraping off more than just the soft black soot on the surface. The harder material was difficult to remove once it had dried on the wooden slates, and this is what had happened in my case. I had scrubbed the stubborn surface with all my strength but had not realised that the wet surface concealed the faint characters which, I must admit, were clearly visible after I had dried the slate.
>
> Teacher was furious...He pulled both my ears and I crawled on the ground towards him...With my two ears firmly in his hand he could balance me on either side of him as he pleased. He swayed me to the right at arms's length, and when I tried to recover my balance, he closed in with a powerful left-hand swipe. Then he grabbed me by the ears again, pinched me tightly and shook me firmly as if to test his grasp on the substance of power.[22]

Sanneh also records that this type of treatment was supported by his father, who felt that one of the chief purposes of the Qur'anic school was to instil discipline and respect. Such an attitude, one might add, is not uncommon.

Nevertheless, harsh aspects of discipline have not always been approved. Al Ghazali, who was one of the greatest of all Islamic educational theorists, stated that the Islamic teacher was the spiritual father of his students and should give advice rather than reproof, correcting moral lapes `through hinting rather than direct prohibition'.[23] Likewise Ibn

Khadldun felt that: `Severe punishment in the course of instruction does harm to the student, especially to little children....It makes them oppressed and causes them to lose energy. It makes them lazy and induces them to lie and be insincere.'[24] Ibn Khaldun did not rule out corporal punishment entirely, but recommended that `if children must be beaten, their educator must not strike them more than three times'.[25] Many present-day educators agree with this view, and would like the atmosphere of Qur'anic schools to be based much more on confidence than fear.

The Status and Public Role of the Islamic Teacher

Teachers are obviously indispensable in Islamic societies, because the transmission of knowledge of the Qur'an, hadith, Shari'a and Arabic is essential to the Islamic religion and way of life. Islamic teachers generally hold a high social status because of their learning their ability to make charms and to divine. At the same time, however, Islamic tradition expects them to live simply and without ostentation. Of course the situation could hardly be otherwise, given that that Islamic teachers have a duty to teach religious knowledge without being paid for it.

In the past, and still in many parts of Africa today, very few books existed. This meant that the Islamic teacher was effectively the only library available to students. Even where there are books today, the teacher is widely seen as the only one capable of guiding students to and through them. Knowledge, it is widely believed, requires a mediator who has thought about it and internalized it in his memory. Among Muslims there exists a belief that `an independent approach to the written word is fraught with mystical dangers'.[26] The teacher is therefore needed to interpret and transmit the knowledge.

The status of Islamic teachers may be illustrated by comments made by some young men in Northern Nigeria. These youths stated that when their teacher was present, they never drank alcohol, smoked, roamed about with women, or wore European or tight clothes. Tight clothes, they explained, were unacceptable because `by wearing them you show your body'. They said that if their teacher found them out, he would scold them tell their parents, and inform the whole village of their bad behaviour.[27]

This situation is changing, however, and the status of the Islamic teacher is generally deteriorating. The decline is being slowed by the work of a few institutions. The Islamic Institute in Dakar, for example, was opened in 1974 and has greatly improved the qualifications and skills of teachers in the Islamic schools of Senegal. However, many youth are affected by Western culture and technology, and in general they do not give Islamic teachers as much respect as their counterparts did in former times.

The Goals and Relevance of Islamic Education

Although we have already said a great deal about the goals and relevance of Islamic education, it is useful to enlarge on some issues and to pull threads together. First, we should distinguish between three types of goals in the system: instrumental, expressive and normative.

Goals are instrumental when they are merely the means, or instrument, for achieving something else. For example, pupils may see education just as a way to get certificates, which in turn they can use to get jobs. Education becomes simply a means to a particular end for the individual concerned. Thus instrumental goals generally encourage students to be individualistic and competitive rather than to cooperate and work in groups.

In contrast, expressive goals seek to create unity, cohesion, equality and common identity among students. They are expressive because they express some ideal. And normative goals are concerned with the development of standard beliefs and patterns of behaviour through learning.

We have already mentioned that the Islamic system places less emphasis on examinations and diplomas than does the Western system. In general, therefore, it places less emphasis on instrumental goals and more on expressive and normative ones than does the Western system. Ibn Khaldu stressed the importance of normative goals when he stated:`The basis of all the traditional sciences is the legal material of the Qur'an and the Sunna, which is the law given us by God and his messenger.'[28]

Secondly, we should ask what relevance, if any, the Islamic education system has for modern African states striving to overcome the problems of underdevelopment. Several authors have argued that Islam hinders development, and we should consider whether their views are reasonable or not.

Max Weber was one critic of Islam. He arguments were partly based on the low priority that Islam places on instrumental goals.[29] He suggested that the religion was dominated by a warlike morality, and felt that its emphasis on conflict and its rigid hold over its members restricted the growth of capitalist attitudes and business activities. He contrasted this with the outlook of Protestant Christianity which, he said, was likely to be much more competitive and individualistic. Weber also felt that Islam encouraged conservative economic and political systems to remain so and that many of the systems suffered from contradictions which were only occasionally challenged by radical forces.

This view was largely shared by Marx and Engels, who described Islam as `anti-developmental' and `anti-modernizing'. Engels maintained that the French conquest of Algeria was `an important and fortunate fact for the progress of civilisation', and he claimed that the French brought `industry, order and at least relative enlightenment', to a `barbarous' society.[30] Marx and Engels described capitalism as a dynamic force which introduced necessary changes into stagnant societies in danger of extinction. They viewed Islamic administrative structures as rigid and inflexible, in contrast to what they considered the progressive and civilised structures of the colonising powers.

More recently, Claude Lévi-Strauss has criticised the legal and inflexible philosophy of Islam. He has argued that Islam is set in contemplation of a society which only existed many centuries ago, and that it attempts to solve the problems of the modern world with arguments, logic and solutions which are no longer relevant.[31]

These views should not necessarily be accepted, however. Weber's idea that Islam is dominated by a warrior class whose life-style and interests determine its philosophical and religious outlook is certainly a misinterpretation. As Ali Mazrui has pointed out, the reason why Islam did not encourage attitudes similar to the Christian capitalists was not because it was dominated by a warrior ethic but because it was dominated by the expressive goals of communal loyalty to members of the family and to members of the same religious group. Mazrui also points out that the Islamic laws of inheritance prevented accumulation of capital and the growth of large estates in a way that did not occur among the Christians.[32]

Moreover, these factors do not necessarily make Islam an `anti-modernizing' force. Certainly the religion discourages individualism and accumulation of wealth and property. However, if `modernity' is considered to include socialism and communalism, Islam is very progressive.

Further, not all historians and sociologists agree with Marx and Engels. Two Nigerian historians, for example, claim that Islam, albeit unintentionally, `brought to Nigeria the concept of a nation state transcending the personal bounds of loyalty to clan, a traditional ruler, or particular locality'.[33] The aim of the nineteenth-century Muslim reformers in West Africa—Usuman dan Fodio in Northern Nigeria, and Al-Hajj Umar and Ma Ba Diakhou in the Senegambia to name but three—was `ecumenical'. Their objective was to re-create the Muslim community of the time of the first four Caliphs, which was an era known as the `Golden Age of Islam'. One consequence of their work was the emergence of `larger political systems with new economic opportunities and the establishment of new religious obligations and social values'.[34] From this perspective, Islam in West Africa was a more significant revolutionary force than was the attempt inspired by Christian ideals to substitute legitimate commerce for the slave trade.[35]

In the Senegambia there has also existed a strong alliance between the Islamic brotherhoods and the government, which has helped develop the groundnut economy, the transport network and the system of cooperatives. The leader of Mouride brotherhood, Ahmadu Bamba, transformed senegambian Islam in the early years of the present century by his teaching about the `sanctification of labour'.[36] According to Bamba, work was more important than prayer. This philosophy also influenced the Tijaniyya brotherhood, who comprised over a million people.

Finally, it is worth summarizing the way Muslims expect the Islamic education system to encourage community and national development in Africa. First, they suggest that the real problems of nation building and underdevelopment have an important moral dimension. As one Nigerian Muslim expressed it when commenting on the proposal for a new constitution in his country: `the bitter truth is that our nation is in dire need of complete mobilization more than anything else....I bet even if "Operation Feed the Nation" results in plenty of food in the country, the nation at large will never benefit from it unless and until attitudes change. And it is only through moral and spiritual training that the people can change for good.'[37] Many Muslims thus believe that Islam can make a major contribution to development by strengthening the morals of the nation.

Secondly, many Muslims argue that Islam can provide community, society, dignity and personal identity in the chaos created by industrialization. The education system, they suggest, is an essential instrument for achieving this. Thirdly, many people claim that Islamic Law is an effective weapon against such crimes as murder, theft and rape, which are becoming more common with industrialization. They also claim that Islam's commercial, financial and economic code of practices would, if implemented, rid Africa of the worst abuses of the capitalist system. Finally, emphasizing that Islam is independent of both Marxism and Western capitalism, some Muslims claim that the divinely inspired Islamic socialist system is the most appropriate one of the developing nations of Africa. This, they say, is because people will only accept a socialist ideology that contains a supernatural dimension. These arguments may not be universally applicable, but they are important and should be noted.

We can now turn to a detailed consideration of the development of Islamic education in Nigeria, which has a very large and diverse Muslim population. It is instructive to see how Islamic education has responded to the challenges posed by Western education and modernization.

Case Study: Islamic Education in Nigeria

The Islamic education system has a long history in Nigeria, especially in the north. For example, it has existed for many centuries in the northern districts of Borno, Kano and Katsina, and was only seriously challenged in recent times. N'gazargamu, the former capital of the Borno Kingdom, had four central mosques in the seventeenth century, all of which ran Qur'anic schools. The rulers possessed excellent libraries, and gave Muslim scholars considerable privileges, including exemption from tax and military service. Islamic teachers had considerable moral and religious authority in the towns and villages.

The Islamic reform movement, also known as the Sokoto jihad (holy war), began in the eighteenth century and contributed a great deal to Islamic education in northern Nigeria. Literacy in Arabic was spread over a wide area, and this made it possible for many more people to read the Qur'an. The reform movement also led to greater concern over the education of women, to the establishment of Islamic schools, and to the training of Islamic teachers.

In northern Nigeria a sound Islamic education became one of the principal vehicles of upward social mobility, through which many people became clerks, scribes and judges. This has to be taken into consideration when assessing the Muslim response to Western education. So also does the fact that for Muslims an Islamic education system was not simply an option that could be replaced with another system, even if the latter appeared to be more relevant and effective. The establishment and maintenance of Islamic schools was a divine obligation. Moreover, the institution were considered an integral part of Muslim society and the most important means of sustaining Islamic faith and culture. For these reasons a very large proportion of Nigerian Muslims, especially in the north, continue to put great emphasis on Islamic education.[38]

In the mid-1960s there were 27,600 Quar'anic schools in northern Nigeria, and 2,800 Ilm schools.[39] Some of them were long established, dating back to the time of Shaikh Usuman dan Fodio (1754-1817), and many, like the Gwarrio Fara Ilm school in Zaria city, had gained a reputation for excellence that drew pupils from all parts of northern Nigeria.

Attempts at Reform and Modernization

Usuman dan Fodio's movement was primarily concerned with improving the religious and intellectual climate in Hausaland, which required the reform and modernization of the education system.[40] This objective was taken up again in the colonial era, and has received considerable attention since then. Reform, and modernization, of course, have meant different things to different people in different historical circumstances.

One approach to modernization and reform adopted by the government during the colonial era was to integrate the Islamic and Western systems of education. The principal idea was to introduce into Islamic curriculum a limited number of new subjects, particularly arithmetic and literacy in the Roman script. This approach, adopted in both northern and southern Nigeria, was considered to have two main advantages. First it avoided the expense of operating the Islamic and Western education systems separately, and second the system remained recognizably Islamic and it was therefore much easier for at least some Muslims to adapt to Western education.[41] The government also felt that the strategy was a good way to introduce new teaching methods into the Islamic education system.

In southern Nigeria, the government at the end of the last century attempted to avoid the close association of Western education with the work of Christian missionaries by sponsoring several schools for Muslims in which Western subjects were taught alongside the Islamic sciences.

Schools were opened in Lagos in 1896, at Badagry in 1898, and at Epe in 1899. Before this date no Epe Muslim had ever attended a school in which Western subjects formed part of the syllabus, but 150 enrolled when the government Muslim school was opened.[42] The system was not given adequate financial backing, however, and collapsed within a few years.

More important efforts at integration have also been made by several Islamic societies. In some respects, Muslims have found themselves in a dilemma. If their children attend Western, Christian schools they might abandon Islam. On the other hand if they attend Muslim schools which teach only Islamic subjects, their children would not have the skills demanded in a society undergoing rapid modernization. To resolve this dilemma the Ansar-ud-Deen society was established in 1923. By 1960 it had a membership of 50,000 and had opened over 200 primary schools plus several secondary schools and teachers' colleges.[43]

The ahmadiyya movement, which emerged in India in the 1880s and made its first contacts with Nigeria in 1911, has similar educational objectives to the Ansar-ud-Deen society and has also had a major impact.[44] The movement has inspired its followers to respond positively to the challenge of Western education by establishing Islamic schools which include Western subjects in the curriculum and use Western styles of teaching. Ahmadiyya schools have been open in Lagos, Ibadan, Ijebu-Ode, Jos, Kano and other Nigerian cities, and the movements' influence in education has spread to Sierra Leone, Liberia, Ghana, the Gambia and Mail.[45]

However, the Ahmadiyya movement is regarded by Sunni Muslims as heretical, because it teaches that its founder, Ghulam Ahmad, was the promised Messiah and Mahdi. This belief is unacceptable to orthodox Muslims, who believe that Mohammed was the last of the prophets. The rejection of the Ahmadiyya beliefs has been one reason why some orthodox Muslims have also rejected attempts to integrate Western and Islamic education, for they associate one with the other. Other leaders have focused on the curriculum, and have criticized what they consider to be the neglect of Arabic and Islamic education. Ādam 'Ab Allah al-Ilūri from southern Nigeria, and Ibrahim Niass, who was himself Senegalese but who led the `reformed' Tijaniyya movement which has many followers in northern Nigeria, were among the critics.[46]

It was, moreover, especially clear in the case of the unorthodox Ahmadiyya movement that the reform and modernization of the Islamic education system was not simply a matter of educational method and the introduction into the curriculum of Western subjects. It also involved doctrinal issues and questions concerning the correct practice of the faith. In other cases, as we shall see, it would involve political matters.

We can now turn again to northern Nigeria, where the government at first decided to leave the Islamic education system intact and to build up alongside a separate government-controlled Western education system. Then in the 1920s the attempt at integration got under way. Arabic became part of the curriculum in most government middle schools in the early 1930s, and at the same time provision was made for Qur'anic instruction in all schools in northern Nigeria. Integration at a high level of the education system began with the establishment of the Shahuci judicial school in Kano in 1928. This institution aimed to broaden the education of malams from Kano and elsewhere, many of whom were employed in the Shari'a courts. Instruction was in Hausa and Arabic, and arithmetic and a small amount of English were taught alongside the traditional Islamic subjects. Then in 1934 the government opened the Kano Law School, which in 1947 became the Kano School for Arabic Studies. At the outset the Kano Law School taught all the Islamic sciences and arithmetic, and drew its students from all over norther Nigeria.

It was after the Second World War that some of the most interesting and significant efforts were made to reform and modernize the Islamic education system in the north. Once again it was Muslims themselves who led the way. Aminu Kano, for example, was a qualified teacher in both the Islamic and Western education systems, and for many years until his death in 1983 was a prominent politician. Aminu opened a school in Kano in 1950. Persuaded that `modern' teaching methods could achieve better results in much less time, he provided his pupils with lessons in the Qur'an and Abrabic in the first year, and in the second year alongside these subjects he introduced arithmetic and literacy in the Roman script. This made it unnecessary for children to transfer from the Qur'anic school to an elementary or primary school.

These schools proved popular at first, and in the 1950s around 60 were established throughout northern Nigeria. However political opponents came to see them as a challenge, and through hostile campaigning forced the majority to close down.[47] The situation improved when Sir Ahmadu Bello, premier of Northern Nigeria (1960-1966) set about the reform of the Qur'anic school system. A special ministerial committee, set up to consider the reform recommended that Qur'anic schools be organized into classes according to age, year of entry and ability of the pupils, and that arithmetic and literacy in the Roman script should be included in the syllabus alongside the study of the Qur'an and Arabic. Schools which complied with these recommendations were given financial incentives to improve their buildings and equipment, and an honorarium for the teachers (malams). Very little further development took place after the assassination of Akhmadu Bello in 1966, however, and in practice only a few schools benefitted from the financial assistance.

Reforms were also attempted at the level of the Ilm schools. These reforms were in many respects simply an extension to the secondary level of the educational model developed by Aminu Kano. They formed part of what has come to be known as the Islamiyya school system, a system proposed by the Northern Muslim Congress (NMC) which was established in Kano in 1950.[48] Later in the 1960s Ahmadu Bello's reforms included a provision for the payment of grants to Ilm schools that included English and Hausa in the curriculum. Small grants were also made available for the building of classrooms and the partial payment of salaries of qualified teachers.[49]

By the late 1970s some 65 Islamiyya schools had been established in northern Nigeria, a majority of them in Kano, by individuals, societies and whole communities concerned for the education and general welfare of the young. They adopted a five day week from Saturday to Wednesday. Some Islamiyya schools offered four year courses while others made provision of courses lasting six or even seven years. In this way they replicated the middle school and the secondary school systems. The schools tended to attract a relatively large number of female students, for they offered an acceptable alternative to many parents anxious about the values of the other school systems.

In some instances the problems encountered in educating girls were overcome by the establishment of single sex schools such as the Girls' Grammar School in Ibadan founded in the 1950s by Alhaja Humana Alaga, leader of the Isabatudeen (Band of Religious Enthusiasts) society. Included in the curriculum alongside Islamic knowledge were Arabic, English language and literature, history, geography and domestic science. Elaborating on the reasons for establishing this school, Alhaja Humana spoke of the difficulties she encountered in getting her own daughters into mission-run schools, of the need to give Muslims greater confidence in themselves, and of her desire to raise the status of Muslim women.[50]

In both the north and the south, however, attempts at modernizing the Qur'anic and other tiers of the Islamic education system did not meet with the approval of the Muslims. Ibrahim Niass, the Senegalese Muslim leader with a large following among members of the `reformed' Tijaniyya brotherhood, saw no need for Western education and insisted that Arabic literacy and religious education alone were indispensable for achieving the aims of the brotherhood.[51] Niass and his representatives in Nigeria did much from the 1950s, onwards to encourage Islamic education, the education of Muslim women, and the spread of literacy in Arabic and Hausa.

An institution which played a central role in this spread of literacy in Arabic and Hausa in northern Nigeria was the Zawiya system developed by both the Tijaniyya and Qaderiyya brotherhood. The Zawiya serves a number of functions and is to be found in both urban and rural areas. It is in essence a centre where members of a brotherhood, travelling from one town or village to another can obtain acommodation. It also functions as a school. In the urban areas like Kano city the Zawiya may provide advanced classes in Islamic studies, and in rural areas a basic training in the fundamentals of Islamic faith and practice. Moreover, in both cases the Zawiya may also function as a library and an extremely important channel of communication. To take as an example the `reformed' Tijaniyya led by Ibrahim Niass, an extensive Zawiya network was established across northern Nigeria and indeed throughout West Africa, making possible the spread of literacy in Arabic, and Hausa in the Nigerian context, on a very wide scale.[52]

The Response to UPE

One of the strongest recent challenges to the Islamic system of education has come from a campaign for Universal Primary Education (UPE), which was launched in 1976. Here we will concentrate on the Muslim reactions in northern Nigeria, particularly in Bauchi, Gongola, Sokoto and Kano States. While discussing this reaction it is worth bearing in mind some of the observations already made about the long and respected tradition of Islamic education in these areas. The section is chiefly based on research by Clarke and by Bray during the 1970s.[53]

In all northern states, there had been considerable educational expansion in the decade before the launching of UPE. In the North Eastern State 200,000 children were attending primary school in 1975, which was a 42 per cent increase on the 1968 figure. The number of secondary school pupils increased by an even greater percentage, for in 1975 11,000 pupils attended 48 secondary schools, compared with 3,400 pupils in 19 secondary schools in 1968. The same upward trend was observed in the teacher training sector. Both Bauchi and Gongola States, therefore, which formed part of North Eastern State until 1976, had experienced rapid educational development and expansion. The picture was duplicated in the other states.

When UPE was launched in 1976, even more people entered primary schools, secondary schools and teacher training colleges. In Bauchi State, for example, 300,000 primary school pupils enrolled in September 1976 compared with 132,000 in September 1975. In Sokoto State about 40 per cent, i.e. about 80,000 of the state's six-year-old children signed on for UPE. In Kano Sate Grade 1 enrolment in 1976 was nearly five times as big as it had been in 1975. In these states and throughout the federation, huge sums of money were spent on the scheme. This fact reflected the high priority attached to it for national development.

Many Muslims interviewed felt that the effects of the scheme on Islamic society would be deep and widespread. They maintained, for example, that the Qur'anic education system, the Islamic ethical and religious system, male and female roles, the nature of parenthood, and models of marriage and authority would be changed. It was argued that different types of knowledge, of work ethic and of educational psychology would be introduced. In turn, these could threaten the role and livelihood of malams.

The common practice among many Muslims in northern Nigeria, especially in the rural areas, is for a father to give his daughter in marriage when she is about twelve years of age. A girl, ideally, should experience her first menstruation in her husband's home and should be married before her sexual potential is fully developed. Underlying this attitude is the fear of a possible conception outside wedlock. Lost virginity and illegitimacy are considered to be more the result of parental irresponsibility than the outcome of `uncontrolled' sex. Thus the implication for a father of such developments can be serious. He may, for example, be prevented from acquiring a position of authority in the community, for a man is often chosen for such a position on the basis of his ability to control, manage and rear his family correctly. To send a daughter to school—the Western-type school—increases in the minds of many Muslim parents the risk, if she stays at school beyond Primary 4, of losing her virginity. Loss of virginity makes it more difficult, many argue, to find a husband for a girl. A venerable malam in Bauchi State stated that to send a girl to school beyond Class 4 of primary school was `not a safe practice'. His three daughters would not, he affirmed, continue on at a school beyond this stage.

`Western' education would not only lead to a higher incidence of loss of virginity and its attendant consequences, but also, it was argued, undermine the system purdah, which is a fairly widespread practice in norther Nigeria. Muslim girls who went to schools attended by pupils of variety of different religions, it was argued, would want to imitate the ways of non-Muslims and thus would refuse to accept early marriage and seclusion. Muslims in other parts of Nigeria have no such fears on this score, for they have never accepted seclusion as an integral part of the Prophet's teaching or the tradition of Islam. In the north also, some of the educated Muslim élite argue against the practice of purdah, stating this it has no basis in `pure' Islam. What the `purists' contend is that women should not be confined to the home or prevented from engaging in occupations such as teaching and nursing outside the home. This does not mean, however, that there should be unrestricted intercourse between men and women or the indiscriminate adoption by the latter of `masculine roles and functions to which they are not naturally suited'. The idea of a person being fashioned by nature was widespread among the Muslims interviewed.

Many rural and urban Muslims did not accept the opinion of some of the educated élite with regard to purdah. For the former, sending girls to school would destroy a valuable tradition. Secluded women play a very significant role in rural communities with the aid of their children. These women carry on house trade in food stuffs such as groundnut oil, boiled cassava, hard-boiled eggs and other snacks. Some engage in the retail trade in such items as pepper, salt and vegetables. In both types of trade children act as `go-betweens', playing a crucial role in linking the secluded women with their customers and suppliers. Placing the children in school meant depriving women in purdah of their `go-betweens' for a considerable part of every day. The family could thus suffer a considerable decline in income, and the village community could be deprived of important `social services'. The bicycle mechanics, the blacksmiths, the cobblers, butchers and tailors in many village communities have come to rely on such `house trade' for their breakfast, lunch and supper.

Western education can lead to certain other unacceptable `innovations'. It is already altering the accepted view held by the male members of society of the `ideal' wife and bringing about a change in the prescribed roles of women which have been rigidly defined by religion and custom. Educated male members of society, for example, frequently say that they cannot mary an illiterate: they require a `social wife'. As some students expressed it: `a wife must be able to entertain friends, speak to them, talk about current affairs, talk sensibly at parties, purchase the books one needs, etc.'Thus women must be educated—though not to the same level as the men—and must appear in public. Some parents, fathers in particular, and malams view of all these changes with alarm. Women, they claimed, would begin to behave like men, to determine their role in society, to regulate the dispensing of their services, to act independently. Thus, they felt UPE would radically alter the male-held conscious model of the ideal woman and wife. Muslim men, particularly in the rural areas as has been indicated, saw the ideal woman as submissive, obedient and content to enjoy reflected status from her husband. It is the men not the women who have the right to participate in public life and who monopolize public affairs. Women are almost entirely excluded from public ritual, worship and politics. According to some Muslim men, however, an educated woman would want to enter public life, thus usurping male roles and functions, and undermining the social order.

Islam is considered to be a blueprint of the social order. As one Muslim graduate stated, `the Islamic religion totally organizes society'. He suggested that it sets out the criteria for the correct relationships between ruler and ruled, between parents and children: `Islam maintains order and unity and lays down strict guidelines for what is considered to be good and bad. Changes brought by the introduction of a Western system of education will lead to alterations in the entire life style of Muslims.'

Though they are not opposed to education *per se*, and indeed they highly value the Qur'anic system of education, many Muslims interviewed found it difficult to see what beneficial effects Western education might have on their society. The Muslim chief of Luishi village near Bauchi town thought that his daughter might have an easier and better life as a result of her Western education. However, he was an exception. Some malams still regarded the Western-type school as an instrument of Christian evangelization. This, it would appear, is not simply on account of the sometimes real sometimes apparent alliances between missionaries and colonialism, but also a consequence of the different theory of knowledge, educational psychology and pedagogical approach held by Muslims.

With some exceptions,[54] UPE also threatened the specific livelihood of the malams. As have noted, malams have had strong control over Muslim children to the extent of being able to take them from place to place without the permission of parents. Traditionally, children have also worked on their malams' farms, and to replace this with paid labourers would be very costly. With the full implementation of UPE, which would eventually become enforceable by law, many malams believed that the number of pupils attending Qur'anic school would drop considerably, thus depriving them of their responsibility, weakening their authority, and leading indirectly to a decline in their standard of living.

In 1977 indeed, when the UPE scheme was barely a year old, some malams stated that they had already experienced some of these effects. Malam Dahiru had only three pupils that year. They were supposed to attend his Qur'anic school after primary school classes, but the malam reported that they were too tired either to learn anything or to work on his farm. Malam Ahmadu, a colleague of Malam Dahiru, had only 12 pupils in his Qur'anic school in 1977, whereas he used to have 40. He explained that with the introduction of Western education and the other social and economic changes taking place in society, Qur'anic education was now seen as non-functional and irrelevant in relation to job opportunities and the new expectations of the young.

Malams reacted to these threats in different ways. Some launched a mini-jihad against the UPE scheme, while other offered to participate in the scheme after the adoption by the authorities of an `appeasement strategy'. Provisions were made for malams to give instruction in Islam and Arabic Studies in the primary schools. However, the teaching in primary schools posed problems for the malams. Few of them were trained in the educational methods and techniques used by other teachers, and they suffered problems of status with the other staff. Though the policy both ensured that Islamic religious knowledge was taught in schools and helped provide teachers for UPE, therefore, it encountered problems.

Finally, we should consider the extent to which the widespread resistance to the UPE scheme, which the national and state government politicians considered to be a key instrument in nation building, can be viewed as reactionary and hindrance to national development. There would appear to be an inverse relationship between the response of many Muslims to UPE and the process of nation building. Many older Muslims appear to be convinced that traditional Islamic education can produce better Muslims that the Western system, and that it ought to be a part of whatever future educational system is imposed.

This view is supported, though not without qualifications, by third generation Muslims who have been educated along Western lines. They acknowledge that the Islamic system of education produces a good Hausa Muslim but they believe that the education system should also produce full Nigerian citizens and that the traditional system cannot do this on its own. Likewise, second generation Muslims educated along Western lines do not want to be Hausa Muslims only but also to be Nigerian citizens. Both of these groups add that some of the protests against UPE are unfounded. Many muslims who have been educated in Western schools are, they say, leading exemplary lives, teaching in rural areas and spreading Islam by example and learning. Muslim girls who have attended primary and secondary school, they maintain, are no more lax or promiscuous than those who have not. They also point out that the belief that a girl who is married off at twelve accepts her role in life and is faithful to it without protest is misleading.

Second and third generation Muslims and others educated in Western schools hold the view that if the nation, and Islam too, is to develop, the skills and techniques required for organizing and administering a modern state must be acquired. In the past Muslims possessed these assets, but now things have changed and the historical process cannot be reversed. They argue, with force, that the Islamic and Western systems of education must be integrated.

Questions and Project Work

1. Why in your view have Muslims placed so much emphasis on Islamic education?

2. What are the distinguishing features and goals of the Islamic education system?

3. Discuss the Muslim response to Western education in Nigeria.

4. Suggest ways in which the Islamic and Western education systems might be more fully integrated. Where possible discuss this matter with teachers, parents and educational planners in your area. As well as putting forward proposals, discuss the obstacles to integration.

Notes

1. Handun, S. and King, N. *Ibn Battuta in black Africa*. Rex Collings, London 1975, p. 12.
2. Clarke, P.B. *West Africa and Islam. A history of Religious Development from the 8th to the 20th Century*. Edward Arnold, London 1982, Chaps. 1 and 2.
3. Johnson, R.W. `Educational Progress and Retrogression in Guinea (1900-1943)' in Brown, G.N. and Hiskett, M. (eds.) *Conflict and Harmony in Education in Tropical Africa*. George, Allen and Unwin, London 1975, p. 223.
4. Hodgkin, T. `Scholars and Revolutionary Tradition: Vietnam and West Africa'. *Oxford Review of Education*, Vol. 2, No. 1, 1972, p.122.
5. Tibawi, A.L. *Islamic Education*. Luzac, London (2nd edition) 1979, p. 38.
6. Ibid., p. 24.
7. Ibid.
8. Ibn Khaldun *The Muqaddimah: An Introduction to History*. Translated from the Arabic by Rosenthal, F., edited and abridged by Danwood, N.J., Routledge and Kegan Paul, London 1967, p. 426.
9. Hiskett, M. *The Sword of truth. The Life and Times of Shehu Usuman dan Fodio*. Oxford University Press, New York and London 1973, p. 23.
10. Tibawi, op. cit., p. 40.
11. Wilks, I. `Islamic Learning in the Western Sudan' in Goody, J. (ed.) *Literacy in Traditional Societies*. Cambridge University Press, Cambridge 1968.
12. Sanneh, L. *The Jahanke*. International African Institute, London 1979, Ch. 7 and passim.
13. Tibawi, op. cit., p. 41.
14. Ibid., p. 43.
15. Sanneh, op. cit., p. 154. See also Sanneh, L. `The Islamic Education

of an African Child: Stresses and Tensions' in Brown, G.N. and Hiskett, M. (eds.) *Conflict and Harmony in Education in Tropical Africa*. George, Allen and Unwin. London 1975, p. 170.
16. Ibn Khaldun, op. cit., p. 423.
17. Ibid., pp. 423-4.
18. Wilks, op. cit., p. 166.
19. Quoted in Hodgkin, T. (ed.) *Nigerian Perspectives*. Oxford University Press, Oxford 1975, pp. 254-5.
20. Bray, M. *Universal Primary Education in Nigeria. A Study of Kano State*. Routledge and Kegan Paul, London 1981, p. 120.
21. e.g. Tibawi, op. cit., pp. 79-80 and passim; Adamu, Haroun Al-Rashid *The North and Nigerian Unity*. Daily Times Press, Lagos 1973, p. 36.
22. Sanneh, `The Islamic Education of an African Child', op. cit., pp. 179-80.
23. Tibawi, op. cit., p. 40.
24. Ibn Khaldun, op. cit., p. 425.
25. Ibid.
26. Goody, op. cit., p. 13.
27. Clarke, P.B., Research notes. Baunchi, Nigeria, 1974-75 and 1981.
28. Ibn Khaldun, op. cit., p. 344.
29. Turner, B.R. *Weber and Islam*, Routledge and Kegan Paul, London 1974.
30. Engels, F. `Defence of Progressive Imperialism in Algeria' in Fever, L.S. (ed.) *Marx and Engels: Basic Writings on Politics and Philosophy*. Fontan Collins, London 1969, pp. 488-9.
31. Lévi-Strauss, C. *Tristes Tropiques*. Plon, Paris 1958, p. 438.
32. Mazrui, A.A. *Political Values and the Educated Class in Africa*. Heinemann, London 1978, pp. 139-42.
33. Ade Ajayi, J.F. and Oloruntimehin, B,O, `West Africa in the Anti-Slave Trade Era' in 'Flint, J.E. (ed.) *Cambridge History of Africa*, Vol. 5. Cambridge University Press, Cambridge 1976.
34. Ibid.
35. Ibid.
36. Cruise O'Brien, D. *The Mourides of Senegal*. Oxford University Press, Oxford 1971.
37. *New Nigerian*, 11/5/1976.
38. Bishop, V.S. `Language Acquisition and Value Change in Kano

Urban Area' in Paden, J.N. (ed.) *Values, Identities and National Integration: Empirical Research in Africa.* Northwestern University Press, Evanston 1980, pp. 191ff.

39. Paden, J.N. *Religion and Political Culture in Kano.* University of California Press, Berkeley 1973, p. 58. See also Bray, op. cit., pp. 56ff; and Stephens, D.G. `A Study of teacher Education and Attitudes over Two Generations in Kano Metropolitan Area of Northern Nigeria'. Ph.D. thesis, University of Exeter 1982, pp. 55-66.
40. Usman, Y.B. (ed.) *Studies in the History of the Sokoto Caliphate.* Dept. of History, Ahmadu Bello University, Zaria/Sokoto State History Bureau, Sokoto, n.d.
41. Clarke, op. cit., p. 225.
42. Gbademosi, T.O. *The Growth of Islam among the Yoruba.* Longman, London 1978, pp. 102ff.
43. Clarke, op. cit., p. 225.
44. Fisher, H.J. `The Modernization of Islamic Education in Sierra Leone, Gambia and Liberia: Religion and Language' in Brown, G.N. and Hiskett, M. (eds.) *Conflict and Harmony in Education in Tropical Africa*, George, Allen and Unwin, London 1975, p. 187.
45. Ibid., pp. 188ff.
46. See Ryan, P.J. *Imale: Yoruba Participation in the Muslim Tradition.* Scholars Press, Missoula, Montana 1978, pp. 201ff. for reactions to modernizing trends in western Nigeria. See Paden *Religion and Political Culture in Kano* op. cit. pp. 140ff. for reaction in the north.
47. Bray, op. cit., p. 60.
48. Paden, *Religion and Political Culture in Kano*, op. cit., p. 141.
49. Bray, op. cit., p. 62.
50. Clarke, op. cit., p. 225.
51. Paden, *Religion and Political Culture in Kano*, op. cit., p. 140.
52. Ibid., pp. 141-2.
53. The research by Clarke was carried out over a number of years, beginning in Bauchi State in 1974. It has been partially reported in Clarke, P.B. `Islam, Education and Development Process in Nigeria'. *Comparative Education*, Vol. 14 No.2, 1978. The research by Bray was carried out over a number of years, beginning in Kano State in 1976, and has been mostly reported in Bray, op. cit.
55. See Bray, op. cit., pp. 147-8.

— 4 —
An African Initiative in Education

Felix K. Ekechi

Introduction

Scholarship on the evolution and development of Western education in Africa, especially since the nineteenth century, has appropriately revolved around Euro-American Christian missionaries. This is so because it was the foreign missionaries who introduced formal education or schooling into Africa. Thus, the emergence of the African educated elite is generally attributed to the work of the missions. "Everywhere [in Eastern Nigeria]," wrote Professor K. O. Dike of Nigeria, "the opening of a missionary outpost was accompanied by the erection of a school....Throughout the [twentieth] century of their existence the Voluntary Agencies...dominated the educational scene in this Region; as a result, all Eastern Nigerian leaders in Church and State, in business and education, owe their training in whole, or in part to missionary enterprise...."[1]

Yet, the African role in education must, also, be acknowledged. For Africans, to be sure, were a critical factor in the popularization of education. In fact, as the European missionaries themselves generally admitted, it was the Africans who made the evangelistic and educational work of the missions possible. For example, as teachers and catechists, the African staffs tirelessly "devoted themselves to...the teaching of the rudiments of reading and writing to young school and church enthusiasts."[2] In the words of a Roman Catholic missionary in Nigeria, the African teachers "were the corner-stone of the [burgeoning] African [schools].... They never spared themselves...." [3] In addition, African chiefs, played their part as well.

> They [and their people] built the schools; many times they...themselves supported the village school teacher; they...brought boys and girls into the schools; they...[showed] the keenest interest in the progress of the scholars; they...made valuable suggestions for the better management of the schools; [and] they...afforded invaluable help as members of the Board of Education.

Were it not for the favorable attitudes of African chiefs, this missionary's report concluded, the educational work of the missions might not have been a success. "One has only to contrast the condition of a country where the chiefs are indifferent or hostile, to realize the immense gain of having chiefs wholly sympathetic to the educational efforts of Christian missions."[4]

Certainly, any discussion of the development of modern education in Africa would be incomplete without reference to the important contributions made by Africans themselves. Hence, in this chapter, we focus attention on the African initiative in education, a theme that is often neglected in the study of education in Africa. More specifically, this essay will be concerned with the pioneering work of Rev. M. D. Opara of Nigeria, who, in 1942, founded the Zion Mission. By the time of his death on August 8, 1965, the mission had over thirty primary (elementary) schools in various parts of Nigeria. In addition, there were two postprimary institutions, namely, the Zion Commercial Secondary School and the Elementary Teacher Training College (ETC). Thus, within a period of about thirty years, the Zion Mission had developed into an enviable educational center, entirely under African control. As will be demonstrated later, by emerging as an indigenous missionary pioneer, Rev. Opara inexorably altered European missionary predominance, both in missionary evangelization and education. Consequently, he was widely acclaimed as the biblical Moses, who had come to liberate his people from European cultural imperialism. In the words of the Zion Mission newsletter, *The Zionist*, "Rev. Dr. Moses Dialaneme Opara...was a great leader who spent all his life fighting for the freedom of his people.... Indeed he was in every aspect like the prophet Moses of old, who led the Israelites from Egypt to the land of Canaan." [5]

Although Zionism ultimately gained a foothold in the region, it was actually education that became the centerpiece of what Rev. Opara proudly proclaimed as "my work for Africa." Thus, right from 1942, Rev. Opara committed himself to the social and economic advancement of his people through education. His preoccupation, said *The Zionist*, was the emancipation of his country "from ignorance, [illiteracy], poverty, spiritual darkness and... political bondage." [6] Progress via education, therefore, was Rev. Opara's "work for Africa," as he once intimated to a Nigerian friend. [7] Essentially, then, it is this African initiative in education that will form the main focus of the discussion below.

However, before we do so, it might be instructive to provide a brief historical account of Rev. Opara himself. First and foremost, it is important to note that Rev. Opara was an Igbo man. He was born about 1905 in the village of Obazu Mbieri, Owerri in Eastern Nigeria (now Imo State). He received his early education in the missionary schools, namely the Church Missionary Society (CMS) schools at Mbieri and Egbu, Owerri, and the Presbyterian Hope Waddell Institute, Calabar. After a few years of secondary education at the latter institution, Opara was employed by the CMS as a teacher and catechist. He held this dual position from 1930 to 1941, when, for reasons that are still unclear,[8] he resigned from the CMS, and, in 1942, founded his own church, the A. M. E. Zion Church. In 1949, however, the church was officially registered in Nigeria under the name, the Christ Methodist Zion Church. Thus, from 1942, a new mission was born (hereafter the Zion Mission), whose central mission was the spread of the Gospel and the promotion of Western education. In fact, education was the key to the social acceptance of the new mission; for it was derisively termed the "grass church," because the church building was initially constructed with grass. Thus, the popularity of the Zion Mission derived largely from its educational program. [9] Correspondingly, Rev. Opara's fame and reputation in Nigeria stemmed from his educational institutions.

For our purposes, it is important to point out at this juncture that Rev. Opara was not, in fact, only a clergyman, rather, he was also an educator, being a certified teacher. In addition, he was a politician and a nationalist. From 1948, for example, he turned his attention to politics, partly, as we shall see, so as to use his political position to advance the interests of the Zion Mission. Besides, as one of his associates inform us, he (Rev. Opara) wanted to be in the vanguard for liberation of Nigeria from British colonial rule.[10] Therefore, Rev. Opara served as a member of the Eastern House of Assembly from 1953 to 1965. While there, he rose to prominence, and gained the reputation of a nationalist agitator, largely because of his fierceless campaigns for political freedom, the Africanization of the colonial civil service, and the provision of modern social amenities to Nigerians. Besides, Rev. Opara proved himself to be an ardent advocate of social reforms."[11]

Nevertheless, as discussed below, it was Rev. Opara's educational endeavors, and particularly his pioneering work in secondary and teacher training education, that catapulted him into national and international prominence. To most of his Nigerian compatriots, Rev. Opara was, indeed, a great fighter, and hence his local reputation as *oweta ihe oma*, literally "the bringer of progress and development."[12]

Of course, Rev. Opara was by no means the only shinning example of the African initiative in education. On the contrary, there were several others, among them Rev. Samuel W. Martin of Issele Ukwu, from the Western Igbo people (Anioma). Like Opara, Rev. Martin established the Pilgrim Baptist Mission, and, as an ardent advocate of education, he established several schools and colleges, including the Teacher Training College at Issele Uku. [13]

Yet another African example was John Chilembwe, the Malawian nationalist, who, in 1900, established the Providence Industrial Mission (PIM) in Nyasaland (Malawi). This mission, we are told, marked "the first wave of Ethiopianism in British Central Africa."[14] Frustrated by European racism, oppression, and cultural dominance, John Chilembwe not only started his own church, but, like Rev. Opara, he opened several "fully independent" African Baptist schools, infused with a new political consciousness. These schools, as Chilembwe remarked, were "[to give] the children of Africa good training [that would] lift them from [the colonial] state of degradation, and [thus] make them suitable members of the Great human family."[15]

European racism, of course, gave birth to separatist churches and schools in various parts of Africa. In fact, as a former British colonial official in Nigeria acknowledged, the "root source of all sedition" in colonial Africa was racism. "The African may condone individual cruelty or injustice, he may put up with what appears to him oppressive laws and taxation...but racial prejudice hurts his sensitivities, rancours in his heart and becomes the root source of all sedition."[16] Thus, in Kenya, the racial/cultural clash between the Protestant missions and the Kenya Central Association, over the female circumcision question, resulted in the establishment of independent African churches and schools in the 1930s.[17] These African initiatives had one thing in common: they symbolized African reactions against European racism and cultural imperialism. In short, the educational initiatives reflected African nationalism, illustrating the Africans' thirst for spiritual and cultural freedom.[18]

Let us now turn to Rev. Opara's educational initiative. For all practical purposes, Rev. Opara may be regarded as a visionary. For he saw himself as destined to make a difference; that is, he envisioned the transformation of Nigeria into a modern society, using education as the vital instrument of modernization. This was his lifelong dream, "my work for Africa," as he described it. And although Rev. Opara appreciated the utilitarian values of education, inasmuch as education is perceived as the key to individual and/or group socio-economic upliftment, he nevertheless viewed education as a potent force against European imperialism. Thus, viewed from the perspective of colonial liberation, he saw education as perhaps the most expedient means through which "we shall free our country from colonial bondage."[19] It is not surprising, therefore, that education formed part and parcel of Rev. Opara's nationalist agenda.

By all accounts, Rev. Opara was an ardent nationalist. His overriding ambition was to make education as widely accessible to as many Nigerians as possible. Hence, according to his eulogist, Rev. Opara established many schools and colleges, and also awarded several scholarships to a large number of students. To quote the eulogist,

> Rev. Opara was not selfish. He believed in the education of everybody. This was what forced him to establish schools and colleges. To encourage this liberal education for all, he gave both primary and secondary and university scholarships to hundreds of people. [Furthermore] Rev. Opara never liked the African [to be] rated a second class citizen anywhere [in the world].[20]

By democratizing education through his liberal education program, Rev. Opara invariably opened "the door of progress" to his compatriots. Of course, he prided himself as "a nationalist and a humanitarian by blood;"[21] hence, his liberal education policy (more fully discussed later) reflected his nationalist consciousness. Records clearly show that Rev. Opara offered numerous scholarships, as well as fee-waivers, to a large number of students in Zion schools and colleges, most of them from relatively poor families. As *The Zionist* put it, "Rev. M. D. Opara throughout his life believed in charity," exemplified in the "many personal scholarships [he provided to people] in his life time."[22]

More specifically, as Zion Mission records reveal, a large number of Zion school students were allowed to attend school without paying fees. These were the "non-fee paying" students that occupy considerable space in Zion school records. According to one estimate, perhaps an exaggeration, about twenty five percent of the total student population in Zion schools did not pay school fees at all, thanks to Rev. Opara's liberal education policy.[23] In fact, some individuals within the Zion Mission complained about his liberalism, obviously because it tended to create perennial financial shortfalls.[24]

But Rev. Opara's liberal disposition was not to be constrained; rather, it extended to students in both the secondary and teacher training institutions. Interestingly, many of the recipients of fee-waivers were the wards of Zion teachers and administrators, as well as Rev. Opara's relatives, friends, and acquaintances. In addition, to promote advanced education, which actually formed a part of his "work for Africa," Rev. Opara awarded a large number of university scholarships. In the process, he invariably enabled students to study in Nigerian and overseas institutions of higher education, including the United States. However, it must be noted that Opara's liberalism invariably drained his resources. Thus, he felt compelled to call upon friends at home and abroad for assistance, so as "to help me carry on the work for Africa." Indeed, he added, "the [burden] that I am now shouldering is beyond my endurance and skill."[25] But despite dwindling resources, Rev. Opara never abandoned his liberal education policy. As a matter of fact, he even embarked on an ambitious educational expansion, with the aim of also penetrating into the Roman Catholic and Protestant enclaves. Thus, the intense denominational or sectarian competition and rivalry of the 1950s and 1960s, provided the impetus for the educational expansion. Indeed, just as the other missions were invited by towns and villages to come and open schools or colleges, so also was the Zion Mission. These two invitations from Orlu and Uyo (Calabar), respectively, are perhaps typical: "Our people," wrote E. Emerenini of Orlu, "are in great need of those who will come to our place and establish a college of any type that will bring progress." And from Uyo came this "urgent" invitation:

> There is a school at [our] place which is being run by the Catholic mission. The Rev. manager has been making vain promises...for many years...to raise the school up to standard four.... Our people are really annoyed and want a manager who can take over the school and can raise it up to standard four next year.... The natives will unfailingly wheel over to [your] mission without delay because they are not [happy with] the

Catholic mission.[26]

Unfortunately, lack of resources militated against the honoring of the invitations.

The Resource Problem

From its very inception, the Zion Mission faced a variety of problems, chief among them being denominational opposition and hostility, and a dire shortage of resources. In the area of education, the mission's most enduring problems were inadequate funds and lack of qualified staff. Let us, therefore, briefly look at the Zion Mission's financial state of affairs, with particular reference to education. To begin with, the earliest Zion school at Obazu Mbieri began in 1942 as a Bible school. By 1947, it had grown into a full-fledged primary school, having been raised to a standard six status. It was therefore eligible for the Nigerian First School Leaving Certificate examination. Also, by 1947, several other Zion schools had been opened in various parts of Eastern Nigeria. Unfortunately, Zion schools were not popular, largely because they lacked qualified staff, that is, trained teachers. In the words of a Zion schoolteacher, "when we [make] mention of Zion [schools] at our place people used to laugh, they did not call teachers under Zion real teachers."[27]

Several other factors contributed to this negative image, including low school enrollment, shortage of space, and lack of school equipment. Of enrollments in Zion schools, even up to the 1950s, a former teacher also remarked: "Schools are relatively small in enrollment. Parents seemed reluctant to send their children to Zion schools. [Thus] Some teachers had to bribe parents to send their children to school."[28] In fact, government school inspectors continually pointed to the small enrollments in the Zion schools, as well as the lack of trained staff, and inadequate equipments. Consider this critical inspection report by the Provincial Education Officer (PEO) of a Zion school in 1958:

> Teaching equipment is very weak.... Seating is inadequate in all classes, and in all Junior and Infant classes [there] is deplorable accommodation.... There must be an area board for each class space. At present there are no [black] boards at all.[29]

To relieve the overcrowding in the school, the PEO suggested that "When the [proposed] new building is complete two Senior Primary classes should occupy it and Infants IA and IB should occupy the main school building at the old site. This is preferable to overcrowding the main school building."

Even the two Zion colleges fared no better in terms of resources, at least as reflected in this letter by the principal of St. Catherine's College, who complained about shortages of essential school materials. "I am tired of reporting that there are no chalk, ink, marking pencils, chairs, desks, [and] benches for the college."[30] Indeed, Zion schools were plagued with inadequate resources, especially funds, throughout their several years of existence. (Zion schools, like all other mission schools, were taken over by the government in 1970.) Thus, as we shall see, the quality of education in Zion schools was adversely affected by lack of funds. For example, when students at the premier Zion school at Obazu Mbieri sat for the Nigerian First School Certificate examination in 1948, the result was far from being satisfactory, as only ten, out of the thirty six candidates, passed. This high failure rate prompted Rev. Opara to question the fairness of the grading given, as he said, that some of the brightest students failed. But the PEO called his bluff: "You are extremely fortunate to [even] have any certificates at all issued to you, in view of the deplorable paper set and general administration of the examination. As a concession, the ten candidates with the highest marks were given passes. Your statement that none of the most of the brilliant boys was in the pass list is therefore absurd."[31]

This "deplorable" performance may have been the result of lack of adequately trained teachers, or perhaps due to the admission of very weak students, or even both. Whatever the case, the Ministry of Education took a serious view of the results. It felt compelled to reexamine the position and status of Christ Methodist Zion School at Obazu Mbieri. First, it ordered that the school must be reduced to Standard Five. Second, Rev. Opara was warned that, unless education regulations were strictly adhered to, particularly with respect to qualified staff, the school would be closed down entirely.[32] It is important to point out here that performance in examinations had become an important basis for the continued existence of schools, or for securing government grants. Hence, the different mission societies (Voluntary Agencies) had to concern themselves with improvements in the quality of education. "The increasing entry of Governments into the sphere of education," wrote a Protestant official, "means that new and higher standards will be demanded. Mission schools can survive only if they meet those standards."[33]

Of course, schools needed official government approval before they could be granted a Standard Six status. Inspection results also determined the eligibility for education subsidies. Besides, a Standard Six school required government approval before students could take the First School Leaving Certificate examination. Approval from the Ministry of Education was therefore crucial for schools. Conditions for approval were clearly stated in the Eastern Nigeria Ministry of Education regulations thus:

1. Approval will depend not only on the work of the Senior Primary classes, but also of the Junior Primary, if these exist in the same school.... Handwork and farm work will also be taken into consideration.

2. Application for approval must be made during the year before the addition of Standard VI to the school is proposed. The inspection for approval will take place in the year before Standard VI is added, and approval will be granted on the condition that the necessary staff for the addition of Standard VI will be supplied, without robbing another approved school.

3. Approval will not be granted to any school...[which] is inadequately staffed with fully qualified teachers.[34]

Given that most Zion schools were "inadequately staffed with fully qualified teachers," and that they also lacked adequate infrastructure, it is not hard to see why they faced many difficulties in their attempts to secure government approval and grants-in-aid. As already noted, government approval was necessary before schools could be raised to standard six status. "The representative of the Voluntary Agency making the application must satisfy himself that the school is up to the required standard and that the necessary staff will be forthcoming."[35] But when, in 1951, Rev. Opara applied for the restoration of Standard Six to the Obazu Mbieri school, the Ministry of Education, after its routine inspection, turned down the request. The explanation was the lack of adequately trained staff, as well as the school's "appalling standard of work." Here is part of the letter from the Acting Inspector-General of Education:

> The standard of work shown by Obazu Mbieri Zion Methodist School in 1951 can only be described as appalling. This allied to the fact that the inspection report shows many unsatisfactory features, plus the fact that the school has been understaffed all the year.... [Therefore,] *The school is not approved for First School Leaving Certificate in 1952.* You have no permission to have Standard Six next year (1952).... I am tired of the constant unsatisfactory conditions which prevail in your Voluntary Agency.[36]

Not only was the school not approved for standard six, it was also denied grants-in-aid. Several other Zion schools had a similar experience. Yet, Rev. Opara remained undaunted. But he nevertheless complained. "The Government assists most of the schools run by apostate churches but has not, after many years application, given us a mite."[37] In fact, Rev. Opara blamed the "enemies" of the Zion Mission for the Zion schools' approval problems. "The modernistic [Protestant], the Catholic and the apostate churches, whose members are the leaders in the Nigerian...administrative departments, victimize our institutions everywhere."[38] Years later, other Zionists expressed similar sentiments about denominational persecution and victimizations.[39]

There is no question, of course, at least as available evidence suggests, that denominational prejudices towards the Zion Mission existed, and might have played some role in the negative assessments of Zion schools. Yet, Zion schools' approval problems stemmed largely from institutional weaknesses, namely, the lack of adequate resources. It was in fact this realization that ultimately impelled Rev. Opara to seek financial assistance, "no matter how small," from the government. Admitting that "we have been [previously] warned" of school deficiencies, he pleaded with the government for "a little help" to enable him rectify reported school deficiencies. "You know, your honour," he wrote to the Deputy Director of Education, "that to maintain efficient schools, we should be helped," adding, "If a little help is given to even one of our schools, we shall be very grateful." Furthermore, "we have tried the best we could to rectify things."[40] Unfortunately, these pleas fell on deaf ears, at least until the mid-1950s. (School subsidies were provided from 1954, largely because, as a legislator, Rev. Opara was able to exert political influence on the authorities.) In the interim, virtually all Zion schools remained unapproved, and so ineligible for government grants-in-aid.

Agonized over the failure to secure school approval and funds, Rev. Opara adopted another strategy of action. He sought government recognition of the Zion Mission as a Voluntary Agency, just as the other missions had. Such a recognition, of course, would qualify Zion schools for education subsidies. But again, the applications were rejected, ostensibly because of Zion schools' "general inefficiency." Wrote the Provincial Education Officer, Mr. P. C. Harmond: "I regret I cannot recommend this [Zion Mission] for approval [as a Voluntary Agency]. None of its schools are of approved efficiency.... Unless and until the Manager can show willingness to cooperate with the Department to a great extent than in the past, I am not prepared to recommend that Christ Zion Methodist Church be granted approved status."[41]

But despite repeated rejections, Rev. Opara continued to pressure the government for financial help, arguing (rightly) that neither "the school fees collected [from the pupils]," nor even "local contributions from the natives," could cover the yearly expenses of the schools. Therefore, he pleaded, "a little special [financial] aid...to enable us to maintain our schools more efficiently at this time [is urgently needed]."[42]

Again, nothing came of these requests. Thus frustrated by repeated government's refusals for aid, and worried about the possibility of the closure of his schools for lack of resources, Rev. Opara turned to America for possible succor. His visit to the United States in 1950 proved fortuitous; indeed, it opened the gates for material assistance. While in America, Rev. Opara established a close relationship with the Evangelical Methodist Church (EMC), whose headquarters was in Altoona, Pennsylvania. From all accounts, he made a great impression on his hosts. In the words of the General-Secretary, Rev. Conn, "Rev. M. D. Opara...thrilled our people [with] word pictures of his past life" and his work in Nigeria.[43] Upon his return from America, Rev. Opara wrote several letters to the EMC authorities, apprising them of the progress of his work, and also the many hardships he faced. "We are having a very hard time in everything," he wrote, adding, "We lack workers. We lack finance. I rely very much on you brethren over there for every help." On the school question, Rev. Opara wrote, "We have an arduous work to do in this country. You will be sorry to hear that owing to lack of funds we...may, unless God turns the tide, close some of our schools."[44]

Not only did the EMC's General-Superintendent, Dr. Breckbill, proffer moral support, he actually promised material assistance in funds and personnel. "Stand assured that we are behind you and the work there [in Nigeria] and will do all in our power to keep the wheel moving in your favor.[45] And from the General-Secretary came this soothing reply: "May the Lord lead you to continue your own good work.... I would say that...the Mission Board was very favorable toward the Nigerian work."[46] Indeed, funds from the EMC, which amounted to about $11,400 in 1952,(47) enabled Rev. Opara to pay teachers' salaries, as well as to aggressively pursue his evangelistic work.

Politics and Economic Survival

Although funds from America, as noted above, provided considerable financial relief, Zion Mission's money problems remained. A possible solution to the "financial exigencies," as Rev. Opara himself described it, was entry into politics. Thus, in 1953, Rev. Opara made a calculated decision to contest in the election to the Eastern House of Assembly. He won, and so served as a member of the Eastern House of Assembly until his death in 1965.

While there, Opara campaigned strenuously for changes in government policy regarding school grants-in-aid. Speaking on the matter in 1954, he drew attention to the official discriminatory attitude towards schools owned by Africans. He therefore demanded policy changes which would make it possible for schools owned by Africans, such as Zion schools, to be granted education subsidies. Amidst applause Opara stated:

> I would suggest that something be done for African-owned schools. (*Hear! Hear!*). There are some schools owned by Africans, as I said before, which are neglected. Assistance is not given to them. They are required to run their own schools to efficiency before they are assisted. I think the wisest thing to do is to assist these schools and watch their progress.[47]

As a result of the positive response in the Eastern House of Assembly, and the Africanization of the Ministry of Education, changes in policy were effected. Hence, Zion Mission schools, as well as others owned by

Africans, began to receive education grants. Equally significant, a large number of Zion schools thereafter were granted approval status, and others raised to standard six. In this connection, it is perhaps safe to conclude, as Whitaker has correctly observed, that "Politics will always rule the day."[48]

Change and Continuity

Surely, the infusion of funds from the government and from America significantly improved the financial status of the Zion Mission. Yet, all was still not well with the Zion schools. For practically all of them continued to experience financial difficulties. For example, the payment of teachers' salaries was irregular, ostensibly for lack of sufficient funds. Nor did the staffing problem disappear. On the contrary, Zion schools continued to suffer from shortages of trained teachers. But it was the non-payment of salaries that gave Opara the greatest headache; for the teachers naturally protested. For convenience, I shall only reproduce a few letters of protest to illustrate the seriousness of the financial crisis. First, this letter from an obviously frustrated female teacher, whose salaries had remained unpaid for four months. "One might think you ought to know," she wrote to Rev. Opara, "that there is a point beyond which human patience cannot go. You have stretched my patience too far and it has snapped." She therefore demanded to be paid "as soon as [possible]," since it was not possible to continue to teach "on an empty stomach."[49] Similarly, a male teacher from the secondary school complained: "It is three months since I was last paid.... [I] am [therefore] badly in need of money now," adding, "If the full salary cannot be available, I think a part of it will suffice as I hope to go home...for the County Council election nominations."[50] Finally, there was this letter, purportedly written by the Zion school committee, to the Ministry of Education: "We want to report this thing too. Some teachers, especially young girls, come to us to ask us to go [and] beg the Pastor to pay them their salaries. He never listen[ed] to us.... In fact, he drove us out of his compound at Zion [Mission] Mbieri.... We are vexed about all those things. They are spoiling our good name."[51]

Although Rev. Opara dismissed this petition as a "false and malicious report," emanating from "the enemies of progress and patriotism,"[52] yet, the fact of the matter was that the Zion Mission was not regular in the payment of teachers' salaries. In fact, members of the Eastern House Assembly expressed deep concern over the irregular payment of teachers' salaries.[53]

Rev. Opara, however, rationalized the delays in the payment of staff salaries in terms of shortage of funds. "I am appealing to the Members to desist from rising up in this House to shout that teachers are not paid.... I am appealing to the Hon. Members to go home and ask their people to pay the Assumed Local Contributions [ALC] in time so that the teachers will be paid regularly." And he added,

> The grants-in-aid the Government is paying to Voluntary Agencies is not sufficient and Voluntary Agencies have to collect money to subsidize the Government grants. When... you cannot collect the exact amount required by the Government to subsidize the payment of teachers...the Manager will not be regular in paying the teachers.[54]

But, as Zion Mission records clearly reveal, shortages of funds did not all occur because of inadequate grants-in-aid. Rather, the embezzlement of funds by schoolteachers, headmasters, and administrators, as well as the mismanagement of funds by Rev. Opara himself, contributed to the persistent financial crisis.[55] In fact, Zion school headmasters were publicly reprimanded by the Zion Financial Committee, for their habitual embezzlement of school funds. And they were also sternly warned to be of good behavior.[56] Not surprisingly, mismanagement of funds left most Zion schools poorly staffed and ill-equipped; and hence, the schools continued to receive negative reports up to 1970, when the East Central State government took over all mission schools.

Although some schools received good reports, especially with reference to school discipline, tone, and "good classroom work,"[57] several others, however, were ordered to be closed because of numerous deficiencies. And Rev. Opara was personally blamed for the schools' predicament. "Almost all the defects and certainly all the serious defects lie within the province of the proprietor and management for remedy. Teaching equipment is very weak and there is little evidence that any equipment money has been spent." In most of his schools, remarked the inspecting officer, "Seating is inadequate in all classes."[58] With particular reference to St George's Zion School at Okigwe, which was inspected in 1961, the inspecting officer, W. R. Taylor, wrote:

> Except in Standard 5 seating is inadequate even for the

> ridiculously low enrollment [of 50 students]. Textbooks have not been supplied to almost all the teachers. There is no rain gauge, wind vane, cupboards, and teaching apparatus is non-existent.... In short, the school is miles away from being properly equipped and one wonders what the manager has done with the equipment grant over the years.... Physically and economically, this is the most unsatisfactory school I have inspected in Eastern Nigeria in ten years.[59]

The inspector thus warned, "if upon reinspection in December, 1961, this school does not show adequate and satisfactory improvement in all respects, I shall recommend to the Minister [of Education] that it be removed from the grant assisted list and/or closed as not being in the best interest of the people to be served."[60]

Uncomplimentary reports, such as the above, abound. Take for example, the case of St. Silas School in Orji Uratta near Owerri, which was inspected in 1962 for possible upgrading from Standard Five to Standard Six. But the small enrollment, coupled with other "unsatisfactory" state of affairs at the school, militated against the proposal. In fact, Rev. Opara was asked to reduce the school to a Junior Primary status.[61] Similarly, several other Zion schools, including the one at Atta, Ikeduru, were streamlined. "As a result of a recent survey," wrote the Permanent Secretary to Opara, "C. M. Zion School Atta Ikeduru under the proprietorship of your agency was considered to be so uneconomic as to be no longer viable. You are therefore requested to reduce the school to Junior Primary status until approval by the Provincial Education Officer to develop further."[62] A far more drastic action was taken with regard to Zion schools in Ubaha Orodo and Umuogosi Umulolo: "Both schools must CLOSE."[63]

Enduring Legacy

It would of course be mistaken to conclude from the foregoing that the Zion Mission's educational enterprise was a failure; far from it. In comparative terms, to be sure, other mission schools, including those of the Roman Catholics and the Protestants, faced, to some degree, similar difficulties. In his report on education in the Owerri Province, decades earlier, the district officer (DO) at Owerri once remarked, "There are new developments;" namely, "the rapid spread of the Missions. The only

Mission School doing serious educational work is the assisted Roman Catholic School at Emekuku." And he added, "The Niger Delta Pastorate schools [a branch of the CMS] are in a deplorable condition. They obviously have no... capable men to direct and inspect the teachers (if they deserve the title) and their work."[64] By the 1950s, many CMS schools in the Owerri Archdeaconry were, like the Zion schools, in dire financial straits, largely because of declines in school grants-in-aid. The financial shortfall, according to the authorities, stemmed from "too many small schools with very poor attendance." Unless the situation improved, and government regulations strictly adhered to, warned the local CMS bishop, "poor or no grants at all would be the result for Anglican schools." The education secretary concurred, adding, "the Owerri Archdeaconry needed to put its house in order," so as to attract government grants.[65] In fact, the Ministry of Education issued a strong warning that grants, to even "assisted" CMS schools, might be withdrawn, unless the staffing, enrollment, and other school problems were rectified.[66] Seen in a comparative perspective, therefore, Zion schools were not unique in the lack of adequate resources. Most mission schools certainly faced similar problems, including shortages of trained staff and equipment, as well as low enrollments.

As far as education is concerned, the Zion Mission certainly performed a valuable function. It provided educational opportunities to a large number of Nigerians, and particularly "the refused members of various [Voluntary] Agencies," who might otherwise have been left out in the lurch. Here, in fact, lies Rev. Opara's enduring legacy. He may have lacked adequate funds to operate Zion schools at optimal efficiency, yet, he contributed significantly to the spread of education in Nigeria. Therefore, from the perspective of African nationalism, it can safely be said that Rev. Opara's work in postprimary education illustrated a successful African initiative. On the other hand emergence in the missionary scene challenged the "hegemony of colonialism," that is, the dominance of both education and missionary evangelism. Hence, "In the annals of missionary enterprise and modern education in Nigeria, Rev. M. D. Opara will always be revered.[67] Specifically, Rev. Opara must be remembered for his patriotic efforts to democratize education. For it was through education that Africans could be freed from an inferiority complex of the Europeans. Indeed, since Rev. Opara reportedly "never liked the African rated a second-class citizen," it means that the eradication of illiteracy, ignorance, and poverty, as he hoped, would enable Africans to stand on the same level as their counterparts elsewhere. It was through pursuit of this nationalist agenda that Rev. Opara apparently allowed hundreds of school children to attend Zion schools free. In addition, he awarded a large number of scholarships, which enabled students to study in both Nigerian and overseas institutions, including the United States. As a result, a good number of Nigerians, who today hold important positions in the country owe so much to Rev. Opara's extraordinary largesse.[68]

Requests by parents and students for admission to either the secondary school, or the teachers's college often accompanied with solicitations for scholarships. This letter of 1961, from a parent from Uyo, is perhaps typical. "This comes to remind you of...the letters of appeal I sent with regards to my boys and girls that we are wishing to send to your Schools next year. Brother Opara, please take notice that you are my only saviour in this struggle of ours to send these students to school in 1962."[69] The influx of "thank you" letters from parents and/or students suggest that Rev. Opara invariably obliged them,[70] and, thereby, endeared himself to solicitors and others. Of course, "charitability confers prestige, earns the attention of community members and commands their respect." Not surprisingly, therefore, students, including those from Rev. Opara's hometown, showered him with extraordinary expressions of endearment, gratitude, and appreciation. In the eyes of Mbieri students, to be sure, Rev. Opara was certainly the quintessential patriot and philanthropist. Hence, they thanked him profusely for all his "kindness to us." And further acknowledging that Opara was "the most generous and God-fearing philanthropist in Mbieri," they added, "Today you are the father and God of Amaogwugwu."[71] Others agreed, including a student, who was then studying in England under Rev. Opara's sponsorship. "I feel I should write to thank you very much for what you have been to our boys as far as fostering education is concerned. To my own mind that is the *chief* service anybody can do for Mbieri in general and Obazu in particular. There is nothing greater."[72] Yet another student at Lincoln University in America wrote: "By writing me...and sending me this money [L150], you have once more demonstrated to the world that your unequalled integrity can neither fall nor waver. This is an unequivocal manifestation of your love to me which cannot quench or succumb before the forces of criticism and bad fate [Sic]."[73]

Most of these letters of appreciation, which actually came from far and near, portrayed Rev. Opara as "somebody in whose blood it has been to help the needy."[74] Thus a grateful correspondent, in thanking Rev. Opara for offering a scholarship to his relative to study at the Zion ETC, stated, "Your good deeds shall never die; you will always be fondly remembered."[75] An ex-student of the ETC wrote in a similar vein: "I must have to say that your goodness and the roll[sic] you play[ed] to the needy ones [among us] is applauded.... Though reward might always be impossible but the Good Lord will pay you in [several] folds." His colleague agreed; "Without you, I would not have [had the opportunity] to further...my Educational career."[76] One Sylvanus Anokwuwa, also a graduate of the Commercial Secondary School, perhaps spoke for all the others, when he wrote to Rev. Opara in these most endearing words:

> No human being can sufficiently reward you for all your good deeds...to the helpless and fatherless Citizens of the Country [Nigeria] except that you will doubly get [your reward] from the Alfa and Omega. Our College has been a fish that fed over [a] million people and will continue to feed [others] as long as those concerned will realise her importance. I assure you, as long as some of our grateful Pioneers live in any place of the country, they must never fail to represent both their college and her Patriotic founder (THE HON. M. D.).... Thank you for your Sympathetic and Patriotic spirit which you have for the refused members of various Agencies.[77]

Also viewed as "a great son of Mbieri," and as "a great patriot [who] brought honour and glory to Mbieri" on account of the work of his Zion Mission, Rev. Opara's "patriotic efforts" in liberal education received high praise. Consider this letter from one B. U. Anyasodo:

> I write [to thank you for] your activities to enlighten our folks at home in the modern way of life. In fact, I am proud that you are doing your best to let our people share from your learnings abroad. It is not everybody that will appreciate your remittances for the town, and even many may turn to sabotage them, I am assuring you that time will kill all such diabolical movements...."[78]

Similarly, a staunch Protestant from Mbieri, who taught briefly at St.

Catherine's College, expressed special pride in "the good work" Rev. Opara had done for the town.

> It is true our Education Secretary offered me [a] place to teach, yet I felt my first duty was to my home town. It is also true I had to work...more than I could have done elsewhere for the same pay, yet I was doing it for the mere joy of working in my own college. I must confess I was much impressed with your efforts; my opinion about your colleges changed very much for the better. From outside the college, and with ignorance of your work, people misjudge your efforts and deprecate your labour, but believe me, my previous wrong opinions were corrected after the four months stay with you.[79]

In summary, this essay has attempted to present a classic case of an African initiative in education. It argues, among other things, that, in spite of the shortage of resources, Rev. Opara succeeded in playing a critical role in the advancement of education in Nigeria. For all intents and purposes, he opened the "door of progress" to his people. This is why he is still fondly remembered. In my several years of field work experience in Mbieri, the pervading image of Rev. Opara that I came away with is that of a man with a social vision. In essence, he was a visionary. "Had Rev. Opara lived much longer," an informant told me, "we would have been better off today."" As discussed above, students extolled his virtues, and particularly his non-discriminatory school admission policy, which was in marked contrast to, say, the "discriminating Irish imperialists," meaning the Irish missionaries, who dominated Roman Catholic schools and colleges. It is perhaps appropriate to conclude this essay with this epitaph, representing St. Catherine's College anthem:

> God bless the School that M. D. Opara founded.
> Long may she stand,
> though by foes of truth surrounded.
> May she not be vanquished
> Keeping true to God and man,
> her glories over yonder![80]

Notes

1. Cited in S. N. Nwabara, *Iboland. A Century of Contact with Britain 1860-1960*. Atlantic Highlands, NJ: Humanities Press, 1978, p. 76. See also J. F. A. Ajayi, *Christian Missions in Nigeria 1841-1891: The Making of a New Elite*. Evanston: Northwestern University Press, 1969.
2. Felix K. Ekechi, *Tradition and Transformation in Eastern Nigeria. A Sociopolitical History of Owerri and Its Hinterland 1902-1947*. Kent, Ohio: Kent State University Press, 1797, p. 72.
3. Ibid., p. 78.
4. Church Missionary Society Archives, London (CMS): *The Church Missionary Reviews*, Vol. LXXII (1921), pp. 299-300.
5. *The Zionist*, No.27 (August l978), p.1.
6. Ibid.
7. Zion Mission Archives (ZMA): Opara to Onyido, 14 Sept. 1948.
8. Based on oral testimonies. It has not yet been possible to locate documents relating to Opara's resignation from the CMS. One version of the oral evidence states that Opara was "repeatedly passed over" in the selection of candidates for training at the CMS Awka Training College; and hence, his resignation. The other version, perhaps more plausible, votes that Opara resigned because his fiancee was pregnant before their church wedding, conduct then seriously frowned upon by church authorities.
9. For details about the Zion Mission see: Felix K. Ekechi, "The Ordeal of an Independent African Church: The Case of the Nigerian Zion Methodist Mission, 1942-1970." In *The International Journal of African Historical Studies*, Vol 20, No.4 (1987), pp. 691-720.
10. Interviews with Chief:;. B. C. Ekeanyanwu at Owerri, Nov. 1989. See also his hand-written notes, Nov. 1989, p. 9
11. See F. K. Ekechi, "'For God and Country'" Portrait of Rev. M. D. Opara of Nigeria 1905-1965." (Forthcoming)
12. Based on interviews at Obazu Mbieri, Nov. 1994.
13. I am indebted to Dr. Jonathan Nwomonoh for this reference.
14. See George Shepperson and Thomas Price, *Independent African. John Chilembwe and the Origins. Setting and Significance of the Nyasaland Native Rising of 1915*. Edinburch: The University Press, 1958, pp. 116-125.

15. Ibid., p. 127.
16. The Nigerian *Daily Times*, 15 Nov. 1929.
17. For discussions on the circumcision question see: Jomo Kenyatta, *Facing Mount Kenya*. New York: Vintage Books, 1965, p. 263; Carl G. Roseberg and John Nottingham, *The Myth of Mau Mau": Nationalism in Kenya*. New York: New American Library, 1970, Ch. 4.
18. Adrian Hastings, *A History of African Christianity 1950-1975*. Cambridge: Cambridge University Press, 1979, p. 175.
19. ZMA: Unpublished memo (? 1962).
20. Ibid., Rev. R. C. Onuekwasui, "The Life of the Late Rev. M. D. Opara." Unpublished essay (1971).
21. See note 19.
22. *The Zionist*, p. 1.
23. ZMA:
24. *The Zionist.*
25. Ibid., Opara to Onyido, 14 Sept. 1948.
26. Ibid., Emerenini to Opara, 14 July 1961; Ndem to Opara, 23 March 1961.
27. Ibid., Caleb Aguigbo to Opara, 4 Dec. 1958.
28. Ibid., Edmund D. Opara to President [Opra], 19 may 1959.
29. Ibid., School Inspection Report (Enugu Nwo), 7 Nov. 1958.
30. Ibid., A. J. Okoro to General Manager, 13 Feb. 1959.
31. Ibid., Lloyd to Opara, 11 January 1951.
32. Ibid., Chairman, Board of Education to Proprietor, 16 March 1949.
33. CMS: J. H. Oldham "Christian Education in Africa." In *The Church Missionary Review*, Vol. XXV (1924), p. 309.
34. *Approval of Schools for the First Leaving Certificate in the Eastern Region* [Nigeria]. Enugu, Government Printer, 1045, p.1.
35. Ibid.
36. ZMA: Acting Inspector General to Proprietor, 14 Dec. 1951.
37. Ibid., Opara to Breckbill, 6 June 1953; also 10 Nov. 1953.
38. Ibid., Opara to Conn, 2 July 1951.
39. Interviews with Bishop Lambert Osita Opara at Owerri in 1983 and 1986 respectively.
40. ZMA: Opara to Deputy Director of Education (DD), 4 Feb. 1950.
41. Ibid., Harmond to DD, 4 Jan. 1950.
42. Ibid., Opara to DD. 9 Feb. 1950; also to PEO, 13 April 1950.

43. *Evangelical Methodist Conference*. Friday, 16 Oct. 1950, p. 13.
44. ZMA: Opara to Conn, 1 Sept. 1951; Opara to Breckbill,, 6 June 1953.
45. Ibid., Breckbill to Opara, 24 July 1951.
46. Ibid., Conn to Opara, 22 Feb. 1952.
47. *Evangelical Methodist Conference* (1952), pp. 47, 52-53.
48. Nigerian National Archives, Enugu (NNAE): *Debates of the Eastern House of Assembly* (hereafter referred to as *Debates*), 23 March 1955, p. 284.
49. Jennifer Seymour Whitaker, *How Can Africa Survive?* New York: Council on Foreign Relations Press, 1988, p.65.
50. ZMA: C. Rosetta Aguta to General Manager, 26, Oct. 1952.
51. Ibid., C. W. O. Ajaegbu to Opara, 1 Sept. 1961.
52. Ibid., Petition to the Ministry of Education, by the Ahaba Orodo Zion School Committee, 17 July 1958.
53. Ibid., Opara to the PEO, 7 July 1958. The petition was found to have been written, not by the committee, but by a teacher, who had been dismissed from service.
54. NNAE: *Debates*, 23 March 1955, p. 284.

Part II
Adult/Women and Environmental Education

— 5 —
An Overview of Women's Education in Africa

Dorothy L. Njeuma

Illiteracy among women in Africa stands at more than 70 percent on the average and more than 90 percent in rural areas; the drop out rate for girls is higher than it is for boys, especially at the secondary level; and girls are underrepresented in crucial fields of studies, especially in mathematics, the sciences, and technology, areas that are critical to their full participation in the development process.[81]

Generally, the majority of women in Africa live in rural areas, where they constitute the bulk of the population. With the advent of industrialization men have moved to urban areas in search of work and have sometimes even migrated to other countries in search of better-paying jobs. Rural women are engaged primarily in the production of food.

In principle, women in Africa are not thought of as heads of households, especially since most African households are not only patriarchal and patrilocal but also, in many parts of the continent, polygynous. It is assumed that, as girls are dependent on their fathers, women are dependent on their households, carrying the burden alone of caring and providing for their children.

But the phenomenon of migration of men from rural into urban areas and also into neighboring countries leaves many women to look after themselves and their children, especially in the rural areas. It is reported that in Zambia, Lesotho, and parts of Senegal and Burkina Faso migration of men has left about 50 percent of women responsible for managing their households and for farming.[82] Even in polygynous unions in which the husband is physically present, women still bear the responsibility of the care, up bringing, and education of the children.

The Education of Women

Tremendous strides have been made in educating women and girls in Africa, especially since the 1960s. At that time the newly independent nations of the continent realized that development could only come about through the education of their citizens, both male and female. The overall enrollment of girls in primary school increased from 26 percent in 1960 to 69 percent in 1984. From negligible numbers in 1960 the enrollment of girls in secondary schools throughout Africa reached 13 percent of total students in 1984.

Throughout the continent girls are attending tertiary-level classes in significant numbers. Although Africa's rate of general adult literacy is still the lowest in the world, among African women the literacy rate increased from 16 percent in 1970 to 35 percent in 1985.

The Problems

Although considerable progress has been made in educating women and girls in Africa in recent years, it has come at considerable cost. In some cases, up to one-quarter of national budgets has been allocated for primary education alone, often to the detriment of other sectors of the economy.[83] In Cameroon the state has consistently invested up to one-fifth of its budget on education. Primary schools have sprung up everywhere, even in the most remote villages. Secondary schools have been built in almost every region of the country. The effect has been to bring schools nearer to the children. Similar policies have been embarked upon in other countries, including Zimbabwe.[84] Everywhere there has been a growing awareness, not only on the part of governments but also on the part of parents, of how important education, for both boys and girls, is for national and individual development. If parents were reluctant to send their daughters to school because of cost or distance, these difficulties have gradually diminished. The result is that, at least at the primary level of formal education, the gap in the enrollment ratio between girls and boys has narrowed very significantly.

But even with expenditures at these levels there are clearly factors that reduce women's participation and serve to make the transition from primary to secondary education especially difficult for girls. In Cameroon, for instance, it is natural for only a third of those girls entering primary school to continue to the secondary level. Of those who enter secondary school only one-fifth remain in the senior years of high school. This pattern is similar across the continent and is in marked contrast to the experiences of boys, some 40 percent of whom finish high school. Obviously, such differentials perpetuated over time will serve to enhance gender inequalities and limit the role women can play in African society outside the rural sector.

The problems that still plague the education of women in Africa can be summarized as follows:

- very low literacy among women, especially in rural areas;
- underrepresentation of girls and women at all stages of the formal system of education (this problem worsens as one moves up the education ladder);
- greater repeat and attrition rates among girls, especially at the secondary level; specialization of girls and women in certain areas of study (humanities, teaching, etc.); very low representation of women and girls in mathematics, physical sciences, and technical studies.

Each of these phenomena are complex and any attempt at an analysis of their causes at best can be only partial. Nevertheless, the following factors are among the most significant.

Poverty

The single most important factor that contributes to the high rate of illiteracy among Africa's women is poverty. As has been underlined above, illiteracy among African women is highest and the education level of girls lowest in the countries that count among the poorest and least developed. In these countries the overall rates of school attendance and of adult literacy are very low. Of the thirty poorest countries in the world, twenty are in Africa.[85]

To provide universal education requires that schools, teachers, and equipment are available to all children, boys and girls. In spite of the fact that some African countries are spending up to one-third of their budgets on education, they have not succeeded in providing even primary education for all of their children. With the economic crisis of the 1970s, which continued and worsened in the 1980s and 1990s, African governments have been forced to make serious cutbacks on public spending and social services. This creates enormous problems for educational systems at a time when, with increased population growth, there are more children for whom education should be provided. The education of all children has become a growing concern, and in this situation it is difficult to pay special attention to the education of girls and women as a group apart from boys and men.

Division of Labor

The social structure of African societies also creates impediments to the education of women. Labor has come to be divided along lines of gender, which society considers to be acceptable. African societies expect women to be responsible for growing food crops, fetching water and fuelwood, raising children, and doing domestic work. Society and women would not find it acceptable if men should take on these responsibilities. These tasks are not only burdensome but they also make heavy demands on women's time. Women are so overworked that they can hardly find time for education.[86] Also, in many African societies, girls are often required to help their mothers look after younger children and with household chores and farm work. This means that girls have less time to spend on schoolwork and sometimes have to drop out of school entirely.

Social Patterns and Attitudes

In many African societies the expectations of parents for their daughters are not as high as those for their sons. Education is not considered to be as crucial for girls as it is for boys. Until a girl is married her natal family wants her unpaid labor in agriculture and in the home. If school attendance interferes with this significant contribution to the household economy, girls will drop out of school. When a choice has to be made for economic reasons between educating a son or a daughter, preference is given to the son. Parents see in the son the perpetuation of the family name, whereas a daughter will invariably be married off into some other family. The education of girls is therefore seen as a less worth while investment.

There is also considerable reluctance on the part of parents to send daughters to school if they will be forced to live away from home in uncertain circumstances. Because secondary schools tend to be located in distant places, this attitude contributes to the low enrollment of girls at this level. Related to this is the wariness of parents to send teenage daughters to school, where they interact with boys and male teachers.[87] The systematic rape of girls in a Kenyan boarding school vividly underscores the concerns of parents.[88]

In many African societies girls are still married off early. This custom, in addition to the labor value of girls in the family economy and teenage pregnancies, accounts for the high dropout rate of girls, especially at the secondary school level. Frequent pregnancies and childbearing are also high among African women, which seriously impedes women's availability for educational pursuits. Preoccupations about marriage on the part of women and girls may also sometimes limit their educational attainment and determine the type of studies they undertake. Although African women sometimes feel that education improves their chances of getting a "better" husband and therefore of living a more comfortable life, they are also wary of being too educated or of entering fields of study that may limit their choice of a husband.[89] While many African men prefer to marry women who can obtain salaried employment and contribute to the household budget, very few will marry women who are more educated than themselves. Many men also prefer to marry women whose jobs leave them time to attend to children and the household—hence, their preference for nurses and teachers as wives.

The School System, Curricula, and Methods

The school system itself, curricula, and teaching methods have contributed to the shortcomings in the education of girls. Girls' schools tend to be less well staffed and less well equipped than boys' schools. Nevertheless, it may be argued that the performance of girls at the secondary level tends to be better in single sex segregated schools than in mixed schools. Some evidence from Kenya and Cameroon suggests that girls do better in all-girls' schools because the competition is keener, and sexist behavior and discrimination occur less.

In technical schools reserved for girls the curriculum covers mainly home economics and commercial and secretarial studies. Technical schools for boys have a much broader curriculum, which includes carpentry, welding, mechanical drawing, plumbing, electricity, mechanics, electronics, leatherwork, pottery, etc. This disparity contributes to the notion that certain types of studies and therefore certain jobs are reserved for men and that others are reserved for women. Paradoxically, the hotel and tailoring industries are dominated by men, and a substantial number of domestic servants in Africa are men.

The stereotyping of roles in textbooks, in teaching methods, and in the attitudes of teachers limits the achievement of girls. Girls come to accept certain fields of study as being "soft" and therefore "more feminine." Mathematics, physics, and technical subjects are considered to be "hard" and therefore more suitable for boys than for girls.

Employment

The degree to which employment possibilities limit the education of women and girls in Africa is not clear. There is no evidence of discrimination against the employment of qualified women and girls. If it is true that the majority of women in salaried employment are teachers, nurses, and secretaries, this is a reflection of the career options they choose. Women's obligations as wives and mothers prevent them from taking on certain types of work and also account for the reluctance of employers to hire women in these salaried positions. Such responsibilities also seem to reduce the efficiency of women in certain types of employment. Official working hours are not flexible enough to cater to the double load—domestic and professional duties—of many working women. This factor also impedes women's progress in highly demanding careers. It also appears that stricter guidelines are applied to women when it comes to promotions. Although women are now found at significant levels of responsibility in many African countries (and this has been increasingly the case since 1975), they often have to be of exceptional ability to be recognized.

African governments have become increasingly aware of the need to promote the participation of women in their overall development efforts. A good number of countries have taken concrete steps to enhance the status of women and to provide better opportunities for the education of women and girls. It is toward this goal that there now exist separate ministries charged with women's affairs in some African nations. Measures are being taken through extension work and the development of appropriate technologies to lighten the burden of women's work, especially in rural areas. In some countries, such as Burkina Faso, early marriages are now prohibited by law.

In order to curtail the damage done to the education of girls by pregnancy some countries, such as Cameroon, now allow girls who become pregnant to return to school after they deliver. In some instances, too, laws exist to prohibit the abuse of minors. And, in addition to the efforts made to educate both boys and girls, more educational opportunities are now available to girls specifically. For instance, in many places technical schools are no longer segregated, so girls have the chance to receive instruction in a wider range of subjects than before. Careers in organizations such as the army and the police, which were hitherto the reserve of men, are now open to women. In the area of employment women receive the same pay as men for equal work. They are entitled to paid maternity leaves of fourteen weeks and are allowed an hour off work each day until their babies are fifteen months old.

Possible Lines of Action

In order to resolve the many problems that still hinder the education of women and girls in Africa certain lines of action need to be followed. First and foremost, the poverty of African countries needs to be tackled squarely. Poverty breeds illiteracy, and literacy among women and girls will rise if the general literacy rate is improved. This implies the provision of better and increased facilities for formal and nonformal education, which in turn requires more funds than are presently available. Governments will also have to decide, in the face of the growing economic crisis, how best to allocate and utilize meager and dwindling resources.

The problem of poverty is closely related to that of population. The population of Africa is young and expanding rapidly. More than 53 percent of Cameroon's population is under twenty years of age. So far most African governments have been reluctant even to consider policies to limit population growth. Obviously, family planning cannot be dictated; the need for it has to be felt, then implemented, by families themselves. It can, however, be encouraged. It is clear that deteriorating economies cannot cope with increasing populations, for which better services should be provided. A correlation has been drawn between fertility and the level of education: women who are better educated tend to have fewer children.[90] A general improvement in the level of literacy of women (and of men) in Africa should lead to greater acceptance of family planning programs. This also implies that the burden of women's work in Africa should be lightened sufficiently to allow women time to participate in literacy programs. In order to achieve this men will have to share some of the tasks that are now performed by women.

The majority of parents in Africa today are aware of the benefits to be derived from educating their children. They want their children—sons as well as daughters to live better than they do, and they see education as fundamental in bringing this about. If in the past parents saw potential profit only in the education of sons, it is becoming increasingly evident that the education of daughters is also important. For one thing girls tend to be more conscious than boys of the need to cater to aging parents. Governments, too, are becoming increasingly aware of the contributions that women, who after all make up at least half of their populations, can make to the global development effort.

* * *

I wish to express gratitude to Carew Treffgarre of the University of London Institute of Education for assistance with suggestions and access to some of the documentation used in this essay as well as to Elizabeth Fitzgerald and Patricia Wright of the Medical Research Council Cell Biophysics Unit at King's College London for their help in typing it.

Notes

1. UNESCO, *Statistical Yearbook and 1975-1985: Ten Years Toward Equality—UNESCO's Programme for the Advancement of Women* (Paris: UNESCO, 1985).
2. UNICEF, *Within Human Reach: A Future for Africa's Children* (New York and Geneva: UNICEF, 1985).
3. UNICEF, *Within Human Reach*; and World Bank, *Accelerated Development in Sub-Saharan Africa: An Agenda for Action* (Washington, D.C.: World Bank, 1981).
4. Fay Chung, "The Situation in Zimbabwe" (Paper presented at the Mount Holyoke Workshop to prepare for the conference on the Worldwide Education of Women, Nairobi, January, 1987).
5. World Bank, *Accelerated Development; Sub-Saharan Africa: Progress Report on Development Prospects and Programs* (Washington, D.C.: World Bank, 1983); and Organization of African Unity, Lagos Plan of Action for the Economic Development of Africa, 1980—2000, *Organization of African Unity*, 2d rev. ed. (Geneva: International Institute of Labour Studies, 1982).
6. The obstacles that lack of time places in the way of the education of women in Africa have been brought out by Brenda Gail McSweeney and Marion Freedman, "Lack of Time as an Obstacle to Women's Education: The Case of Upper Volta," *in Women's Education in the*

Third World: Comparative Perspectives, ed. Gail P. Kelly and Carolyn Elliot (Albany: State University of New York Press, 1982), in their study of women in Burkina Faso.

7. See also Marie Thourson Jones, "Educating Girls in Tunisia: Issues Generated by the Drive for Universal Enrollment," in Kelly and Elliot, *Women's Education in the Third World.*
8. See the reports in the *New York Times* dealing with the rape of 71 schoolgirls and the death of 19 students at the St. Kitzo's coed boarding school near Meru: Jane Perlez, "Kenyans do some soul-searching after the rape of 71 schoolgirls, *New York Times*, July 19, 1992; and "Boys at Kenya school rape girls, killing 19, *New York Times*, July 15, 1991.
9. See Jeremy D. Finn, Janet Reis, and Loretta Dulberg, "Sex Differences in Educational Attainment: A Process," in Kelly and Elliot, *Women's Education in the Third World.*
10. Susan H. Cochrane, "Education and Fertility: An Expanded Examination of the Evidence," in Kelly and Elliot, *Women's Education in the Third World*; Audrey C. Smock, *Women's Education in Developing Countries: Opportunities and Outcomes* (New York, Praeger Special Studies, 1981).

— 6 —

ADULT EDUCATION AND THE AFRICAN STATE IN THE POST COLD WAR ERA

J.R. Minnis

Introduction

This paper explores the tentative and emerging relationship between adult education and the African state in light of the development of powerful pro-democracy movements from 1989 to the present. In a continent where institutionalized democracy is virtually unknown (Jackson and Rosberg, 1985), one country after another is now struggling to cope with internal and international demands for greater openness and democracy.

Before the collapse of the Berlin Wall in 1989, 38 of Africa's 50 countries were governed by single-part regimes of varying authoritarian hues. Eighteen months later, half had pledged competitive elections and placed severe limits on executive powers (Decalo, 1991).

Despite this, Africa's democratic strides are too recent to be properly assessed and may yet prove to be cosmetic or temporary. The fact remains that in the span of a few years, many countries have for the first time embraced democratic or quasi-democratic systems which may have long-lasting effects on the planning and organization of adult education provisions.

While the struggle to democratize will inevitably follow distinct nationalistic and cultural norms unique to each country and region, the process of democratization carries with it certain philosophical and programmatic implications for the practice of adult education. Goodwin (cited in Griffin, 1987:86-87) for example, has identified the basic "ingredients" of liberal democracy as constituting a "coherent, self-consistent model of society." Her list of ingredients are: individualism, contract and consent as the political basis of individual freedom, constitutionalism and the law as limiting the power of the state over the individual, freedom of economic choice, equality of opportunity, a meriocratic theory of social justice, tolerance of dissidence and the distinction between private and public life.

However, in Africa these principles will be locally interpreted and defined depending on local circumstances. In situations where there are divisions between ethnic or other similar groups, and political parties divided along ethnic lines, multi-party democracy may increase conflict when the real need is to increase cooperation between groups. It would also be presumptuous to equate democracy with multi-party governance as practised in Britain or America. There are doubtless many other forms of democracy which maybe far more appropriate in multi-ethnic communities.

The implications of liberal democracy for adult education practice is best summarized by Griffin (1987:87): "liberal adult education policies are likely to advocate both the freedom of the individual from interference by the state and...state support for adult education." By accepting this broad ideological framework, adult educators in Africa can strive to respond to the needs of individuals, diverse groups and the society as a whole.

Because adult education has been historically marginalized and often poorly financed by the majority of African governments (the major provider of adult education), it remains a "poor cousin" to the formal schooling of youth from the point of view of resource allocation. The same cannot be said from a social policy perspective. Many African governments have used adult education extensively as a means of achieving what might be labelled "liberal" social policy objectives—particularly in the area of housing, health and human resource development. Some states have successfully redistributed resources in a relatively fair and equitable manner to rural areas and to the urban poor.

It is also true, however, that educational policy-making tends to be highly centralized in African countries, carried out by ministries of education and their subsidiary agencies. A "social control" model has been the norm resulting in a state monopoly on adult education provision. The overriding objective of the state is to use adult education as a means to maintain and conserve the traditional ordering of society however unjust and inequitous these policies turn out to be. Undergirding adult education provision in Africa is a collective, communitarian ethos which is often at odds with the ethos guiding the formal education sector. Adult educators tend to be more focused on such issues as unemployment, illiteracy, women's education, human rights and the plight of refugees. Adult education is conceived of as a means to minimize the dislocation resulting from social and economic change by extending individual options via educational opportunities. Thus adult education's liberal tendencies are at times incompatible with the state's objectives.

Purpose of the Paper

The demise of single-party rule in Africa represents an opportunity for adult educators to influence the future shape, ethos and direction of the state along liberal democratic lines. The balance of the paper focuses on how this might be achieved and is divided into three sections. First, we discuss a new role for the African state examining changes that are taking place in the economic and political sphere. Second, an overview of the present relationship between the state and education is presented highlighting areas of conflict and tension. Third, we focus on the need to integrate adults into the new economic and democratic structures being formed in Africa, suggesting that existing adult education providers can play a positive role in this regard.

A New Role for the African State

What is currently being worked out in Africa is a new democratic charter for the state; a new mandate to govern, but this time with constitutionally-entrenched political conditions, human and civic freedoms and political accountability within broadly defined market economies. Under the single-party state, rarely are "national" policies truly espoused let alone openly debated (Legum, 1985:35). With public policy-making under the control of hand-picked elites, governments are accountable to no one but themselves. Under single-party rule there has been neither democracy nor economic development; more often there has been both authoritarian government and economic decline (O'Connor, 1991).

Overspending and economic mismanagement along with reductions in foreign aid have placed severe limits on the state's ability to generate long-term economic growth. Not surprisingly, the long-term dependence on foreign aid has had the effect of strengthening the state at the expense of civil society by increasing and consolidating resources in the hands of the state. (Griffin, 1991) argues that rather than pass these resources on to private sector enterprises, NGOs or private households, governments over the years have used the additional resources to enlarge the state by increasing recurrent expenditures (military and civil), by increasing public investment infrastructure, and by expanding the number of state enterprises including the civil service.

Thus the state has been promoted at the expense of the rest of the economy. To complicate matters further, most African economies are close to bankruptcy because of their enormous debt burden, which is by no means identical from one country to another either in its nature or in its intensity. O'Connor (1991) conservatively estimates that the total debt of tropical Africa, excluding Egypt, the Maghreb countries and South Africa, was roughly $150 billion by the late 1980s. More important than the actual amount is the fact that the African debt represents such a large proportion of GNP—over 90 percent compared with 60 percent for Latin America. Nearly all states have a chronic balance of payments deficit with the value of imports far exceeding that of exports.

The consequence of the debt burden for adult education is considerable. In so far as the debt is owed by governments, it will lead to cuts in public spending on adult education provision and other social services. Although there has been considerable restructuring of debt in most countries, this may only bring short-term relief. It merely increases the amount that has to be repaid at a later stage thus limiting the state's future ability to underwrite social and educational programs. Insofar as accumulated debts will have to be paid off, they inevitably mean intensified poverty and reduced expenditures on social services.

There are certain steps states might consider taking to prevent further economic stagnation and possible decline. First, the structure, processes and procedures of the institutions managing the economies could be strengthened. The central banks could be made autonomous; legal limits could be set on the debt to be incurred by central governments and monetary policy need not be subordinated to fiscal policy.

Second, there is a need to abolish economic controls to effectively de-link patronage from politics. If they wish to become democratic, African countries must begin to utilize the expertise of its intellectuals in the solution of national problems. The state requires not only democratically-based stability, but also internal technical capability in all the key sectors of the economy.

And finally, the new realities of the post Cold War era suggest that Africa must learn to reduced levels of foreign aid. Some observers (Griffin, 1991) suggest that in the next decade the definition of aid will be changed from an emphasis on economic growth into one of self-reliance. The latter is a far more feasible notion in today's international climate than at any previous time because the strategy of self-reliance relies more on a reallocation of existing resources than on injections of aid from abroad. Thus African states will either "sink or swim" depending on their ability to adjust to reduced levels of aid.

Education and the State: Present Realities and Tensions

In the present order, the state plays a dorminant, overwhelming role in educational policymaking. The status assigned to the state is important because it is at the level of the state that decisions are made with regard to both the grassroots and to other states, NGOs, and international organizations.

In Africa, teachers and students make up a good proportion of the educated elite in any one country. To prevent the possibility of political disaffection spreading throughout the country, it is imperative that students and teachers be controlled, co-opting them when possible. The resulting dilemma for the state is aptly described by Ki-Zerbo (1990:78), " ... the state struggles under an overload of responsibilities derived from its control over the highest, most sensitive reaches of the educational pyramid. There is only oneway out of this trap: the state has to share some of its responsibilities with grassroots organizations and with inter-African agencies."

In addition to the state's need to maintain control over educational policy and resources, there is also the tendency for formal education to get blatantly monopolized by privileged minorities or regions skilled in the manipulation of power. This struggle over scarce resources creates tension and fuels interethnic antagonisms. According to Ki-Zerbo (1990:70), education, "becomes subject to power struggles unregulated by meritocratic criteria."

A third source of tension lies in the unequal distribution of educational resources between rural and urban areas. Urban areas tend to get the lion's share of resources. Capital cities are especially well placed and often account for 50 percent or more of the secondary school intake (World Bank, 1988). Universities are more often than not located in urban areas, often in capitals, close to the seat of governmental power, the headquarters of NGOs and influential international donor agencies. Paradoxically, farmers who make up 75 to 80 percent of the population of many African countries, and who are responsible for generating a significant portion of national income, are virtually excluded from the policymaking process. This group tends to have the highest illiteracy rate and their children constitute only 25 percent of the secondary school intake (Ki-Zerbo, 1990:70).

A fourth source of tension between the state and education derives from the states tendency to overinvest in formal education, particularly tertiary education, at the expense of vocational-technical training and adult education (World Bank, 1988). The result is high unemployment and educational inflation. Moreover, the state's incapacity to absorb into the labour force large numbers of educated youth is partly responsible for the alarming growth of unemployment in Africa. There were roughly 100 million people unemployed in 1989—four times as many as in 1979. The majority of those withoutwork are women and young men, and for those employed, real wages fell by 30 percent between 1980 and 1989 (Education for All, 1992:5-6).

The scramble for status and job security has fuelled competition among the elites of many countries for advanced training, and for certificates and diplomas to which it can lead, out of all proportion to the country's ability to provide commensurate employment.

These realities pose serious challenges to adult educators concerned with human-centred development. What must be achieved through political dialogue and other means is to establish the legitimacy of public participation and debate; and second, to convince policy-makers of the critical need to engage in shared decision-making with grassroots organizations, women's groups, NGOs, and inter-African agencies in an effort to find creative solutions to these problerns. The task is to impress upon government leaders the need to reallocate existing resources toward the education of women, the rural poor, and the unemployed not only on the basis of social or gender equity, but also from a cost-benefit standpoint. Such policies need not represent an expansion of educational facilities or result in increased expenditures. What is called for is a reallocation of existing resources to the nonformal adult education sector which complements and supplements activities in the formal sector.

An Expanded Role for Adult Education The Economic Dimension

The move to market economies and privatization of state enterprises can act to the mutual advantage of both state and civil society. If, as scholars of democracy suggest, there is a clear link between political freedom, a free market economy and economic development (Lindblom, 1977), then worker education and training opportunities in all sectors of the economy ought to receive urgent attention. However, it is also true that under conditions of highly dependent manufacturing production and a marginal economic infrastructure—conditions that are evident today in Africa—it would not be desirable for the state to direct a disproportionate amount of scarce resources into certain specialized positions whose long-term productivity is dubious (for example, positions in the civil service and management posts in foreign companies). Persons in mid-to high-level managerial positions currently receive the lion's share of training dollars. What is required is a reallocation of resources directed toward the upgrading of semi-skilled and skilled workers. This may prove instrumental in creating conditions for democratic selection and advancement procedures within industry. The private sector must accept its share of responsibility and join forces with the state to plan and underwrite new training policies.

It is also important to point out to policy makers that the creation of workplace educational opportunities not only enhances worker productivity, but instills in the worker a sense of self-worth which extends to the wider network of family and kin relations. New and more expanded definitions of the individual and the self are created; new categories of professional personnel and specialized elites are constructed; the use of education-related rules for the allocation of jobs and promotions is intensified; the corporate identity and authority relations of the family are restructured; and the flow of wealth in the family economy (from wife to husband and from child to parent) changes direction.

In economic terms, educating adults in the workplace carries with it the potential to construct and legitimate new categories of economic value, de-legitimate "traditional" economic pursuits (usually isolated from the wage economy), and redefine formerly private or communal pursuits as deserving remuneration. In this way, adult education contributes to economic growth—independent of individual-level effects—by redefining the economic value attached to a wide range of economic and social activities that, ultimately, become incorporated in aggregate measures of national wealth, such as gross national product (GNP).

Adult education can respond to the needs of individuals, groups and society itself without necessarily taking on a social engineering role. Large-scale economic and political change is well underway in Africa. Adult education, properly planned and organized, is a strategy for managing it, and helping individuals cope with it.

The Political Dimension

Populations in Africa are obviously no longer reverent of politicians nor are they likely to be lulled into acquiescence in the future. They possess larger pools of educated youth who are more aware than previous generations of the need for political and economic reform. Various civic and ecological pressure groups have sprung up monitoring local events and violations for parent bodies overseas. They serve as powerful links between internal and external pressures for democratic change.

African states seriously contemplating democratic change can facilitate the process if they acknowledge the need to support programs designed to educate citizens in the philosophy, processes and procedures of democratic government. Of late, too many governments, often for the wrong reasons, hastily call for elections knowing full well that opposition groups and citizens at large are unprepared and lack adequate resources to cope with the demands of organizing political campaigns. Such efforts simply undermine the right of citizens to meaningfully participate in setting up their own political structures.

Admittedly, the goals of integration and participation of the masses in the political process is by no means simple to achieve and cannot be completed overnight. Adult education's role is to become actively engaged in the task of political socialization and promotion of a national political consiousness that transcends ethnic and linguistic boundaries.

It is widely held that one of the defining characteristics of a democracy is that the rules governing political activity encourage all the varying shades of public opinion to be expressed. If political participation can be thought of as a democratic norm, then it would be logical to expect the state to encourage socialization patterns that maximize participation. One of adult education's immediate tasks will be to sustain an informed citizenry though dissemination of information and knowledge by creating awareness of political, cultural and economic issues. An expanded role for adult education agencies such as museums, libraries, social clubs and the mass media is vital to the accomplishments of this goal (Spaulding,1987:163).

The move toward democracy demands that the mass media in particular be allowed to play an expanded role in the informal education of adults without fear of censorship. Individuals must understand the value of changing their beliefs and behaviour on the basis of new information, and be receptive to the proposition that sustainable democracy demands their time and effort. This is not to imply that all Africans require explicit political education. However, in those countries without democratic traditions, even those citizens who have a degree of awareness and some meaningful interaction with the political system think more of their potential influence rather than their specific and direct impact upon policy making.

Conclusion

The African state will remain one of the main actors involved in adult education policy and practice. The collapse of single-party rule opens the door for new democratic and pluralistic structures. The "political space" created during the transition from autocratic to democratic governance offers a rare opportunity for the state to optimize the use of human resources, support and facilities for the development of work in adult education devoted to promoting democratic norms and values.

By encouraging broader community partcipation in decision-making regarding social policy, the state has an opportunity to redraw the boundaries between itself and civil society in a way that benefits society as a whole. In part, this can be achieved by: (1) relinquishing its hegemonic claim on educational and social policy making, and (2) abandoning policies of containment which have historically disenfranchised the unemployed, women, and ethnic minorites.

References

Decalo, S. 1991. "Back to square one: the re-democratization of Africa." *Africa Insight*, 21, (3): 153-161.

Education for All. 1992. *South Africa Economist*, 5, (2): February/March: 5-6.

Griffin, C. 1987. *Adult education and social policy*. London: Goom Helm.

Griffin, K. 1991. Foreign aid after the Cold War. *Development and Change*, 22: 645-685.

Jackson, R.H. & Rosberg, C.S. 1985. Democracy in tropical Africa. *Journal of International Affairs*, Winter. 285-296.

Ki-Zerbo, J. 1990. *Educate or perish: Africa's impasse and prospects*. UNESCO-UNICEF.

Legume, C. 1985. "Africa's search for nationhood and stability." *Journal of Contemporary Afrian Studies*, October: 31-42.

Lindblom, C.E. 1977. *Politics and markets*, New York: Basic Books.

O'Connor, A.M. 1991. *Poverty in Africa: a geographical approach*, London: Bellhaven Press.

Spaulding S. 1987. "Policy and planning in adult education: the international dimension" In W.M. Rivera (Ed.) *Planning adult learning; issues, practices and direcions*. London: Croom Helm.

World Bank 1988. *Education in sub-Saharan Africa: policies for adjustment, revitalization and expansion*. Washington, D.C.

J.R. Minnis can be contacted at the Department of Educational Foundations, Chancellor College, University of Malawi, Box 278, Zomba, Malawi.

— 7 —
THE ROLE OF ENVIRONMENTAL EDUCATION IN AFRICA'S SUSTAINABLE DEVELOPMENT

Valentine Udoh James

Introduction

As we approach the twenty-first century, one thing is vivid about Africa's environment—it is still being degraded at a much faster rate than it can be sustained. There are several reasons for this unprecedented decline. The major reasons that are often discussed in the literature are the exponential population increase, deforestation due to poor resource management practices such as shifting agriculture, haphazard development such as natural resource extraction. The mining of natural resources devastate the environment drastically and in some cases the impacts are irreversible because of the diminution of the biodiversity.

The least discussed aspect of sustainable development is the possible impact of environmental education on resource management on the continent. In this chapter the importance of environmental education in the sustainable development of Africa is discussed. The primary, secondary, and university curricula, it is argued, must reflect serious inclusion of environmental training. It is argued that conservation and preservation innovations must be integral parts of development and appropriate education has a role to play in sustainable development.

The current political and institutional instabilities in Africa present serious problems for effective education plan which could be instrumental in tackling environmental problems to be implemented. Stable institutions and political environment would enhance the process and attempts to equip the people of Africa with relevant education that could speed up recovery on the continent. There are those who argue that instability in economic, social, and political systems make it impossible to establish an education system which uses a local language (lingua francas) for education in regions of Africa. The success of such a system would lead to advancement on several fronts which include environmental protection, population, and health and more important enable Africans to continue to be culturally creative in their education system.

Brief Assessment of Environmental Conditions on the Continent

Africa, like many parts of the developing world, is facing a grave environmental degradation that is predominately due to unsustainable resource management techniques which have exacerbated land degradation process. Because large scale comprehensive planning is absent and small scale planning is inadequate environmental problems abound wherever development is taking place. In discussing the environmental problems of Africa, four topics are normally covered in the literature: 1) population, 2) deforestation and decertification, 3) degradation induced by development, and 4) natural resource extraction.

Population and Resource Distribution

The most discussed of the four problematic areas of development is human population explosion. Economists, anthropologists, sociologists, and natural scientists have argued their understandings of problems induced as a result of population growth. Table 1 shows the data pertaining to the social and economic conditions of some African countries. The Gross National Product (GNP) per capita for many African countries is significantly low when compared to the average GNP of countries where the standards of living are higher.

The column on infant mortality in Table 1 indicates that between 1977 and 1993 significant progress has been made in improving the mortality rate on the continent. The substantial drop was due to improvement in health services, some educational services on prenatal care and a host of other preventive efforts.

The majority of the African population does not receive adequate education. Illiteracy is a major problem which hinders development. Countries that have invested significant percentage of their GNP into directing education development of their societies have benefited enormously from such an investment. These countries have been able to encourage private interest in education planning in order to improve the quality of education and also to make available choices for different education opportunities. Table 1 (part 2) shows the primary school enrollment rate for 1975 and 1992. For countries with available data, although the rate of enrollment has increased, the illiteracy rate is still significantly high in many countries of Africa. The last column of Table 1 (part 2) clearly indicates this fact. This problem of not being able to provide education to the people is due to the rapid rate of population growth on the continent and since the majority of the people of Africa are below the age of fifteen, this group represents the largest group of uneducated and a potential problem for the future of the continent as a whole. A creative population is an educated one.

TABLE 1: SOCIAL AND ECONOMIC CONDITIONS OF SOME AFRICAN COUNTRIES

Part 1

Current Conditions					
	Population (millions) 1993	GNP per capita (US $) 1993	Share of Agriculture in GDP (%) 1975	Share of Agriculture in GDP (%) 1993	Child Malnutricion (%) 1991
Sub-Saharan Africa	558.9	520	23	19	119
Angola	10.3	—	—	—	160
Benin	5.1	430	31	36	108
Burkina Faso	9.8	300	38	—	162
Burundi	6.0	180	61	47	127
Cameroon	12.5	820	29	29	102
Central Afr. Republic	3.2	400	35	47	122
Chad	6.0	210	43	41	154
Congo	2.4	950	15	11	91
Corte d'Ivoire	13.3	630	28	33	117
Ethiopa	51.9	100	—	—	149
Ghana	16.4	430	48	48	103
Guinea	6.3	500	—	24	167

	Population (millions) 1993	GNP per capita (US $) 1993	Share of Agriculture in GDP (%) 1975	Share of Agriculture in GDP (%) 1993	Child Malnutricion (%) 1991
Kenya	25.3	270	30	25	82
Lesotho	1.9	650	29	8	121
Liberia	2.8	—	25	—	167
Madagascar	13.9	220	30	32	150
Malawi	10.5	200	35	36	177
Mali	10.1	270	61	42	191
Mauritania	2.2	500	27	25	125
Mozambique	15.1	90	—	31	160
Niger	8.5	270	50	39	157
Nigeria	105.3	300	31	33	105
Rwanda	7.6	210	49	37	133
Senegal	7.9	750	30	20	97
Sierra Leone	4.5	140	33	—	192
Somalia	9.0	—	49	—	149
South Africa	39.7	2,980	8	4	72
Sudan	26.6	—	38	—	97
Tanzania	28.0	90	37	49	117
Togo	3.9	340	27	49	117
Uganda	18.0	180	0	49	114
Zaire	41.2	—	17	—	117
Zambia	8.9	380	13	34	94
Zimbabwe	10.7	520	16	13	86

TABLE 1: SOCIAL AND ECONOMIC CONDITIONS OF SOME AFRICAN COUNTRIES CONTINUED

Part 2

Current Conditions					
	Infant (per 1,000) live births 1993	Child Malnutrition (%) 1991	Primary School Enrollment rate (%) 1975	Primary School Enrollment rate (%) 1992	Percent Illiterate (aged 15+) 1990
Sub-Saharan Africa	93	—	56	—	51
Angola	122	20	—	—	58
Benin	85	—	50	—	77
Burkina Faso	129	—	16	31	82
Burundi	101	—	22	69	50
Cameroon	61	14	97	—	46
Central Afr. Republic	101	—	73	—	62
Chad	120	—	73	—	62
Congo	84	—	—	—	43
Corte d'Ivoire	91	—	62	—	46
Ethiopa	117	47	24	22	—
Ghana	79	36	71	—	40
Guinea	132	18	30	42	76
Kenya	61	22	95	—	31
Lesotho	77	—	100+	100+	—
Liberia	123	—	62	—	61
Madagascar	93	39	95	—	20
Malawi	142	27	—	—	—

	Infant (per 1,000) live births 1993	Child Malnutrition (%) 1991	Primary School Enrollment rate (%) 1975	Primary School Enrollment rate (%) 1992	Percent Illiterate (aged 15+) 1990
Mali	157	—	24	—	68
Mauritania	99	—	19	—	66
Mozambique	146	—	—	60	67
Niger	122	—	20	—	72
Nigeria	83	43	51	—	49
Rwanda	109	29	56	—	50
Senegal	67	20	41	58	62
Sierra Leone	164	—	39	—	79
Somalia	120	—	59	—	76
South Africa	52	—	—	—	—
Sudan	77	—	47	—	73
Tanzania	84	28	53	68	—
Togo	83	—	—	99	57
Uganda	114	23	44	71	52
Zaire	92	25	88	70	28
Zambia	103	27	97	—	27
Zimbabwe	67	—	73	100+	33

Source: Adapted from World Bank (1995) p.x.

The General Condition of Education

The pre-colonial era in Africa was a time when formal education was absent. Education was informal but wholesome. The family was the basic provider and educator of children in social, political, cultural, economic, and agricultural matters. The village unit began to take hold of informing and providing the general etiquette for public conduct and general affairs of governance in the village. The small units of the villages and the use of local languages were instrumental in making these informal education very effective and efficient.

The colonial eras in Africa were marked by the introduction of new languages into Africa. New international, regional, and local boundaries were drawn in order for the colonialists to govern and manage the newly formed countries. The sudden interruption set the natural evolution of education back. Formal education was necessary in order for the colonial operations to function effectively in the interests of colonial rulers (James 1991).

There is no doubt that the indigenous systems of resource management suffered a tremendous set-back during the transitional periods (from pre-colonial to colonial) before the formal education became the main form of education in Africa. Natural resource management strategies through foreign methods gradually began to gain a strong hold in Africa. More organized and technical Western style management of African institutions which depended, on and required Western education was introduced into Africa.

The African education system is comprised of primary, secondary, technical, and university education. All the levels of education have been impacted by tight budgets due to economic problems, national emergencies which have been exacerbated by civil strife and in many cases by neglect and mismanagement. The elementary education must be refocused in order to teach the basics of education which are reading, writing, and mathematics; but more importantly the use of modern technologies so that the products of African school systems can be as good as those of other school systems around the world. In a changing world where competition is intense education policy or education planning as it used to be called twenty-seven years ago must address concrete issues or problems facing Africa's primary, secondary, vocational, and higher education systems. The mission of these systems must be clearly stated and implemented. The policy statement must clearly include ideas about how the environmental decline can be addressed in the twenty-first century.

Primary Education Planning

For several decades, the intentions of primary education in Africa has focused on increasing the coverage of education. The idea behind the universal primary education (UPE) has been to increase coverage. It has been the objective to ensure that every child receives free primary education. Countries such as Lesotho, Ethiopia, and Nigeria have attempted this idea. In 1962, Zambia attempted to implement "compulsory primary education." The efforts encountered some difficulties because the education was not totally free (Psacharopoulos 1990). In many African countries, the education situation at the elementary or primary level is one of increasing illiteracy because of limited access, inequity, and poor quality. The rapid population explosion has compounded the problem associated with not being able to provide primary education to every child.

Improving the Quality of Primary Education

Many countries in Africa have concentrated extensively on the training of teachers, construction of schools, and ensuring decent student/teacher ratios in order to improve the quality of education. One of the major problems confronting the schools in Africa is the condition under which the students learn. In many cases the school buildings are poorly constructed. The facilities for both the faculty and students do not enhance the teaching and learning experience. For instance, during the rainy seasons, the classrooms become filled with rainwater since they do not have windows and the surrounding environment have standing water which becomes infested with water borne diseases and young people are exposed to these terrible conditions. To make things worse, in Nigeria and many rural parts of Africa, students have to bring chairs to school. Otherwise, they have to sit on the floors. Teachers have to scramble for materials to instruct. The 1966-70, Zambia's First Development Plan had as its main priority the ambitious goal of making sure that primary education was improved by expanding the training available to teachers so that they could be effective classroom teachers and managers (Psacharopoulos 1990).

The floundering of the promotion of basic education in Africa dates back to the 1960s. For instance, in 1963, the Uganda educational system was experiencing the problem of teachers leaving the profession for other more lucrative jobs. Morale was low because teacher salary was not sufficient to live by and was not keeping up with the inflation rate.

Swaziland's Second Development Plan between 1972 and 1978 had little impact in raising the quality of education although it focused on reducing dropout rate. Student performance on Swaziland's Primary Certification Examination was poor (Psacharopoulos 1990).

There is the general agreement that teacher improvement is necessary in order to improve the quality of education but additionally curriculum improvement is imperative. This aspect must include the addition of a curriculum on environmental education. One that deals with identifying the country's natural resources, the quantity of biodiversity, the threat that confronts the natural resources as a result of growth, the significance of citizen as the protectors of the natural resources and the ecological systems and the importance of ecological principles in the protection of the world's habitats. Strengthening and improving the curricula on science would certainly enhance the involvement of children in the plan to protect the African environment. Practical experiences such as an out-door trip to a National Park to observe the country's wildlife could be very useful in inculcating in young people the concept and practice of conservation. The awareness brought about as a result of having the wilderness or natural ecological setting as a classroom forms a lasting impression which lasts a lifetime. A curriculum on environmental studies/science that is built on such fundamental environmental and ethical training is bound to be beneficial to the natural resources of Africa.

Before the environmental studies or natures studies curriculum is added at the primary/elementary school level, it is important to address the root causes of the decline in the standard of education in Africa. Many Africans of different political persuasions would agree that wrong priorities, poor planning, poor economy, and the use of foreign language for instruction are the root causes of the stagnation or decline in the standard of education on the continent. Educating primary school students in the native languages has had mixed reviews in Africa. It presents a special challenge given the fact that in any one country, there are as many languages as there are linguistic groups. For example, devising a lingua franca for a country such as Nigeria is difficult because there are about two hundred and fifty ethnic groups. A country such as Sierra Leone has had no education policy since 1970. There is a necessity for well developed policy which is realistic and relevant to the development of African countries. Countries such as Tanzania and Zambia now have educational policies that emphasize self reliance. The idea of combining education with production would enhance environmental protection and environmental planning ethics. Practical skills linked to production can be learned in the primary schools if the teachers have the skills acquired through proper training in order to teach the school children (Achola 1990). Most of Africa is still rural and many people do not proceed to secondary and the university and as such the elementary schools must prepare students to be engaged in rural development or work which could be mainly in the agricultural profession and agricultural development. This is directly linked to environmental or natural resource conservation and protection.

Secondary or High School Education

This is a very critical level in making sure that education is directly linked to technical and vocational skills while making sure that the social and arts curriculums do no suffer any setbacks. Here like in the elementary school, there must be a focus on combining education with the production aspects of the African societies. The appropriate training necessary for the sort of employment opportunities, job creation, resource management and resource protection must be the centerpiece of the secondary school education. The secondary schools must give students the skills and competencies necessary to perform effectively in the long-range management of African resources—in terms of human and natural/ecological resources. The importance of environmental training is crucial to the management of the natural resources of Africa. Despite the political and civil strife in many parts of the continent, one thing is clear, the natural resources face tremendous stress even at peace time. Thus creating the conditions or necessities for trained personnel in the environmental fields.

In modern Africa, conservation efforts are growing and in many countries protected habitats are being established in order to conserve and protect the flora and fauna of the continent. In countries such as South Africa, Zambia, Zimbabwe, Botswana, Zaire, Tanzania, Malawi, Kenya, and Uganda where there are many protected areas, there is a growing need to have trained personnel who can assist in the management, administration, and planning of the protected areas. The necessity for these trained personnel is more pronounced especially now that there are ambitious plans for "people and parks" concept for park management. In order to resolve the potential and existing conflicts between people and natural resources, African countries must invest in the training of its resource managers. The secondary schools could play a significant role in this regard. Revamping the educational system in order to diversify the course offerings could improve the quality of the secondary school education so as to prepare students for the "real world" that they would confront upon the completion of their education.

Attempts and efforts to encourage harmonious existence between humans and natural resources are continuing in Africa. Western (1982), Marks (1984), Matowanyika (1989), and Anderson and Grove (1987) have all argued about the significance of linking traditional African ways of life with wildlife management. In the face of an exponential increase in the population in Africa, it is important to train people with new skills in order to revitalize traditional relationships between people and wildlife. In order for the African population to benefit from the parks and other protected areas there must be a strong support of the local inhabitants. It is the trained personnel who can help in efforts to inform the public on the importance of their natural habitats. The internationally financed projects in Africa such as presented in table 2 makes it important for new skills to be acquired by resource managers in Africa. Africa has approximately thirty "people and parks" projects out of a total of about one hundred and sixty-seven national parks. These parks offer many opportunities for resource management and land use planning. Africa's parks present extensive biological diversity of great importance to the survival of the cultural diversity on the continent. Mackinnon (1986) notes that some of the worlds largest parks exist in Africa. Examples include Salonga in Zaire which has about 3,656,000 hectares, Etosha in Namibia contains about 2,127,000 hectares and Kafue in Zambia can boast of approximately 2,240,000 hectares. Many of Africa's parks attract foreign visitors who provide the financial base or engine for the establishment of the much needed infrastructures in and around the regions where the parks are located. The Serengeti in Tanzania and the Amboseli in Kenya are excellent examples of spectacular tourist destinations. Trained Africans are needed for the management of the parks and education at the high school levels must address the needs and opportunities offered by the parks. More than 500 protected areas exist in Africa besides the parks. Although these protected areas vary in quality from country to country, their continuous protection depends upon funding and availability of trained personnel. Young high school students must receive the necessary education that has root in environmental sciences, planning and management in order for the urban-rural interface of Africa to be protected. Students must plan important roles. Vocational education at the secondary school level could adequately address the shortage of skilled labor. Leader-Williams and Albon (1988) maintain that although funding for the management of parks and protected areas are slim, there is a lot of room for improvement especially in the staffing. This means that if and when funding are available either through an increase in government subsidy or by the parks becoming self-sustaining through user-fee (visitor charges) more people would be employed by the park system. Making park management styles country specific has its advantages but it should be pointed out that the more the protected areas get closer to the International Union for the Conservation of Nature and Natural Resources (IUCN) standards, the better managed they become and the better protected they are from poachers and conflict resolutions are handled appropriately.

TABLE 2: SOME OF AFRICA'S PEOPLE AND PARKS PROJECTS

PROJECT	COUNTRY	SPONSOR/ IMPLEMENTOR	DEVELOPMENT COMPONENT
AmBoseli National Park	Kenya	World Bank/ Government of Kenya	Waterpoint access, revenue sharing
Mountain Gorilla Project	Rwanda	AWF/ Government of Rwanda	Tourism
Bururi Forest Project	Burundi	AID/Government of Burundi	Agroforestry
Air-Tenere Project	Niger	IUCN/Government of Niger	Management of arid lands
Wildlife Extension Project	Kenya	African fund for Endangered Wildlife	Small scale rural development
Rumonge Forest Project	Burundi	Catholic Relief Services/Government of Burundi	Agroforestry

PROJECT	COUNTRY	SPONSOR/ IMPLEMENTOR	DEVELOPMENT COMPONENT
Nyungwe Forest Project	Rwanda	Swiss, French, EEC, IBRD/Government of Rwanda	Agriculture improvement, rural industry, tourism
Beza-Mahafaly	Madagascar	WWF/Government of Madagascar	Road construction, agricultural improvement
Andohahela Project	Madagascar	WWF/Government of Madagascar	Agricultural improvement
Kafue Flats National Park	Zambia	WWF/Government of Zambia	Wildlife utilization

Source: Adapted from Hannah (1992)

The harvesting of wildlife in protected areas of Africa have been beneficial to the economies of some countries. The controlled culling in a country such as Zimbabwe's Chirisa Safari Area averages an annual revenue of about $45,556,230 (Child, 1984). But in order to continue to enjoy this type of substantial benefit, Zimbabwe must have an education program in place to train needed park managers and to inform its growing citizens the necessity to protect wild habitats and maintain a healthy wildlife population. Management of parks and other protected areas benefits local populations who could be allowed on a seasonal basis to harvest wildlife for consumptive purposes. Such a management strategy calls for the understanding of the reproductive cycles of the wildlife and the successional stages of the habitat as a whole. Thus the diversification of the curriculum at the high school level to embrace new approaches which make the education relevant to a community's resources is essential to the sustainable development of a society. For instance, it is a well known fact that wildlife based industries depend extensively on the availability of wild stocks so that captive breeding can be carried out. Although this idea of maintaining high stock in the wild requires technical training, secondary education which combines a vocational (technical) training can accomplish the goal of providing expertise in order to maintain population of wildlife. Kakum National Park in Ghana could be a source for a diverse population of butterfly and other fauna in the world. Just as Papau New Guinea's butterfly industry has flourished, Kakum's can serve West Africa well in providing laboratories with diverse butterflies for research.

As was previously mentioned, protected areas management provides the opportunity to promote tourism. However, caution must be exercised not to raise expectations that conservation would be the panacea for eradicating the economic problems that a country is facing. The major role of protected areas in providing opportunities for coordinating the general tourism goals and objectives of a community with the land-use development for a region is an ecological and economical imperative. The main reason for such a reasoning is because there are environmental consequences of tourism in protected areas. Table 3 shows some East African examples. Studying the environmental consequences of tourism on natural habitats, species (both flora and fauna) and the surrounding communities requires undertaking an environmental impact analysis. In order to conduct such an analysis, a trained team of experts from different disciplines is necessary. These individuals must be university graduates. Environmental Impact Analysis requires a multidisciplinary team to offer an interdisciplinary technique in providing solutions to the emerging problems due to tourism and associated development.

African universities must prepare graduates with skills necessary for them to conduct the research necessary for the protection and maintenance of healthy ecosystems in the parks. The physical/chemical, and biological parameters of the protected areas must be assessed in terms of their existing and projected conditions. Environmental inventory must be conducted in order to know the number of wildlife and flora of the protected area. The degree of the impact of a proposed project must be studied and projection made in order to understand the carrying capacity of the area. The different science and policy related disciplines in the university must be involved in the training of Africans. The skills must be linked to employment opportunities available in Africa. For instance in providing the necessary land use management strategies in park areas around the world, buffers are necessary to shield a protected core.

TABLE 3: IMPACTS OF TOURISM ON PARKS AND COMMUNITIES

Activity/Condition	Environmental Consequences	Explanations	Parks/Protected Areas
Overcrowding	Environmental stress, animals show changes in behavior	Irritation, reduction in quality, need for carrying-capacity limits or better regulation	Amboseli
Over-development	Development of rural slums, excessive man-made structures	Unsightly urban-like development	Mweya, Seronera Keekorok, O1 Tukai
RECREATION			
Powerboats	Disturbance of wildlife and quiet	Vulnerability during nesting seasons, noise pollution	Murchison Falls
Fishing	None	Competition with natural predators	Ruaha, Nile
Foot Safaris	Disturbance of wildlife	Overuse and trail erosion	Mt. Kanya, Kilimanjaro
POLLUTION			
Noise (radios, etc.)	Disturbance of natural sounds	Irritation to wildlife and other visitors	Many areas
Litter	Impairment of natural scene	Aesthetic and health hazard	Many areas
Vandalism	Mutilation and facility destruction	Removal of natural features, facility damage	Sibiloi
FEEDING OF ANIMALS			
Feeding of animals	Behavioral changes of animals	Removal of habituated animals–danger to tourists	Masai Mara, Ruaha
VEHICLES			
Speeding	Wildlife mortality	Ecological changes, dust	Amboseli, Mikumi
Off-road driving, night driving	Soil and vegetation damage	Disturbance to wildlife	Ngorongoro, Amboseli

Source: Adapted from John and Kathy MacKinnon (1986) p. 87.

It is necessary to understand the biophysical conditions of an environment in order to adequately plan for a buffer. John and Kathy MacKinnon (1986: 90) argue that in order to determine the type and extent of buffer zone needed to protect a threatened resource the following factors must be taken into consideration.

- Needs of threatened wildlife species for use of additional habitat outside the reserve boundaries. Knowledge of the size and habits of the species will give some indication of the extent of an adequate buffer zone.

- The need for the buffer zone to serve other protective functions, such as soil and water conservation or fire-break protection.

- The need to contain wildlife species likely to move out of the reserve.

- The reasonable needs of local people for land, forest products, grazing areas or meat.

- The amount of land available for buffer use, whether it is currently under natural or other vegetation, and whether it is vacant or being used.

- The suitability of possible buffer crops for the particular land type and climatic conditions and the interests of local wildlife.

Creating and implementing the condition advanced in the ideas put forward by the MacKinnons requires studies in land use planning and landscape architecture. These are definitely university disciplines and as such African universities must provide adequate training in these disciplines which have strong and rigorous environmental components.

Conclusion:
Setting the Agenda for the Mission of Education in Africa

In this chapter, the future of environmental education in the education systems of Africa has been explored. There are many challenges for education in Africa given the difficult economic,political, and social circumstances of the continent. The political instability and social problems have compounded the problems of education for the citizens of many African countries so that they cannot adequately address the development problems confronting their societies. The elementary, secondary, and university management have all responded to the unrest and instability in the countries by not functioning effectively and properly. There have been strikes by students and faculty because of lack of subsidies, tuition hikes, lack of basic education support materials, poor student housing and infrastructure, poor salaries, and the generally bad educational situation.

These problems have resulted in a search for new primary, secondary, and university management strategies to deal with the problem that education systems in Africa are facing. Many African countries are experimenting with the idea of privatizing education. The fact remains that realistic goals must be set so that education is attainable by the majority of the people in the countries of Africa. Education has always been the primary responsibility of government and as such a mix of publicly and privately managed schools would be appropriate. The quality of publicly supported schools is questionable because they are plagued with innumerable problems which result in students receiving poor and inadequate education. Certainly privatization will improve the quality of education of those who can afford it. There is a need for a diversification of the financial bases for education in Africa. This could be achieved through the establishment of money making activities. Students should share in the costs of managing the schools. Any non-academic expenses should not be subsidized by the government. The students should be charged for non-academic expenses. The retention of faculty and staff must be top priority for maintaining the quality of education and private entities as well as the governments of Africa must invest in educational resources such as books, computers, and laboratory equipment. At the university level, donors who focus on enhancing the education in Africa must rethink their role to address the root problems of education. Africans must rethink what is really at stake if the standard of education continues to decline on the continent. Certainly the end result would be the loss of biological diversity due to haphazard development, poor land use practices, inadequate management and mismanagement of the natural resources. There is no doubt that a loss of cultural diversity would follow the loss of biodiversity. Thus, it is imperative to focus on environmental education in Africa.

References

Achola, P.P.W. 1990. Implementing Educational Policies in Zambia. World Bank Discussion Paper No. 90. The World Bank: Washington, D.C.

Anderson, D. and R. Grove. 1987. "The Scramble for Eden: Past Present and Future in African Conservation." p. 1 in Conservation in Africa: People Policies and Practice. O. Anderson and R. Grove (Eds.) Cambridge: Cambridge University Press.

Child, G.F.T. 1984. "Managing Wildlife for People in Zimbabwe." In J.A. McNeely and K. R. Miller (eds.), National Parks, Conservation and Development: The Role of Protected Areas in Sustaining Society. IUCN/Smithsonian Institution Press, Washington, D.C.

Hannah, Lee. 1992. African People, African Parks: An Examination of Development Initiatives as a Means of Improving Protected Area Conservation in Africa. United States Agency for International Development (USAID): Washington, D.C.

James, Valentine. 1991. Resource Management in Developing Countries. Bergin and Garvey: Westport, Connecticut.

Leader-Williams. N. and S. Albon. 1988. "Allocation of Resources for Conservation." Nature v336:533.

MacKinnon, J. and Kathy MacKinnon. 1986. Managing Protected Areas in the Tropics. Gland, Switzerland: IUCN.

MacKinnon, J. and Kathy MacKinnon. 1986. Review of the Protected Areas System in the Afrotropical Realm. Gland, Switzerland: IUCN.

Matowanyika, J. 1989. "Cast Out of Eden: Peasants versus Wildlife Policy in Savanna Africa." Alternatives. v16:30.

Marks, S. 1984. The Imperial Lion. Boulder: Westview.

Psacharopoulos, George. 1990. Why Educational Policies Can Fail: An Overview of Selected African Experiences. World Bank Discussion Papers: Africa Technical Department Series. World Bank:

Washington, D.C.

Western, D. 1982. "The Environment and Ecology of Pastoralists in Arid Savannas." Development and Change. v13:183.

World Bank. 1995. Social Indicators of Development. John Hopkins University Press. Baltimore, Maryland.

— 8 —

INTEGRATING GENDER INTO ENVIRONMENTAL EDUCATION IN AFRICA*

Eva M. Rathgeber

Abstract

This paper argues that the integration of a gender dimension into environmental education curricula will promote both environmental conscientization and environmental responsibility among African school children. The paper focuses on the environmental education curriculum in the African context, arguing that, to some extent, the emphasis on environment has been donor-driven. The paper provides a brief overview of the current teaching and content of environmental education, with special focus on gender issues. Attention then turns to some key past decade, using the example of forestry to illustrate the complexity of African women's interaction with the natural environment. The paper concludes with a discussion of the potential of gender analysis as a methodology to enable children to achieve better understanding of human management of the natural environment.

Résumé

Bien que la femme africaine soit celle qui a la fois utilise et gère les resources naturelles, sa contribution fait rarement partie du curriculum des écoles en Afrique. La thèse de l'auteure est que l'intégration de l'analyse de genre dans les cours d'écologie servirait a la fois a conscientiser les enfants a cette question et a les rendre plus aptes par la suite a conserver les ressources naturelles. L'accent mis sur l'importance de l'éducation a l'environnement provient, selon l'auteure, des pressions exercées par les pays donateurs. Après un survol du contenu des cours d'écologie dans les écoles primaires et secondaires, l'auteure utilise l'exemple de la foresterie pour illustrer la complexité des rapports

---

* This article is based on a keynote address given to the International Association of Social Studies Educators meeting in Nairobi, Kenya in June 1994. The author is grateful to an anonymous reviewer of the *Canadian Journal of Development*

qu'entretient la femme africaine avec l'environnement. L'article conclut sur une discussion du potentiel de l'analyse de genre comme méthodologie permettant aux enfants de mieux comprendre la gestion humaine de l'environnement naturel.

Introduction

Despite women's central roles as users and managers of the environment, analysis of their contribution is rarely incorporated into environmental education in African schools. Environmental education (EE) programs put great emphasis on multidisciplinarity, on issue analysis, and on problem-solving but this is mostly done from a "gender neutral" perspective. Most frequently it is assumed that all persons in the community (men, women and children) have more or less the same relationship with the surrounding environment. This has impeded the effective teaching of environmental concerns because it has denied children the opportunity to analyze realistically the responsibilities and constraints faced by poor women and men in Africa in both the urban and rural sectors and to understand why environmentally-harmful choices are often made both by individuals and by households.

This paper argues that the integration of a gender dimension into environmental education curricula will promote both environmental conscientization and environmental responsibility among school children. The paper begins with an analysis of environmental education from a global perspective and then focuses on an examination of the EE curriculum in the African context. It provides a brief overview of some of the current teaching and content of environmental education in Africa, with special focus on gender issues and argues that to some extent environmental concerns have been imposed from outside Africa. Attention then turns to a few key findings that have emerged from research on gender and environment during the past decade, using the example of forestry to illustrate the complexity of African women's interaction with the natural environment. The paper concludes with a discussion of the potential for gender analysis as a methodology to enable children to achieve better understanding of human management of the natural environment. It will be shown that integration of some of the findings of gender-sensitive research and utilization of gender analysis as part of the methodology and content of EE would enhance the understanding of African children of their environment and give them more adequate preparation to contribute to on-going conservation efforts.

I. Environmental Education in the Global Context

In Africa as elsewhere during the 1980s, educators placed increasing importance on teaching children to observe and become sensitized to the compexities of the physical environment around them. African educators recognised that in the context of dwindling natural resources there is a need to teach conservation and preservation theories and practices and to instil in school children the requisite knowledge, skills and desire to participate in the achievement of these aims.

This was consistent with prevailing international attitudes towards the importance of environmental education. UNESCO and UNEP both have been central actors in the development of a pedagogy for EE and they have identified the following objectives for formal and non-formal environmental education:

i) the provision of long-term strategies for the prevention of environmental problems;
ii) the development of solutions for environmental problems that arise or already exist; and
iii) the promotion of environmentally sound, sustainable development (UNESCO-UNEP, 1992).

Perhaps the most fundamental component of environmental education is its multidisciplinary nature which integrates the geophysical, biological, socio-economic, sociocultural and demographic variables that have an impact on the environment. In this sense, EE at a global level, has moved far beyond the conceptual boundaries of traditional disciplinary teaching.

Environmental education in the formal school curriculum usually has a number of objectives. When taught by knowledgeable, enthusiastic and creative teachers it allows children to develop in-depth familiarity with issues, to become adroit in analysis and investigation, to learn citizenship skills and civic responsibility, and to acquire a sense of control (UNESCO-UNEP 1992). Environmental educators emphasize problem-solving approaches and the utilization of action research.

II. The African Context

In several African countries efforts have been made since the mid-1980s and earlier to include EE in school curricula. However, environmental concerns tend to be narrowly defined and to be infused into existing subjects (e.g. science, social studies, home economics and agriculture) rather than to be taught in their own right (DaSilva, 1994). To a considerable extent, this is the case because curricula in most African school systems already are overburdened and there is no available time for the introduction of entirely new subjects. Typically, in both primary and secondary schools, environmental issues are introduced through a focus on topics like soil erosion, waste disposal, decertification, conservation, etc.

Although environmental educators globally have emphasized the importance of producing curriculum material that presents the multifaceted nature and the interdependence of humankind's natural and social environment, African environmental educators on the whole have been less successful in giving emphasis to the human influence on the environment and in effecting attitudinal change through environmental education (Bakobi, 1994). Given the fact that in Africa environmental problems themselves are most commonly seen from a technical rather than a cultural perspective, this is perhaps not surprising (Abucar and Molutsi, 1993). However, one negative repercussion of this lack of attention to human and cultural issues, has been a tendency for African educators to assume that people's perceptions of the environment remain static and therefore do not lend themselves to useful analysis. Consequently, curricula have overall emphasized the use of technologies to control the environment rather than impact, focusing on changes in human attitudes and practices. Attention has been on product rather than process (Weekes-Vagliani, 1992), leading for example, to the development of technical strategies for coping with and halting land degradation. Some of these reasons are closely linked with local social systems and power structures which, in turn, are greatly effected by the social relations of gender. The tendency in African environmental curricula to focus on technology at the expense of community attitudes and practices has created an important obstacle to the integration of a gender perspective into EE.

It is difficult to trace the origins of environmental education in Africa. Certainly over the past 15 years there have been committed African environmentalists and educators who have argued passionately and convincingly for the inclusion of environmental concerns into the curriculum. However it is also true that to some extent the push for the inclusion of environment in school curricula has come from the North, often through the intervention of donor agencies. Throughout the 1980s and into the 1990s, donors like SIDA, USAID, UNESCO, UNEP, GTZ and others have supported environmental education workshops, planning meetings, regional surveys, training courses, etc. The North began to place high priority on the promotion of sustainable global development after the publication of the Bruntlandt Commission report in 1987 and in the period leading up to the U.N. Conference on Environment and Development (UNCED) in Brazil in June 1992. This heavy endorsement by donors has driven some of the current African interest in and commitment to environmental education.

The fact that environmental concerns have been somewhat donor-driven in Africa, has meant that there is sometimes only limited commitment to the development of sound environmental practices at both the local and the national levels. Maureen Fitzerald's study of EE programs in Welo Province, Ethiopia concluded that they were premised on "accommodative environmentalism," i.e. on an acceptance of the status quo and a belief that current power structures should remain more or less intact rather than on a desire to effect real change in environmental management. She found that initial pressure for the inclusion of EE in formal and non-formal education in the region came from the World Bank and FAO in discussions with the Ministry of Education after the famine of 1981-85. The donors argued that the effects of the famine had been exacerbated by long-term degradation due to poor land management practices by local farmers and that in the future this could be avoided by teaching children more appropriate agriculture practices in schools. SIDA was asked to become the lead agency in coordinating an integrated rural development program in the region, with some emphasis on EE. Fitzerald found little evidence that sustainable development was a priority for Ethiopia's economic policymakers at the time and that the emphasis placed on EE by the Ministry of Education had little linkage or integration with other aspects of government decision making (Fitzerald, 1990). Consequently, the impact of the program was quite limited.

The Ethiopian experience shows the need for EE to be integrated into overall national economic and social objectives, however if it is to have real impact, such integration must also occur at the community level. Local attitudes to conservation and preservation of the environment must be shaped to be consistent with overall government objectives. In this context, gender analysis provides an effective means for reaching a better understanding of the relationship between environment and local economic and social organization. In most communities both men and women have prescribed productive and reproductive roles that inform the nature of their interaction with the environment. For example, collection of fuelwood and water are usually jobs reserved for women and children, and therefore women are likely to have a strategic interest in the preservation of local water and fuelwood sources. Men, on the other hand, may place lower value on preservation of local woodlots and water sources simply because they are not burdened by a daily need to collect wood for and water. However, such attitudinal differences between men and women and the different natural resource management strategies that they imply are not reflected in African environmental education programs.

A cursory review of some recent literature on environmental education suggests that it is remarkably gender-insensitive. Words like "population," "humanity," and "man" are used to describe the human interaction with environment. Academicians proposing strategies for effective multidisciplinary teaching of EE commonly refer to both teachers and students as "he" thus reinforcing a sense that environmental studies are a male domaine. Much of the material emanating from UNEP, UNESCO and other international organizations tends to take this approach. As illustrated below, it is also reflected in actual curricula used in many African schools.

III. Curriculum Content

An examination of the EE components in Uganda's senior secondary schools' social studies and environment syllabus in 1988 provides a good example of the approach used to impart environmental knowledge. EE was organized into the following units:

Unit 1: Understanding the social and the physical environment
Unit 2: Man develops his environment
Unit 3: Man uses technology to develop and improve resources and the environment
Unit 4: Man is influenced by his social environment and political

organization
Unit 5: Man's search for identity and unity in his environment (UNEP, 1988)

It is striking that the language used is entirely male-focused. By 1988 there was a strong movement towards gender sensitization in Africa. Neighbouring Kenya had hosted the 1985 U.N. Conference on the Status of Women, which drew large African participation. Nonetheless it appears that, at least in Uganda, power over the environment was still seen very clearly as a male preserve. The unit titles give a suggestion of action and of control, i.e. "man develops his environment...man uses technology..." but this positive imaging reinforces existing stereotypes about the secondary roles and contributions of women. It seems evident that the use of such male-focused language would reinforce any predisposition in the minds of the teachers that interaction with the environment is primarily through male interlocutors.

Analysis of the topics under each unit reveals even less likelihood that a gender-sensitive approach would be employed. For example, under Unit 3 the following topics were to be taught:

1. Technology and agriculture
2. Technology and energy
3. Technology and manufacturing
4. Technology and communication
5. Technology and transport
6. Environmental problems arising out of technological advancement and measures to solve them

In each topic, the entry point seems to be a technological, machine—or tool-based approach rather than an examination of human interaction with the particular sector in question. Bernard Bakobi notes that this failure of the EE curriculum to focus on human interaction with the environment is also common throughout the SADC countries (Bakobi, 1994). This is consistent with tendencies noted elsewhere for school science curricula to de-emphasize human or social values in favour of a technology-based approach (which is seen as being more objective) (Rathgeber, 1995). Since girls tend to respond more positively to the discussion of human and social issues, the adoption of the technological focus in teaching about the environment can become another way of discouraging the full interest and participation of female students.

Another example can be drawn from agriculture. Although it is well-known that women are the major subsistence food farmers of Africa, most syllabi give no attention to the sexual division of labour and responsibility and to the limited capacity of women to make decisions about the use of land because of prevailing cultural and social norms. Instead, EE is integrated into the curriculum in a generic way. For example, the topics covered in Kenyan primary schools in Agriculture in 1992 included:

a) land use
b) soil conservation, soil erosion
c) disease and pests
d) water utilization

In secondary, schools the topics under Agriculture were as follows:

a) environmental influences on agriculture
b) soil
c) land reclamation
d) soil and water conservation
e) crop pests and diseases
f) livestock diseases
g) water supply

It is clear that in both the primary and the secondary curricula there is a focus on environmental issues of critical importance in Kenya. However, the entry point for these topics has been depersonalized and emphasis is placed on the geophysical aspects rather than on an analysis of social, cultural and economic factors that effect the capacity of men and women to use their land in an environmentally sustainable fashion. In this way, children will learn, for example, the essentials of soil and water utilization and conservation, but they are unlikely to learn why farmers are sometimes forced to overgraze their land or to deplete their soil of nutrients by planting the same food crops year after year instead of in rotation. These decisions, made by female or male farmers may be based on social and economic circumstances rather than on lack of environmental knowledge. However, the organization of the curriculum solely from a technological perspective will implicitly lead children to assume that poor environmental management is due to farmer ignorance rather than social, cultural and economic constraints.

In general, EE communication in the formal school curriculum has tended to take a theoretical approach, providing general overviews of problems. More over, such problems usually are seen from a one-dimensional perspective. Thus, for example, children may learn about the importance of access to water supplies for agricultural purposes, but they probably will not learn about the potentially harmful health effects of inadequate access to water. Vivian Weekes-Vagliani (1992) notes that it would be pedagogically more effective to make direct linkages with the problems faced by local communities and specifically by men and women within those communities. If local conditions and problems become a starting point for EE, then it will be easier for children (or adults) to relate what they learn in school to their own experience outside the classroom. It is also more likely that attitudes, and in time harmful practices, will be changed.

Ideally, schools should link EE with farmwork and teach effective management of local natural resources. There is a need to focus on local soils and water, including conservation, on deforestation and on how the community and the individual can become agents of change. Again, gender analysis offers one way of approaching such issues in the classroom. All children have observed the different duties and responsibilities undertaken by adult males and females in their families, and this could provide a good starting point for discussion and analysis. Teachers must be trained and the curriculum developed "so that students learn about the agricultural balance sheet of an area" (Brundtland Commission, 1987, p. 113). It seems self-evident that children will feel a commitment to protecting their local environment only if they understand fully the extent to which it is threatened and the implications of this for their own future livelihoods.

IV. The Role of Teachers

Teachers play a central role in effective environmental education. Multidisciplinary EE is dependent on the leadership of creative teachers who are able to analyze situations with their students. However, the use of such approaches puts a heavier burden on teachers than traditional pedagogic methods that place emphasis on textbooks and written materials and which are still very common in African schools (Bakobi, 1994). Unfortunately in many African countries, teacher training in EE is inadequate, both as part of original teacher training and as in-service training (Lindhe et al., 1993). Teachers have little access to books and equipment, and they have not themselves been able to develop the investigative and analytical techniques that are fundamental to effective EE. In East Africa, Ethiopia has one of the best records of providing in-service EE training, particularly for teachers at the primary level. Important topics for training include the concept of environmental education, teaching methodology and the adaptation of content to local needs (Lindhe et al., 1993). However, in most African countries such specialized training is not available and even in Ethiopia, EE teaching materials are scarce.

Because of their lack of training and appropriate instructional materials, most teachers tend to utilize traditional methods to impart environmental education. A survey of the teaching of EE in the SADC countries noted that students most commonly were asked to "list," "prioritize,""describe," etc. (Bakobi, 1994). Emphasis was on memorization and on theoretical approaches. Students were not asked to analyze, explore, understand or discover within a multidisciplinary context, as recommended by trained EE educators.

This tendency appears to hold across Africa. For example, Adara notes that in Nigeria there continues to be a critical shortage of EE specialists as well as a dearth of relevant texts and teaching materials, with the result that environmental information tends to be presented as simple facts rather than as problems or projects which will encourage student involvement (Adara, 1993). Similarly, in Kenya most teachers have no relevant training about environmental issues and are unable to teach the subject effectively, even when it is in the syllabus. Moreover, because teachers are frequently transferred by government departments of education, they often don't have time to develop close relationships with local communities which would make it possible for them to use the local environment as a laboratory for investigation and analysis together with their pupils (Wanaswa, 1993). Responsibility for environmental matters is split among several different ministries and departments, which sometimes leads to conflict of interests and makes it difficult to implement programs to improve environmental education. However, the education syllabus now emphasizes conservation and management of the environment, in contrast with an earlier focus on "exploitation of our natural resources" (Wanaswa, 1993). Moreover, student teachers currently enrolled at Kenya's Diploma Colleges do receive some basic training in EE.

In Uganda, there are similar problems. A study carried out in early 1994 by Adimola et al revealed that there is little institutional capacity to undertake comprehensive environmental education, including inadequately trained teachers and a low level of resources to support environmental education activities both in formal and non-formal sectors. The study also identified a need for research to inform policy formulation and environmental education program design and implementation at all levels. An important part of the problem in Uganda, as elsewhere in Africa, was generally low sensitization to environment issues, even among top policymakers. NGOs have tended to sensitize the Ugandan public around crisis situations like the water hyacinth choking the country's major lakes, droughts and famines. Moreover, Ugandan schools currently teach "from and about" the environment not "for" the environment. There are no prescribed EE curriculum guidelines on which teachers can base their teaching and environmental components are presented for purposes of passing examinations. To teach "for" the environment would involve the transfer of analytical skills that would enable students to recognize problems and to systematically seek solutions through the examination of data. At the same time, it would help to promote desirable values and foster positive attitudes towards the environment.

It appears that while there is some commitment to the development of effective environmental education, most African countries have been unable to implement a truly multidisciplinary approach. In particular, little attention has been given to the relationship between human beings and the environment, and especially the impact of the social relations of gender on the development of natural resource management strategies at the local level. Research on gender and environment has been carried out in Africa over the past 15 years and an examination of some key findings could provide important input into African environmental education curricula.

V. Gender and EE: Some Theoretical Connections

The role of women in the management of natural resources continues to go unrecognized by EE curriculum developers in Africa. A recent review of

African environmental research did not mention gender as an important area for analysis (Filho, 1994). Similarly, African experts at a workshop in Abidjan in 1991 identified key issues for integration into environmental curricula, including drought; desertification; deforestation; pollution; physical quality of life in human settlements; implications of over-population; environment-linked diseases; availability of drinking water; management of natural resources; social and coastal erosion; and bush fires (USAID, 1991). They made recommendations as to how these could better be integrated into the curriculum, but they failed to note that these issues could affect men and women differently. This is particularly unfortunate because gender analysis is based on the use of precisely the type of analytical, multidisciplinary approaches and questions that are advocated by environmental educators. For example, with respect to a topic like "the physical quality of life in human settlements," gender analysis would lead to insights related to access to housing; responsibility for maintaining standards of cleanliness inside and around the house and compound; capacity of the household unit to pay for services like garbage collection, water or electricity, if they are available; preponderance of violence and crime; spread and control of environment-related disease, and numerous other topics. Not only do women usually have specific family responsibilities closely related to these questions, but their limited access to resources and low status in many societies puts severe restrictions on their capacity to respond to such environmental concerns. It is evident that the utilization of a gender analysis approach would add an important realistic dimension to the investigative and analytical skills which are a cornerstone of EE.

The fact that research findings from gender and environment have not been integrated into school curricula in Africa should perhaps not be surprising since there has been resistance even among donor agencies to integrate such findings into their development planning. For example, most of the work done by the World Bank on environmental issues is totally gender "neutral," which, in practice, usually translates into a male bias. There is an implicit assumption that the environment and environmental issues are perceived in the same way by males and females. Given the context of men's and women's differing experiences with the environment and the divergent needs that they have of the natural environment, this assumption may be ill-founded. As argued by Bonnie Kettel (1993) both "gender" and the "environment" are social and cultural constructions, and perceptions of "environment" are dependent on human interaction with and use of the natural landscape. Consequently, perceptions of environment are closely linked with the sexual division of labour.

An emerging feminist analysis of environment has drawn attention to significant linkages between women's productive and reproductive roles, the global commoditization of agricultural production and environmental degradation (Dankelman and Davidson, 1988; Mackenzie, 1993). In face of demands for increased agricultural production and higher levels of efficiency, African farmers are forced to adopt agricultural practices which will have severe implications for the long-term sustainability of their resource bases. Although it has been amply demonstrated that intensified cropping, higher yielding varieties, irrigation, high levels of fertilizer and pesticide use all strip the land of nutrients, structural adjustment policies advocated by the World Bank and the IMF and put into practice by the national governments of most African countries, have led to the large scale adoption of ultimately harmful agricultural practices.

In the context of donor-driven efforts to promote the utilization of technology packages, indigenous knowledge about soil conservation and environmentally sustainable farming practices, passed down through generations to both women and men, has been marginalized. As noted, EE curricula in Africa prefer to stress technological solutions to environmental problems. Therefore, although traditional knowledge systems may sometimes offer useful insights into effective management of local soils, such knowledge has not been integrated into school curricula and consequently has been relegated to an inferior status in the minds of both educators and school children. It should be noted also that the technology-based environmental knowledge currently taught in schools is supportive of both the continued domination of the North over the South and of men over women. Most of the technology comes from the North rather than the South and it is used, or at least controlled, by men rather than women.

To illustrate the potential benefit of the integration of gender issues into EE in Africa, it is useful to consider some specific research-generated knowledge about women's natural resource management practices. The case of fuelwood resources provides a good example.

VI. Women's Work in Fuelwood Management

Collection of fuelwood is considered women's work in virtually all African societies. One Kenyan study estimated that women spend from five to six hours weekly in fuelwood collection (Sunny, 1992), however Mary Omosa found that in the Bura district of Kenya, fuelwood collection took from seven to nine hours per day and that all members of the family, including children were regularly involved. They walked an average of 12 km. in each firewood-searching trip (Omosa, 1992). It is clear that there are great variations in the amount of time and effort required for fuelwood collection, depending on local environmental conditions and levels of deforestation.

Although it is rare for women to collect fuelwood expressly for commercial reasons, there are cases, as in Ethiopia, where this occurs. For example, each day large groups of Ethiopian women climb into the hills surrounding the capital city of Addis Ababa to collect wood in the hillside forests. They carry loads ranging from 15 to 50/kg into the city (10-15 km.) which they sell to slum dwellers for small profits (Haile, 1989). When wood is gathered as a largerscale commercial venture, it is usually undertaken by men. Exploitation of existing wood resources is more systematic and vehicles (animal-drawn carts or even trucks) are used for transport purposes. Environmental protection and tree planting usually is not a priority for commercial wood dealers, and, even for local communities, struggling to survive in hostile environments, environmental concerns are often of secondary importance. Because rural women's needs for wood are constant, they have a vested interest in ensuring that the forest areas in their regions are preserved to ensure a continuing supply of wood. However, although shortage of fuelwood is often a serious problem for women, it is not their only problem and they are sometimes more concerned with other issues, e.g. shortage of water or of food.

As fuelwood becomes more difficult to find or more costly to purchase, poor women tend to cook less often or to cook foods requiring less fuel. In this way, women are the first victims of local wood shortages because their reproductive roles (including cooking of family meals) place them in a situation where they are held responsible for inadequate meals. Omosa found that in Bura district in Kenya, people often did without meals during periods of great fuelwood scarcity (1992). This has long term negative nutritional effects on families, especially young children and pregnant women.

Rural women often collect tree products, sometimes from non-forest areas, as important sources of family protein and income. Elizabeth Ardayfio-Schandorf found that Ghanaian women routinely collect leafy vegetables, honey, fruits, nuts, medicinal plants, fodder, and wood for household utensils and building materials. Some of these products are for domestic consumption but a large proportion are sold and are significant sources of income for the poorest women. A study in Zambia found that of more than 70 traditional vegetable species that were consumed, more than half were gathered in the wild. They formed an important part of household food security. The leaves and pods of dryland trees such as the acacia can contain up to 15 percent pure protein, which makes it a rich source of animal fodder. A study in Zimbabwe found that women routinely incorporated small wildlife (caterpillars, mopani worms, etc.) into the diets of their families and that these were recognized as having a high nutritional value (Chimedza, 1993).

Local knowledge about natural resources is usually specific to regions or areas and focused on livelihood strategies and management of risk. Increasingly, research is showing that rural African women have immense instrumental knowledge bases. For example Elizabeth Ardayfio-Schandorf (1993) found that in northern Ghana women collected different kinds of fuelwood for specific functions or purposes, and their knowledge of tree species and of the properties (intensity of heat, length of burning, etc.) of different types of fuelwood was often very detailed. However, Ardayfio-Schandorf also found that if such knowledge was not used fairly regularly, it tended to be forgotten.

Frequently rural women also have extensive knowledge of the medicinal properties of local flora and fauna, especially ones used during pregnancy, childbirth and the care of young children. Another area of knowledge often dominated by women relates to use of forest products for handicrafts, both for domestic use and for income-generating activities.

Rural women's knowledge also extends to forest and agricultural management. In some cultures women are responsible for looking after small livestock, which graze on forest products. They assume responsibility for teaching children how to protect small seedlings to ensure that they are not eaten by the animals (Williams 1992).

In most African societies, intercropping of trees and shrubs with food crops has been a common practice. Traditionally, intercropping, coupled with crop rotation, has been an important means of building up soil nutrients. Frequently, drought or pest-resistant species have been interspersed with food crops.

Conclusion

The forestry case, illustrated above reveals numerous relevant facts that usefully could be integrated into African EE curricula. It is clear that the interaction of rural African women with the environment differs from that of men and that therefore it is necessary to focus specifically on both men and women in teaching EE. Women have specific responsibilities relating directly to the use of natural resources. These include collection of fuel and water, agricultural production for family subsistence, collection of wild berries and wild herbs for family consumption and medicinal purposes, etc. Each of these tasks carry with them the need for specialized knowledge about natural resources as well as knowledge of conservation. This knowledge, while not couched in scientific terminology, nonetheless provides direction and justification for rural women's prevailing forest management practices.

The knowledge bases of rural women are holistic, drawn from observation of natural phenomena, experience, oral history and tradition, and symbolism. Their knowledge is not categorized in a way which lends itself to easy organization into neat learning units. This is one reason why local knowledge has often been undervalued or ignored in formal education curricula. But equally importantly, and as already suggested above, there has been a tendency for EE to be closely linked with and to give value to the "technical" and the "scientific" rather than the "traditional."

All African children, especially in rural areas, have watched their mothers or female adults engaged in work which involves intensive interaction with the environment. Usually from an early age, children have assisted with some of the lighter tasks and, in the process, have acquired important environmental knowledge. However, when children move into the classroom this "home" knowledge is set aside and replaced with "school knowledge" taken from textbooks or from teachers. One important contribution that could be made by environmental educators in African schools is to close the gap between "home knowledge" and "school knowledge." By developing teaching materials that recognize the daily environmental decision-making undertaken by African women and encouraging children to analyze why their mothers make those decisions, African educators could help to create congruency in the minds of children.

One way of approaching this might be to utilize the Minds Across technique developed in Uganda whereby children were encouraged to write stories and draw pictures relating to a subject under discussion in the classroom. Empty classroom walls were filled with stories and pictures by students and the stories were eventually turned into books, produced by desktop publishing. In this way, poor schools were able to produce their own teaching materials, based on the knowledge and insights of the children themselves.

Use of such innovative and low cost techniques would begin to address some of the current deficiencies in the teaching of EE in Africa. There is a strong argument to be made for the development of a uniquely African environmental education curriculum that fuses both traditional and modern approaches to environmental management. Given the very different roles played by men and women in natural resource management in Africa, it is clear that gender analysis should be a central component of such a curriculum not simply to ensure equity for African women but most importantly to provide children with a more complete understanding of human interaction with the environment around them.

It is evident that there already exists a large information base about environmental issues in Africa. There are many African researchers working on environmental issues with interests varying from highly technical studies of global change to very focused studies about natural resource management at the community level. There is also a renewed interest in indigenous knowledge and in oral history and a great deal of work is being carried out on these subjects. The challenge facing African educators is to make effective use of this knowledge in a way that provides a holistic and relevant framework for the teaching of environmental education to African children.

References

Abucar, H. Mohamed and Patrick Molutsi, "Environmental Policy in Botswana: A Critique," *Africa Today*, 40, 1, 1993.

Adara, O.A. "Environmental Education in the Formal Sector: Problems and Prospects," *in Proceedings of the First National Conference on Environmental Education, Lagos, Nigeria,]7-19 March 1993*, Lagos,

Nigerian Conservation Foundation, 1993.

Adimola, Beatrice, John R.W. Aluma, Daniel Babikwa and Gabriel Obbo Datandi, *The Status of Environmental Education in Uganda*, Report to the International Development Research Centre, Nairobi, Kenya, June 1994.

Agarwal, Bina *Engendering the Environment Debate. Lessons from the Indian Subcontinent*, CASID Distinguished Speaker Series, No. 8, East lansing, Michigan, Center for Advanced Study of International Development, 1991.

Ardafayio-Schandorf, Elizabeth, "Women and Forest Resources Management in the Northern Region of Ghana," Report to Environment Liaison Centre International, Nairobi, Kenya, 1993.

Bakobi, Bernard L.M., "The Status of Environmental Education in the SADC Region," Summary Report to the Environmental Education for Youth "Creating Awareness" SADCELMS Workshop, Windhoek, Namibia, 13-19 March 1994.

Brundtland Commission, *Our Common Future*, Oxford, Oxford University Press, 1987. CHIMEDZA, RUVIMBO, "Wildlife Rcsources and Household Food Security," Report to Environment Liaison Centre International, Nairohi, Kenya, 1993.

Collins, Jane L., "Women and the Environment: Social Reproduction and Sustainable Development," in RITA S. GALLIN and ANNE FERGUSON, eds., *The Women and International Development Annual, Voume2,* Boulder,Co., Westview Press, 1991.

Coulibally, Suzanne, "Women, Migration, and the Management of Natural Resources," WEDNET Final Report, Nairobi, ELCI, 1993.

Dankelmen, Irene and Joan Davidson, *Women and Environment in the Third World: Alliance for the Furture*, London, Earthscan, 1988.

Dasilva, Christian M., "Local or Traditional Environmental Knowledge and Environmental Education in Secondary Schools: Closing the Gap with Research," Paper presented at Workshop on Research Issues in Environmental Education in Eastern and Southern Africa 29 August—2 September 1994. Nairobi, Kenya.

Filho, Walter Leal, "An Agenda for Environmental Education Research in Africa," Paper presented to the Workshop on Research Issues in Environmental Education in Eastern and Southern Africa, 29 August—2 September 1994, Nairobi, Kenya.

_____ and Zena Murphy, "An Overview of Environmental Education in the

Commonwealth," in Walter Leal Filho, ed., *Environmental Education in the Commonwealth*, Vancouver, Commonwealth of Learning, 1993.

Fitzerald, Maureen, "Environmental Education in Ethiopia: The Sources of Decision-Making." in DESH BANDHU, HARJIT SINGH and A.K. MAlTRA, eds, *Environmental Education and Sustainable Development*, New Delhi, Indian Environmental Society, 1990.

Kettle, Bonnie, "Gender and Environments: Lessons From WEDNE," Unpublished paper, Faculty of Environmental Studies, York University, 1993.

Haile, Fekerte, "Women Fuel Wood Carriers in Addis Ababa," in Eva M. Rathgeber and Bonnie Kettel, eds., *Women and Nantural Resource Management in Africa*, Manuscript Report, Ottawa, International Development Research Centre, 1989.

Leach, Melissa, "Traps and Opportunities: Some Thoughts on Approaches to Gender, Environment and Social Forestry with Emphasis on West Africa." Institute of Development Studies, University of Sussex, England. Paper presented for DSA Women in Development Study Group Meeting, May 1991.

Lindhe, Valdy, Miles Goldstick, Stachys N. Muturi and Paul Rimmerfors, eds., *Environmental Education. Experiences and Suggestions. Report from a Regional Workshop*, Nyeri, Kenya, 4-10 October 1992, Nairobi, SIDA Regional Soil Conservation Unit, 1993.

Mackenzie, Fiona, "Exploring the Connections: Structural Adjustment, Gcnder and thc Environment," *Geoforum*, 24, 1, 1993, pp. 71-87.

Omosa, Mary, "Women and the Management of Domestic Energy," in Shanyisa A. Khansiani, *Groundwork. African Women as Environmental Mangers*, Nairobi, ACTS Press, 1992.

Rathgeber, Eva M., "Schooling for What? Education and Career Opportunities for Women in Science, Technology and Engineering in U.N. COMMISSION FOR SCIENCE AND TECHNOLOGY, GENDER WORKING GROUP, eds., *Missing Links: Gender Equity in Science and Technology for Development*, Ottawa and New York, International Development Research Centre and UNIFEM, 1995.

Shiva, Vandana, *Staying Alive: Women, Ecology and Development*, London, Zed Books, 1988.

Sunny, Grace, "Womens Role in the Supply of Fuelwood," in SHANYISA A. KHASIANI, ed. Groundwork. African Women as Environmental

Managers, Nairobi, ACTS Press, 1992.

Wanaswa, E.A., "The State of Environmental Education in Kenya: Past, Present and Future," in Walter Leal Filho, ed., *Environmental Education in the Commonwealth*, Vancouver, Commonwealth of Learning, 1993.

Weekes-Vagliani, Winifred, *Lessons from the Family Planning Experience for Community-Based Environmental Education*, Technical Paper n 62, Paris, OECD Development Centre, 1992.

Williams, Paula J., *Women, Trees and Forests in Africa*. A Resource Guide, Nairobi, Environment Liaison Centre International, 1992.

UNITED NATIONS ENVIRONMENT PROGRAMME (UNEP), *Environmental Education. Strategic Resources Planning in Uganda*, vol. 8, UNEP, 1988.

UNESCO-UNEP, *Environmental Education Newsletter. Changing Minds-Earthwise. A Selection of Articles, 1976-1991, Connect*, Paris. 1992.

USAID and AFRICAN DEVELOPMENT BANK. *Proceedings of the Workshop on Education and the Environment*, Abidjan, Cote d'Ivoire. November 4-8, 1991.

* Eva M. Rathgeber is Director of the International Development Centre's Regional Office for Eastern and Southern Africa, based in Nairobi, Kenya. She was formerly the Coordinator of IDRC's Gender and Development Unit in Ottawa. She holds a Ph.D. in Comparative Education and has published widely on gender, higher education and science and technology issues.

PART III
CURRENT TRENDS IN EDUCATIONAL REFORM

— 9 —

GHANA'S EDUCATION REFORM: HISTORICAL PERSPECTIVE

D. K. Fobih & A. K. Koomson

Background

The education reform of 1987 uniquely stands out as an unparalleled epoch in the evolution of education in Ghana. Its uniqueness stems from the fact that it is the most comprehensive educational package ever to be formulated and implemented in the country since formal education was brought to the shores of Ghana by the Portuguese merchants in the fifteenth century. Its comprehensiveness derives from the fact that it touches the spectrum of Ghana's educational system, thus making it an all-embracing educational package that cuts across basic to tertiary levels of education. One other noteworthy attribute of the 1987 Educational Reform was its eclectic nature. Bits of earlier educational policies and constructive criticisms to past educational systems, which, due to Ghana's perennial problems of political instability and weak economic base, either remained unimplemented or partially implemented, were blended with new educational thinking into a crystallized reform package. The extent to which the Educational Reform of 1987 reflected the foregoing attributes can be seen from a brief account of the past policies on education and how such policies contributed to the chaotic scenarios that paved the way for the on-going reform. The chronology of the past educational policies could be delineated into four eras, namely:

i) The Nkrumah Era: 1951-1966
ii) The Ankrah and Busia Era: 1966-1972
iii) The Acheampong, Akuffo, Rawlings[1] and Limann Era: 1972-1981
iv) The Rawlings[2] Era: 1981-1986

Generally, the policies that characterized these eras had either one or a combination of the following weaknesses. Firstly, they were not backed by strong knowledge-based data or empirical evidence. Secondly, community participation both in policy formation and implementation was either low or non-existent. Thus, reforms could not be sustained when internal and external sources of funding ceased. Thirdly, commitment and leadership were seriously lacking for both policy formulators and implementors. Fourthly, lack of funding rendered the policy implementation strategies ineffective. Finally, the rapid change of government resulted in the abandonment of reform packages for which huge investments had been made.

The Nkrumah Era: 1951-1966

The key problems that were inherent in the colonial educational system prior to the assumption of office of Dr. Kwame Nkrumah as the first black head of colonial government in 1951 were its inaccessibility to majority of the people and the irrelevance of its curriculum to the daily life experience of the local folks. Schools were very few and urban-based.

Dr. Kwame Nkrumah, realizing that the inherent problems in the colonial education legacy could not promote rapid national development, announced sweeping changes in the country's education system prior to the attainment of internal self-government. In his Accelerated Development Plan of 1951, Dr. Nkrumah sought primarily to provide equal opportunity in education by abolishing tuition fees at the junior primary school and replacing senior primary with the middle schools. Then as president of the First Republic of Ghana, he announced and implemented a fee free and compulsory education package in 1961 for all children at the basic level of education.

It needs mentioning also that since the mass of the populace did not know much about the importance of formal education, community participation in the policy formation and implementation processes was not emphasized. Thus, by the top-down approach, the two policies were formulated and implemented primarily by the government. Marginal community support in terms of communal labour for the construction of school buildings was provided. Essentially, ad hoc measures were adopted initially in the implementation of the new educational packages. Lack of infrastructure, especially, school buildings, led initially to the use of church buildings, temporary sheds and even shade of trees as classrooms. Later, most of the communities which had no school buildings managed to put up such buildings with government funds that were provided through the local authorities.

Pupil teachers who possessed Middle School Leaving Certificate (MSLC), which was basic level education, were drafted to teach in the schools. Six weeks and 2-year teacher training programs were instituted for pupil teachers to equip them with basic teaching skills required for effective teaching at least at the primary level of education. Again, between 1951 and 1966 several training colleges that offered 4-year and 2-year training for post-middle and postsecondary graduates respectively, were established to train more qualified teachers to replace the pupil teachers. Since the teaching profession had low image in the country at that time, the government attracted middle and secondary school leavers to the profession by paying stipends to teacher trainees in the training colleges. The most significant outcome of the policies implemented between 1951 and 1961 was the astronomical increase in the number of schools and enrollment from 1,592 schools with 204,262 pupils in 1950 to 10,421 schools with 1,404,929 pupils in 1966.[1]

At the secondary level, several secondary schools and technical institutions were established to cater for the projected increase in demand for secondary education. Since increased access to basic and secondary education has direct implication for tertiary education, two additional universities, namely, the University of Science and Technology (UST) and the University of Cape Coast (UCC) were established during the period. Whereas UCC was given the mandate to initially train graduate teachers for the secondary schools and training colleges, UST was charged with the production of engineers and high level technicians for the numerous industries that were springing up in the country. As a result of the measures undertaken by the government, by 1960, Ghana could boast of 3,000 students in the eight technical institutes compared to 266 students in five technical schools at the pre-policy period. At the basic education level, by 1958, there were about 455,740 children in primary children that were in school in 1951. These children were being taught by 15,000 qualified teachers with an average class ratio of 1 teacher to 30 pupils. Secondary school enrollment also increased to 9,860 students in the 38 government assisted secondary schools as compared to 2,776 students in 11 assisted schools in 1951. Thus by 1957, with the government's new programme, primary, secondary and technical school's enrollment had improved remarkably (Nimako, 1974, M K Williams, Kwamena Po, 1975). In the area of technical education, though the impact was minimal the foundation of what was to remain a permanent structure for technical education in the country had been laid.

The fact that the foregoing educational package was an imposition on the people of Ghana attracted criticism especially from the few elites who did not see the political wisdom in providing universal education that gave rise to mass unemployment. The criticism also focused on the curriculum, which, to the critics, bore little relevance to the needs of the society. Thus, whereas from the international perspective Ghana's education package by 1966 was the most highly developed in West Africa, internally, it was perceived with mixed feelings. The prevailing circumstances to some extent justified the imposition and the large-scale implementation since there was high illiteracy rate at that time and the primary goal of the government was to increase access to formal education.

However, with the expansion of the economy, increased population growth and social services after independence, it soon became evident in the late 1960s that the strides made in the fifties in the education sector needed further expansion. As population doubled school enrollment figures became meaningless and unrepresentative of the school-going age group in the population. Teacher-pupil ratio had similarly fallen. Inspite of the establishment of the technical education division of the Ministry of Education, the educational system still continued to produce mainly literal scholars who had become job-seekers and a burden on the government. The Education Act of 1961 did not seem to have addressed these issues effectively but to commit the government to the provision of free-textbooks supply and fee-free compulsory basic education. The latter policy was partially and ineffectively implemented; the effect of which still haunts the delivery and management of basic education services today.

In an attempt to correct the inherent weaknesses in the Education Act of 1961, Dr. Nkrumah launched his Seven-year Development Plan (1963-1970) in which education was the pivot for the anticipated socio-economic and political changes. The plan also envisaged the conversion of the last two years of the middle school into continuing schools to prepare the products for the labour force and towards occupational opportunities in the area where schools were situated. (E.g. farming, fishing, fishsmoking, shoe making, weaving, woodcraft, dressmaking and hair dressing.) (Seven-Year Development Plan, 1964, Nimako, 1974). The coup d'etat of 1966 strangled all efforts in the plan for reform. Notwithstanding this setback, one significant achievement was made. The low recognition given to vocational and commercial education had been addressed by integrating thirteen privately-owned commercial and business institutions into the public system of secondary education.

The Ankrah and Busia Era: 1966-1972

The overthrow of the Nkrumah government saw the reformulation of part of the existing educational policies. A number of measures emanated from the Kwapong Committee of 1966, which was set up by Ghana's first military government headed by General Ankrah, to review the entire education system and make it cost-effective. The Committee, which was under the chairmanship of Professor Kwapong, the first black Vice-Chancellor of the University of Ghana, had its other members drawn primarily from the tertiary institutions and the Ministry of Education (MOE). The Kwapong report did not only criticize the quality of education during the regime of Dr. Nkrumah as inferior and its curriculum unrelated to the needs of the community, but also indicated that the country was not rich enough to support free basic education. The government, however, did not have the courage to abolish the fee-free basic education because the masses had appreciated the rationale for such a policy and any attempt to repeal the law would attract their wrath. Prominent among the measures taken in respect of the Committee's report were the:

- Conversion of many middle schools into technical and vocationally-based continuation schools;
- Closure or conversion of several training colleges into secondary schools; and
- Withdrawal of allowances or stipends paid to teacher trainees.

These innovations made little impact since there were no qualified teachers to handle the technical and vocational subjects. The withdrawal of the stipends of teacher trainees, coupled with the prevailing poor conditions of service did not only worsen the existing problem of lack of qualified teachers, but also made the teaching profession the least attractive job in the country. The closure of some schools resulted in a steady decline of enrollment at the primary level of education. For example, enrollment at the primary level, which was 1,137,495 pupils in 1965-66 academic year declined to 947,502 in 1970-71 academic year.[2] Despite the advances made over the years, comprehensive change had still not occurred in the curriculum of the schools whereas the available jobs in the economy required personnel trained in business, vocational and technical skill.

The middle schools had become amorphous. Pupils were entering secondary schools at primary grade 6, in most cases middle forms one and two and in few cases by middle form three. It was realized that the GCE ordinary level work could be completed by secondary form four due partly to abundant trained graduates from the University College of Cape Coast and partly to improved teaching methods. Furthermore, the preliminary preparatory course at the University College of Cape Coast had rendered the two-year sixth form work unnecessary and not cost effective. In an attempt to redress these shortcomings, in 1969, the new civilian administration headed by Prof. K. A. Busia set up the Amisssah Education Committee to overhaul the structure and content of pre-tertiary education. The committee made significant recommendations including the categorization of the secondary level into lower and upper schools. Though Dr. Busia, the Prime Minister for the 2nd. Republic of Ghana from 1969 to 1972, set up the Amissah Committee, the vision that he had for education was not allowed to manifest itself.

The Acheampong, Akuffo, Rawlings [1] and Liman Era: 1972-1981

Once again the recommended innovations did not have chance to be implemented. A military take-over suddenly interrupted the education transformation process in January 1972. The drawback was, however, temporary. Soon after assuming office, the new military regime, realizing the importance of the reform proposal and public pressure for reform also set up an education review Committee under the chairmanship of Prof. N. K. Dzobo in March 1972. Before 1972, teaching and learning conditions in the public schools had deteriorated to a point that parents, who could afford higher fees charged by the better staffed and better managed special or private schools, preferred educating their wards in the latter. Several factors accounted for this trend. Among them were:

i) Lack of qualified teachers due to the closure of several training colleges;

ii) Several qualified teachers left the classrooms for better jobs due to poor conditions of service in the education sector;
iii) Lack of textbooks and other basic teaching and learning materials;
vi) Poor management and supervision of public schools;

The foregoing factors gave rise to unequal opportunity in secondary education as it favoured the urban dwellers and the rich more than the rural settlers and the poor. Again, the curriculum was still unrelated to the life of the community with several school leavers, both from the basic and secondary levels of education trooping to the urban centres for the non-existent white collar jobs. By 1972 the state of Ghana's education system at the basic level demanded some form of overhauling to make it more relevant to the people and to solve the observed negative trends from the existing system. Hence the committee was to address the same perennial problems that had plagued education in earlier years. Expansion of primary school enrollment and increased access to secondary education which stood at 70% and 15% respectively were to be improved. Efforts were also to be made to diversify the curricula at all levels to give equal weight to technical, vocational and commercial subjects as prevails for the arts and liberal subjects.

A reduction of the seventeen years duration of pre-tertiary education, review of the two assessment systems, the Common Entrance Examination (CCE) and the General Certificate of Education (GCE) ordinary and advanced level that had hitherto dictated the philosophy and objective of the educational system was also included. It was against this background that the Dzobo Committee was inaugurated in 1972 by the Acheampong military government to review the education system as the basic level of education had proved dysfunctional. Membership of the committee, which was headed by Prof. Dzobo, the then Dean of the Faculty of Education, University of Cape Coast, was composed of intellectuals from the universities and some retired and serving heads of secondary schools.

By June 1973 the committee had completed its work and the government accordingly issued a white paper in February, 1974 outlining the New Structure and Content for education in the country (MOE, 1974). The major features of the proposal approved by the government were Kindergarten education for children between ages 4—6 years; a revised structure of the educational system—6 years primary, 3 years Junior Secondary, 2-year Senior Secondary (Lower) leading to GCE ordinary level, technical and commercial courses as terminal or continuing programme to another 2-year senior secondary (Upper) leading to the GCE advanced level. From senior secondary (upper), students may proceed to either a teachers' training, a polytechnic or a university for a three-year programme (K,6-3-2-2-3). It is apparent that the structure was built around the old one with still the GCE determining success and advancement through the system; a process which has, in the past, favoured students from elite and high socioeconomic background. The three-year university programme also remained intact.

In spite of its limitations the new proposal had significant features, Vocational and technical subjects had been made part of the entire pre-university course and every pupil in the Junior Secondary School was to do at least two of such subjects. For the first time, pre-university education was reduced from 17 years to 13 years (i.e. K, 6-3-2-2) thereby making a saving of 4 years on educational expenditure . This was justified by the fact that most of the students entered the secondary schools through the CEE with eight years of basic education, which was then ten years. The proposed structure was as follows:

OLD STRUCTURE		**PROPOSED STRUCTURE**	
LEVEL	YEARS	LEVEL	YEARS
Basic	Primary 6	Basic	Primary 6
Basic	Middle 4	Basic	JSS 3
Secondary	Lower 5	Secondary	Senior. Sec. Sch SSS (lower) 2
Secondary	Upper 2		SSS (upper) 2
TOTAL	17	TOTAL	13

TABLE 4: RELATION BETWEEN THE OLD AND NEW STRUCTURES OF EDUCATION BY 1975.

The financial gains from the years saved were to be ploughed backed to improve and support the new system so as to ensure quality output. By that arrangement the Ghanaian structure of education was brought in line with other international systems that use grade 12 as the pre-tertiary terminal point or a requirement for entry into tertiary institutions. It was also significant that a recognition was given to the need for all school-going age children to have been exposed to kindergarten experience. This was to serve as the foundation upon which quality control in the contracted educational structure was to be ensured.

In an attempt to implement the reform programme the Acheampong regime initially established, in 1976, Experimental Junior Secondary Schools in every region with three-year programmes based on the new curriculum to replace the continuation schools' concept. A pilot 3-year structure teachers' training programmes with subject specialisation based on the new curricula (i.e. vocational and technical skills) were also initiated to prepare postsecondary pre-service teachers for the main reform implementation.

Furthermore,the Acheampong government, after accepting the reform package, established the Ghana Education Service in 1974, primarily, to ensure effective implementation and monitoring of the New Structure and Content of Education. Before the establishment of the GES, monitoring and management of schools at the pre-university levels were carried out by the Ministry of Education (MOE) through its Regional and District Education Offices. The GES thus became the professional wing of the MOE that was charged with the implementation and monitoring of policies formulated by the MOE on behalf of the government. A Director-General and its two deputies and directors for the Basic, Secondary, Technical, Manpower and Training and Planning divisions worked at the Headquarters of the GES. The staff of the headquarters coordinated and monitored the activities of the Regional and District directorate of the GES.

The implementation of the Dzobo reform was left exclusively in the hands of the staff of the Regional and District directors of the GES whose activities were coordinated by the Director of Basic Education. Large-scale implementation strategy based upon the phase-out and phase-in approach was adopted in putting in place the Dzobo Reform package. The reform started with the phasing out of the old Primary one and the phasing in of the new Primary one (P.I) all over the country in 1975. This was followed in the second year with Primary 2 in that order until Primary 6 was reached in 1980.

Ad hoc measures were adopted in the implementation of the reform. The Curriculum Development Division of the Ghana Education Service

(GES) utilized the services of subject experts in the training colleges, secondary school and universities to write hurriedly the textbooks and instructional materials in 1974. The publication and supply of the textbooks were contiguously done for each level of the primary classes as and when they phased in. Thus, by 1981 the content of the old primary school system had given way to the new. Trainers training workshops were hurriedly organized in the regional centres to orientate the teachers to the new structure and content of education. By means of the cascade approach, these trainers then mounted in-service training programs in the districts and zonal centers to equip teachers with skills for handling the new texts.

The in service training began with all teachers in grade one or primary one (P1) class in 1974 followed by all P2 teachers in 1975, and ended with P6 teachers in 1979. In other words, one clear year of in-service training was held for all teachers of a particular level as and when a new level was phased in. This strategy was adopted on the assumption that the type of training received by the teachers in the system was adequate for handling the primary level of education. As part of the policy on the proposed Junior Secondary School (JSS) level, it was felt that the nature of the curriculum required a new type of teacher capable of handling its relatively higher content. Thus, a three-year post-secondary teacher training programme was started in 1975 to train teachers for the new curriculum. The rationale behind this approach was laudable insofar as it was envisaged that a reasonable number of teachers might have been trained by the time the reform reached JSS1 in 1981. Thus, the foundation upon which a successful change-over depended was gradually being laid.

Like the first government, funding of the reform came, exclusively, from internal sources. Having repudiated all the debts accumulated and loans contracted by former regimes, the government of Acheampong kept and utilized moneys meant for servicing foreign debts for the reform. The government gave a misleading impression that it was economically sound to embark upon a colossal reform of this kind without international support. Again, since the government failed to put in place a cost-sharing device, whereby the public would contribute substantially towards education financing, the government's inability to sustain the reform became an imminent issue of concern when Ghana was caught up in the global economic recession of the mid-70s. As a result, budgetary allocation to education started dwindling. The repudiastionistic strategy adopted by the government eroded its credit worthiness and thus could not negotiate for foreign loans to carry on with the reform to its logical conclusion.

Furthermore, the implementation of the 1974 education reforms coincided with the Union Government philosophy, which was seen as a political ploy by the military government of Acheampong to perpetuate its stay in power by unifying the existing political groupings. This political philosophy, which attracted heavy funding, turned the government's attention from the implementation of the education reform. With the rejection of the Union Government concept in a referendum, and the removal from office of Acheampong's Supreme Military Council [1] by the Supreme Military Council SMC [II] in 1978, the driving force behind the education reform was reduced.

Once again, history repeated itself but this time in a disorganized fashion amidst economic decline and the infra-structure being developed had to be abandoned. In April, 1978, a military palace coup took place under General Akuffo, namely SMC 2 followed in June 1979 by a more radical one with a ruthless revolutionary zeal headed by Ft. Lt. Rawlings (i.e. Armed Forces Revolutionary Council—AFRC) who were interested in their political agenda more than the on-going reform. However, in December 1979 the regime handed over power to a new civilian administration also to be dislodged again two years later, December 31, 1981 by the same military junta. As problems shelved never cease to exist, when the military regime was re-instated, the problems facing the nation in general and the education sector in particular had worsened as a result of ad hoc measures, political instability and frequent change of emphasis in education policy. Thus, in 1984, the new government had to revisit the Acheampong regime's educational agenda.

The unfavourable political environment, coupled with the economic recession and economic mess that characterized the military regimes from 1972 to 1979, made it abundantly clear that the new structure and content of education could not proceed to the JSS level on large-scale as it had been the case at the primary level. Experimental and piece meal approach for an implementation of the JSS component of the basic level of education was a better option for adoption in 1981 by the government of Dr. Limann which assumed the presidency of the 3rd Republic of Ghana in 1979. This strategy was adopted because there was lack of adequate:

(i) financial resources to provide additional school buildings and construct workshops throughout the country, and

(ii) qualified teachers to handle the JSS subjects especially the vocational and technical-based subjects.

Accordingly, extra experimental Junior Secondary Schools were established in several districts in the country. By 1987 when the major or new reform was about to be implemented, there were 118 JSS throughout the country.[3]

The Rawlings Era [2]: 1981-1986

By 1983 when the third level of JSS was in place, the quality of basic education had sunk very low and criticisms had started emerging from the general public mainly from educationists. The structure of basic education was completely devoid of clarity by 1985, insofar as three conflicting distinct systems were operating concurrently. Firstly, after completing the 6 years primary education which was based on the New Structure and Content of Education, a pupil could either enter JSS.1 in areas where such schools exist or enroll at Middle Form 1, which was part of the old structure. Secondly, since the old Senior Secondary was in existence, level of entry of graduates from the JSS was undetermined. In most cases such products were admitted to form one of the old Senior Secondary because the JSS schools were perceived as inferior by the heads of the Secondary Schools. Also they followed different curricula which did not fit easily into the old secondary curricula. Thirdly, pupils from the Middle Schools continued to gain admission to the old Secondary Schools at different levels by way of the Common Entrance Examination (CEE) mechanism, which the 1974 reform sought to abolish. In addition to the above conflicting scenarios, academic standards and supply of logistics for effective teaching and learning had declined to the lowest level. The state of Ghana's education system by 1985 was aptly described as `clinically dead'. The prevailing environmental circumstances, therefore, favoured a more pragmatic reform package to reverse the downward trend of education especially at the basic level.

Prominent among the factors that created conditions for the 1987 Education Reform were:

i) Exodus of trained and highly qualified teachers from the country as a result of the economic decline in the mid 1970s;

ii) Lack of textbooks and stationery items as a result of lack of foreign exchange;
iii) Deterioration of buildings, furniture and equipment resulting from collapse of school management;
iv) Cutting back on levels of funding of the education sector by successive governments. The proportion of GDP devoted by government to education declined from 6.4% in 1976 to about 1.0% in 1983 and 1.7% in 1985.
v) Non-availability of virtually any data and statistics needed for vital planning. This led to decisions being taken on ad hoc basis.
vi) Enrollment growth had declined to 1.5% for Primary; 1.1% for Middle and 1.5% for Secondary levels, whereas school age population grew at 3.6% per year with University enrollment remaining fairly constant over the period;
vii) Poor management and supervision due to the fact that the personnel of the GES had no vehicles to visit the schools at regular intervals.
viii) About two-thirds of the adult population remained illiterate while the drop out rate from the formal sector continued to rise.[4]

It was against the foregoing background that the announcement of the 1987 Education Reform by Rawlings [2] government of the Provisional National Defence Council (PNDC), was seen as a step in the right direction.

The Reform

The Anfom Education Commission, which had come to replace the G.E.S. Council that was abolished by P.N.D.C. Law 42 in the early '80s, had only advisory powers unlike the council it had replaced which had executive powers. Upon coming into being, it was charged with the responsibility of reviewing the state of the educational system and make recommendations to Government.

In 1986, the Anfom Education Commission submitted part of its report to Government. In its report, the Commission noted among other things, that the proposals represented the views of a cross-section of the population and that:

> they do not differ in many ways from those made by the Dzobo Committee on which the 1974 New Structure and Content of Education in Ghana is based. They can be regarded as endorsing, emphasizing and amplifying those proposals, save in some crucial areas where novel proposals are advanced.[5]

The major highlights of the reform, which formed part of the recommendations of the Commission, were:

(i) A nine year basic education followed by a three year senior secondary schooling and a 4 year University cycle (6.3.3.4) as against the 6 year primary, 3 year Junior Secondary Schooling, 2 year Senior Secondary Lower and 2 year Senior Secondary Upper (6.3.2.2) proposed by Dzobo in 1974 (Paragraph 196, 197)
(ii) A philosophy of education which should influence national thinking and planning (Paragraph 19, 20)
(iii) Entrants into teacher training should possess Secondary Education. (Paragraph 69)
(iv) Teacher trainees to be paid allowances and treated on a parity basis with all other trainees. (Paragraph 72)
(v) Local community participation in the provision of Basic Education should be mobilized without waiting for the decentralization to be completely implemented (Paragraph 160).

The Commission recommended that the new scheme should commence in 1990, with entry into class one of the first batch of the 9-year Basic Education pupils. According to the Commission, this arrangement would:

> ...give the country some breathing space (three years) to prepare the teachers, to procure sufficient textbooks and other teaching materials, to have improved the building and other equipment base, and to have obtained prior commitment to the new scheme. By 1999, the old system would have been phased out as the first "Certificates of Basic Education" are awarded.[6]

Thus in 1986 the Government had before it the five year development plan for the implementation of the reforms submitted by the Conference of Directors of Education on behalf of G.E.S. and the report of the Anfom Education Commission for consideration.

The reform implementation process actually began with the speech of the then Secretary of Education, Dr. Mohammed Ben Abdallah, on October 15, 1986. He outlined the factors indicating a decline in educational provision in the country which have been alluded to earlier in this paper and the principles that formed the bases of the reform package for education. The principles reflect:

(a) the affirmation of education as a basic right for every citizen
(b) that majority of Ghanaians do not participate in national development as a result of illiteracy, partial literacy or mis-education.
(c) the need for cultural identity and dignity
(d) wrong type of education leading to unemployment
(e) the need for citizens to acquire scientific and technological skills to cope with the flux of life
(f) a creation of an awareness of one's environment.[7]

In line, therefore, with these major considerations, the Government, within the framework of the Education Structural Adjustment Programme, restructured pre-University Education to meet the over-all national Educational Objectives.

Conclusion

The history of educational reform in Ghana is impregnated with vital lessons for developing countries which continually experience political instability, weak economic base, low living standards and low rate of development. Inasmuch as education remains the main conduit for national development, it stands to reason that devising an appropriate educational package that is both cost-effective and qualitatively affordable as well as relevant to the needs and aspirations of the people must be the over-arching goal of developing countries.

Though the education reform of Ghana is in the infantile stage, its structure, which is consistent with the systems of most of the world powers, has significantly decentralized the delivery of education services and reduced the net expenditure of the government on education. The government is now utilising the reserves that are accruing from this cut in educational spending to improve upon the quality of education and implement a fee-free universal basic education by the year 2005.

Another positive effect emanating from the reform is the active participation of the communities in the provision of education. This cost-sharing approach has increased the level of committment of the communities to the extent that they now exercise some control in the running of the schools in their localities.

On the other hand, the practice of jettisoning an existing educational package when there is a change in government only tends to increase the economic burden of the country. Only problems inherent in the existing system must be addressed when there is a change in government.

References

Djangmah, J.S. (1994), Educational Reforms in Ghana: The Dream and its Implications, A Memorandum to the Education Reform Review Committee, p.13.

Ghana, *Ministry of Education Report*, 1968-1971, Accra.

Ghana, *Report of the Education Review Committee*, 1994, Accra. p.13

Ghana, *Report of Education Commission on Basic Education,* 1986 Accra, (Preamble No. 4 p.iii)

______, 1986, paragraph 193.

Mc. William, H.O.A. and M.A. Kwamena-Poh (1975), *The development of education in Ghana*, Longman Group Ltd. p.145

Ministry of Education and Culture (1986) *The Educational Reforms Programme Policy Guidelines on Basic Education*, Accra, Ghana. pp. 2-3

— 10 —
EDUCATION IN SOUTHERN AFRICA: CURRENT CONDITIONS AND FUTURE DIRECTIONS

David Baine and Tuntufye Mwamwenda

Abstract

This paper provides a concise summary of selected topics of contemporary, primary and secondary education of black students in Southern Africa. The topics reviewed are: a) curricula, b) methods of instructional delivery, c) learning materials and equipment, d) examinations, e) enrollment and class sizes, f) teachers, g) teacher-student ratios, h) drop-out, failure and repeater rates, i) economic considerations, j) rural-urban discrepancies, k) racial and class issues, l) female education, and m) language of instruction. The discussion begins with an acknowledgement of the enormous improvements that have been made in the field of education in Africa despite vast limitations of resources: economic, personnel, technological and material. In spite of these achievements, given the magnitude and complexity of educational development, a number of problems continue to exist. These problems are reviewed as are various recommendations for change.

Zusammenfassung

Dieser Artikel gibt enine knappe Zusammenfassung von ausgewählten Themen über zeitgenössische Primar—und Sekundarbildung schwarzer Studenten im südlichen Afrika. Die behandelten Themen sind: a) Curricula, b) Lehrmethoden, c)Lernmaterialien und—ausrüstung, d) Prüfungen, e) Einschreibungen und Klassenraumgröße, f) Lehrer, g) Leher-Schüler-Quoten, h) vorzeitige Schulabgänger-, Mißerfolgs—und Wiederholquoten, i) wirtschaftliche Erwägungen, j) Diskrepanzen zwischen Stadt und Land, k) Rassen—und Klassenfragen, l) Bildung für Mädchen, und, m) Unterrichtssprache. Die Diskussion beginnt mit einer Anerkennung der Ressourcen, wie z. B. im Bereich Wirtschaft. Personal, Technologie und Material, in der Bildung erzielt wurden. Trotz dieser Leistungen bestehen einige Probleme hinsichtlich der Ausdehnung und komplexitäc erzieherischer Entwicklung weiter. Diese Probleme werden ebenso wie unterschiedliche Empfehlungen für Veränderungen angesprochen.

Résumé

Cet article fournit un bref résumé de quelques sujets portant sur l'éducation primaire et secondaire contemporaine d'élèves noirs en Afrique du Sud. Les sujets ètudiés sont: a) les curriculums, b) les méthodes d'enseignement, c) le matériel et l'équipement scolaire, d) les examens, e) la scolarisation et les effectiifs, f) les enseignants, g) les quotas enseignants-étudiants, h) les taux d'abandons, d'échec et de redoublement, i) les considérations économiques, j) les contradictions entre milieux ruraux et urbains, k) les problèmes raciaux et de classes sociales, l) l'éducation féminine et m) la langue d'enseignement. La dissuion commence par une confirmation des progrès énormes réalisés en Afrique dans le domaine de l'éducation, en dépit de resources fortment limiéesdans les domaines économique, personnel, technologique et matériel. Maigré ces succès, un grand nombre de problèmes persiste vu l'étendue et la complexité de l'extension de l'éducation. Ces problèmes sont étudiés de même que différentes propositions de changement.

South African countries have placed high priority on education as a key to individual and national development (Mwamwenda and Mwamwenda 1992). Correspondingly, large percentages of government budgets have been allocated to education (SAE 1992). As a result, since independence, African nations have made monumental improvements in spite of enormous limitations of resources: economic, human, technological and material. A recent World Bank report (1989) stated that African educational development since independence has been spectacular and impressive. According to Heyneman (1990), the expansion of the educational system is unique in human history. In the past fifteen years, the educational growth rate in Africa has doubled that of other developing countries in Asia and Latin America (Adams and Kruppenbach 1987). Some of the achievements in the field of education in Southern Africa are described below.

- Several countries such as Zambia and Botswana have introduced free education in primary, and sometimes, in secondary levels of schooling (Graham-Brown 1991; Kaluba 1986; Mwamwenda &

Mwamwenda 1992).

- There has been remarkable expansion in the number of primary and secondary schools; in fact, the magnitude of the expansion of primary and secondary education in Zimbabwe has been described as a modern miracle (Mackenzie 1988).

- In most countries school enrollments have shot up (Mwamwenda and Mwamwenda 1992; SAE 1992). For example, in Zimbabwe, primary school enrollment rose from 819,586 in 1979 to 2,260,367 in 1986 (Mackenzie 1988).

- Universal primary education has been achieved in several countries including Botswana, Swaziland, Lesotho and Zimbabwe (Mwamwenda & Mwamwenda 1992; Peil 1990; SAE 1992).

- Equality of access to educational programs for males and females, for children in urban and rural areas, and for various racial and economic groups has been improved; for example, some previously racially segregated schools in Zimbabwe are now integrated (Frederikse 1992).

- Teacher in-service and pre-service training programs have been increased and improved.

- Literacy had been substantially increased in countries such as Botswana, Lesotho, Swaziland and Zimbabwe (SAE 1992).

- Attempts have been made to make curricula more relevant to the agricultural and technical context of the majority of Africans (Jansen 1989).

Present Problems

In spite of these achievements, given the magnitude and complexity of educational development, a number of problems continue to exist. These problems are reviewed, as are various recommendations for change.

Curricula

Pre-primary Level Curricula

Pre-primary readiness or preparatory programs have been initiated in several countries. For example, in Transkei, pre-primary programs have been established for children aged three to five. Currently, there are not sufficient programs for the large number of eligible children, and most of the students enrolled in primary education have not participated in readiness programs. The lack of adequate preparation for formal schooling may contribute to the alarmingly high drop-out and failure rates (Matoti 1990)

In South Africa, during the period 1987 to 1990, positive steps were taken to introduce pre-primary upgrading programs for black children. However, the social and political upheavals in the region caused the entire school system to deteriorate to the extent that few of these programs were actually carried out (Hartshorne 1992).

Primary Level Curricula

In primary schools, the composition of the curriculum is remarkably similar world-wide, regardless of the level of economic and educational development. Curricula have changed little since the early 1960s. In primary schools more than 50% of the time is spent teaching language skills and mathematics. Vocational subjects such as agriculture, domestic science and business are more commonly taught in primary schools in developing countries than in industrial countries, but the time allocated to such subjects is still minimal. During the 1980s, only about 6% of total school time was devoted to teaching these topics (Lockheed and Verspoor 1991).

Generally, curricula in developing countries tend to mimic former colonial curricula, which in primary schools focus on training students for secondary schools (Hartshorne 1992) in spite of the fact that less than 10% of the children entering primary schools reach secondary school. These curricula place their emphasis on literacy and numeracy rather than on the knowledge and skills required to function effectively in rural environments, although 70% of the children living in developing countries live and attend schools in rural areas, and more than 80% of these children will spend their lives living and working in rural areas (Bishop 1989).

In South Africa, from 1987 to 1990, steps were taken to introduce vocational and technical orientation programs at the higher primary school levels. However, as previously mentioned, with the social and political upheavals in the region, school programs deteriorated so much that there could be no guarantee that any of these programs were in fact carried out (Hartshorne 1992).

Secondary Level Curricula

In South Africa, the secondary level of instruction is white-oriented and white-dominated. Major emphasis is placed on matriculation and other examinations intended to assess students' ability to profit from university level study. The secondary level curriculum does not prepare the majority of black students who do not go to university (Hartshorne 1992). The most common criticism of secondary schools is that they fail to prepare young people for the world of work, and that the students fail to develop essential values, attitudes, respect for self and others, social skills and life skills. Unfortunately, most black parents place high value on an academic secondary education and the anticipated social and employment benefits, while devaluing technical education that in many cases may be of greater value to students (Hartshorne 1992).

Secondary education in South Africa is authoritarian, disciplinarian, teacher-dominated, content-oriented and knowledge-based. Often teachers rely on a single textbook; class notes are learned by heart, and students are given little time for questions, discussion, active participation, group work or hands-on activities (Hartshorne 1992).

Secondary Level, Vocational Education

In Lesotho, Botswana and Swaziland, vocational education programs have been developed as a way of overcoming unemployment and facilitating employability of school leavers both at primary and secondary levels (Jansen 1989; Urevbu 1988). In many cases, however, vocational education has been associated with a number of problems. Vocational and agricultural education programs because of the facilities and equipment required:

- are more costly than regular education and are of questionable cost-effectiveness;

- are often associated with students perceived as less intellectually capable;

- have a negative connotation because of their association with black education during colonial times;

- are often not associated with increased employment opportunities or increased earnings; and

- are frequently rejected by both parents and students (Jansen 1989; Psacharopoulos 1987).

The failure of vocational education to enhance employment opportunities arises from a failure to conduct market analyses to determine what skills are and will be in demand in the market place, from an obvious mismatch between what education offers and what exists in the world of work, and from the fact that teachers do not have the knowledge and skills required for teaching vocational, agricultural and technical skills (Bergmann 1985; Psacharopoulos 1985; Selvarathnam 1988).

In general, there is a feeling of disenchantment, a feeling that students, particularly those in rural areas, are not learning skills that would be of value in their daily lives. Some people think that the kind of education received is irrelevant because even if students pass examinations, they cannot find employment and, because of the limited number of places available, students cannot gain admission to higher education (Graham-Brown 1991).

Socialist curriculum models of various forms have been adopted in Angola, Botswana, Mozambique and Zimbabwe. These models are characterized by an emphasis on practical work to eliminate the distinction between mental and manual work, and to promote a strong attitude toward labor. In these communities, education has a strong community orientation, and educational activities are designed to meet demands of productivity (Jansen 1989).

In integrated, white, city schools in Zimbabwe, the curriculum appears to be much as it was when the schools were exclusively white. African customs, culture and language are generally neglected in the curricula (Frederikse 1992)

Examinations

Jansen (1989) described the use of the Cambridge Examinations in a number of South African countries, including Botswana, Lesotho (cf. Tlou and Mantle 1991), and Zimbabwe (cf. Chikombah 1991) as a form of cultural imperialism determining what was taught in the curriculum. In other cases, matriculation examiners are reportedly often ignorant of the syllabi and of the subjects they are marking (Graham-Brown 1991). In Botswana, for example, teachers frequently complain that a significant number of the questions asked in examinations are totally unrelated to the recommended course of studies (Mwamwenda & Mwamwenda 1992). The dominating focus on examinations in schools has led to rote learning of factual information rather than comprehension and application of knowledge and skills.

Teachers

Obviously, teachers play the major role in the educational process. Unfortunately, however, large numbers of teachers in the countries of Southern Africa are unqualified. For example, in 1988, 17% of the South African primary school teachers in black schools outside the homelands, and 28% in the non-independent homelands, were not qualified. In the black homeland of Transkei, approximately 51 % of the teachers in the senior secondary schools and 63% of the teachers in the junior secondary schools were not suitably qualified for their respective levels of instruction, although the majority of them were qualified to teach at the primary school level (Matoti 1990). These teachers were not only not qualified for the secondary level of instruction, but also not qualified to teach specialized subjects (Matoti 1990) such as mathematics, science and technical skills (Cosser 1991; Hartshorne 1992). In 1989, in Zimbabwe, 3,136 teachers were qualified while 6,929 were unqualified (Graham-Brown 1991).

There has been a grave failure to train sufficient numbers and types of teachers (Hartshorne 1992). As a result of the teacher shortage in Transkei, a number of teachers-in-training who had failed college examinations were teaching as unqualified teachers. Employment of unqualified teachers perpetuates the vicious circle of poor teachers producing poor students, resulting in high failure rates (Matoti 1990).

In Transkei, the failure rate among teachers-in-training is quite high. For example, in 1990, 58% of the primary teachers-in-training in teacher training colleges, and 66% of the students training as secondary level teachers obtained less than 50% in their examinations.

Teachers are often poorly paid, lack necessary (instructional materials, work with large numbers of students in crowded classrooms, teach in dilapidated buildings, and have poor living conditions. As a result, it is difficult to attract people with science, mathematics and technical backgrounds into the field of education (Mwamwenda & Mwamwenda 1992). Teacher motivation is often low, and absenteeism and turn-over rates among teachers are frequently high (Graham-Brown 1991). For example, in 1991, teachers in Mozambique went on strike for most of the year (SAE 1992). In Zimbabwe, teachers were less attracted to township than to urban schools because of problems with living accommodation, transportation, fewer resources, and larger numbers of students (Frederikse 1992).

Centralized models of curriculum development have often neglected the most important variable in successful curriculum change, the teacher. For example, in Zimbabwe where ambitious departures in curriculum policy have been declared, there has been little evidence of the required training or implementation which would translate these objectives into practice (Mungazi 1986).

Student-Teacher Ratio

The shortage of classrooms has led to very high student-teacher ratios. For example, the ratios in Zimbabwe were recently 1:55 (primary level) and 1:44 (secondary level) (SAE 1992). In 1992, in Botswana, the average ratio was 1:45 (Mwamwenda & Mwamwenda 1992). In Transkei, conditions were more severe; Matoti (1990) reported the following ratios:

Junior primary : average: 73:1; range: 39:1 to 142:1
Senior primary : average: 51:1; range: 30:1 to 86:1
Junior secondary: average: 22: 1; range 10:1 to 31:1
Senior secondary: average: 26:1; range: 19:1 to 34:1

Based on 1989 statistics, Cosser (1991) estimated that to reduce the teacher-student ratio to an effective level, an additional 93,000 teachers would be required in South Africa. Ironically, although there is a shortage of schools and teachers for black children in South Africa there is a surplus of schools and teachers for white students, and schools for whites are being closed, while white teachers are being retrenched. In addition, in spite of a need for additional training facilities for black teachers, training colleges for white teachers, less in demand, are being closed (Hartshorne 1992) - another of the tragic consequences of apartheid.

Enrollment and Class Sizes

In Southern Africa, school-age children represent a relatively large percentage of the population. In Transkei, for example, children 5-19 years of age comprise 42% of the population (Matoti 1990). In recent years, school enrollments have increased dramatically. In Botswana and in Swaziland for instance, in the late 1980s, approximately 80-90% of the school-age children were in school (Mwamwenda & Mwamwenda 1992; Sargent 1991). In fact, Zimbabwe, Botswana (Mwamwenda & Mwamwenda 1992), Lesotho and Swaziland have achieved universal primary enrollment (SAE 1992). Often, there have not been enough classrooms to accommodate the number of children attending schools. As a result, in Zimbabwe, Mozambique and in other countries, increases in enrollments have led to double sessions in which half the children go to schools in the mornings, and the other half attend in the afternoons. In some cases, even triple shifts have been introduced (Frederikse 1992). In South Africa, the shortage of classrooms is greatest in the homelands.

During the 1980s, one of the major improvements in schooling in South Africa was the near elimination of double-session classes in the first two years of schooling (Hartshorne 1992). There are several disadvantages of double shifting. Firstly, the number of hours of instruction each student receives is reduced; hours of instruction have been positively related to student achievement (Lockheed & Verspoor 1991). Secondly, teachers sometimes work for long hours, for example, in Zimbabwe from 7:15 am to 5:20 pm; in the afternoons teachers are often tired, hot and perhaps, less enthusiastic (Frederikse 1992). Thirdly, when instructional time is reduced because of double-shifting, the number of hours devoted to practical agriculture and home economics is correspondingly reduced; instruction is focused almost exclusively on academic subjects (Lockheed & Verspoor 1991).

Drop-out Rates

Historically, many children have not stayed in school long enough to achieve basic literacy and numeracy. For example in South Africa, at least 300,000 young, black people annually join the ranks of those who are not functionally literate or numerate (Hartshorne 1992). On average, 15% of those entering primary school drop out after the first year; a further 10% drop out the next year; 30% of those entering primary school will complete four years, while less than 10% of those entering primary school reach secondary school (Bishop 1989). The primary school drop-out rates in Angola were recently 76%; in Mozambique 66% and Malawi 69% (SAE 1992). In Transkei, Matoti (1990), observed an 87% drop-out rate over 10 years.

In South Africa, of the four racial groups, the blacks have the highest drop-out rates and the highest failure rates. The whites have the highest pass rates followed by the Indians (Mphahlele 1991). In South Africa, the percentages of students reaching Standard 10 (matriculation) are: whites, 69%; Indians, 43%; coloreds, 11 %; blacks, 4% (Cosser 1991).

There are various reasons for these discrepancies. Usually, the whites have had the best teachers, the best facilities, the highest per student expenditures, and the lowest pupil-teacher ratios (Mphahlele 1991). These factors are discussed in detail later. Cosser (1991) has described a number of other influences. For one, in South Africa, schooling is compulsory and free for all racial groups, except for the blacks (Hartshorne 1992). For the blacks, education at all levels is still a luxury for which all parents must pay (Mphahlele 1991). In rural areas, parental support for schools is very limited because education is not thought to have much relevance to real life situations. Education is seen as failing to fulfill the needs of the local community and failing to provide access to the higher knowledge and status that would enable rural, young people to move into a world of greater opportunity (Hartshorne 1992). Moreover, years of Bantu education, overcrowding, poorly equipped classrooms, and unqualified teachers have adversely influenced both student achievements and the value assigned to education (Cosser 1991).

Failure rate

Given the general absence of school readiness training, the poor conditions in black schools, and the recent social and political disruption in schools in South Africa—essentially, the disintegration of secondary schools—failure rates have been quite high. For instance, in South Africa, failure by black students of the matriculation exams ranged from 44% in Northern Transvaal to 73% in Johannesburg (Hartshorne 1992). In Transkei in 1990, 61% of the black students failed the Standard 7 exam, 56% failed the Standard 10 exam and only 15% qualified for university entrance (Matoti 1990).

Repeaters

Because of the high failure rate, the numbers of students repeating grades is also high. For example, in Transkei, 15% of the total number of pupils enrolled in 1990 were repeaters. These students add to problems of overcrowding (Matoti 1990).

Instructional Delivery

According to Lockheed and Verspoor (1991), many of the teaching practices in developing countries are not conducive to student learning. Ineffective practices include:

- long periods of lecturing and rote recitation: for example, in Botswana, students listened to lectures for 54% of the time, and spent 43% of the observed instructional time on oral recitation;

- having students copy from the blackboard; giving students few opportunities to ask questions or participate in active learning;

- having students memorize texts with few opportunities for hands-on involvement; and

- providing little ongoing monitoring and feedback related to student learning (Lockheed & Verspoor 1991).

Economic Considerations
School Fees

In the past, primary schooling had been free in Zimbabwe (Chikombah 1991; Frederikse 1992), however, the government now charges fees for children at primary schools in urban areas; only rural primary schools remain free. Fees are charged for secondary schools, but the fees for rural secondary schools are half those of urban areas, to encourage people to stay in rural areas (Frederikse 1992).

In Swaziland (Sargent 1991), each child is charged school fees right through primary and secondary school. Parents are also expected to contribute to school funds and other special costs. In addition, as is the case in most Southern African countries, each child must be provided with a school uniform and books by parents. Education is a major expense for many families, and it has been recommended by a government commission in Swaziland that the first four years of primary education should be made free (Sargent 1991).

In Botswana, generally education is free; tuition, boarding facilities and meals are paid for by the government. For secondary level schooling, parents must pay for uniforms and transportation. All schools require uniforms, although no school can expel a student without a uniform (Tlou & Mautle 1991).

In Lesotho, all secondary education is paid for jointly by parents, guardians and the government. Secondary level students whose parents are not able to pay the fees are not able to attend school (Tlou & Mautle 1991).

In South Africa, education is free and compulsory for all white children, for a period of ten years. For Asian and "colored" children, education has been compulsory since 1979 and 1980, respectively. For black children, education has generally been neither free nor compulsory (Mphahlele 1991). Free, compulsory education until 16 years of age has been placed in the Namibian constitution (Graham-Brown 1991).

Fees restrict schooling for some families. For several economic reasons, some families in developing countries must pull their children from school. Demanding money before harvest leads to indebtedness. Prolonged periods of drought in Southern Africa have adversely affected crops and family income; as a result, there is often no surplus to pay school fees (Graham-Brown 1991). Females are usually the first affected (SAE 1992). In Zimbabwe, the main reason given for females dropping out of school is financial (Graham-Brown 1991). Zimbabwean policies state that no students will be restricted access to school because they cannot afford fees, but the process of proving indigence is complicated (SAE 1992).

School Funding

A large percentage of government budgets has been allocated to education: for example, during 1987/88, in Swaziland 27%, and in Lesotho 15% (SAE 1992). In South Africa, the relationship between white and black per capita costs improved from 15.1 in 1972 to about 10:1 in 1980 and approximately 5:1 in 1990 (Hartshorne 1992).

A number of factors have strained government budgets. These include:

- rapid expansion of the number of schools;
- rundown schools require extensive maintenance;
- inflation and devaluation of the dollar;
- high, recurrent expenditures in the form of salaries, equipment and materials;
- competition from other parts of the budget, such as health (AIDS); and
- the recent demands in Eastern Europe and the Soviet Union for financial aid from the West, diverting funds from the South (Graham-Brown 1991).

As a result, less developed countries are experiencing increasing inability to cope with the costs of formal schooling of the present kind. These countries are searching for alternatives that would be of lower cost and yet not bring about a deterioration in the quality of education (Hartshorne 1992). For example, in Namibia, in recent years there has been considerable private sector intervention in secondary level and vocational and technical schooling, mainly by large mining companies (Graham-Brown 1991). In Zimbabwe, 90% of the schools are private, operated by independent trusts, missions, mines, local authorities and farms; in 1989 private school enrollment was 1.9 million; public school enrollment was 280,000; in 1992, there were 40 independent primary and secondary schools (Frederikse 1992). In Lesotho, over 90% of the primary schools are church owned, with the government overseeing curriculum development, instructional effectiveness, examinations, teacher training, and teacher salaries (Matsela 1991).

Learning Materials and Equipment

Textbooks are the major, if not the only definition of the curriculum in most developing countries. Unfortunately, the curricula presented in textbooks are often poorly designed, frequently too difficult or easy for the students, and poorly sequenced. In addition, the focus is frequently on memorization of problem solutions rather on the acquisition of problem-solving skills (Lockheed and Verspoor 1991): In the past, the lack of textbooks was the most serious educational deficit in developing countries; e.g., in Botswana, fewer than 20% of primary school students had access to a science or social studies textbook (Botswana, Ministry of Finance and Development Planning, 1984, cited in Lockheed and Verspoor 1991: 52). Teachers lack not only textbooks but also teacher guides that supplement textbooks. Unfortunately, the mere provision of textbooks does not guarantee their use. A study of 127 primary classrooms in Botswana indicated that the teachers used textbooks only 12% of the time (Fuller and Snyder 1991, in Lockheed and Verspoor, 1991). Many teachers were educated in schools lacking good textbooks and may need assistance integrating textbooks into their instructional programs (Lockheed and Verspoor 1991).

In Zimbabwe, in the integrated schools, it is reportedly difficult to obtain textbooks and exercise books (Frederikse 1992). In Mozambique, during 1988, the supply of textbooks was good in urban areas but poor in rural areas; prohibitive fees impeded student access to books (Lockheed and Verspoor 1991).

Instructional equipment related to science education, agricultural and technical education is also usually in short supply. In some classrooms, there are not enough desks, tables, chairs, chalkboards and other basic school equipment.

Rural-Urban Discrepancies

In South Africa, the essential problems and issues in rural education are reportedly no different in essence from those in the rest of Southern Africa. In rural areas, the problems are generally more extreme and intractable because of greater poverty, geographical and political isolation, fewer employment options, feelings of dependency, exacerbated by additional layers of bureaucracy and traditional authoritarianism, along with resistance to change. The problems of rural education are most pronounced in the homeland areas that the South African government has starved of adequate development resources (Hartshorne 1992). Hartshorne (1992) warned that there is real danger of a dual education system being created in South Africa. Formal schooling would prepare the few in urban areas for mental labor, while non-formal education would prepare the many students in rural areas for manual labor (Hartshorne 1992).

Racial and Class Issues

In South Africa, in the early 1990s, the South African government allowed its racially segregated schools to begin admitting students of all colors. Thus far, however, because of the history of racially segregated living areas, very few black students live close to and have been integrated into white schools. The township schools will remain exclusively African for a long time (Hartshorne 1992).

Zimbabwe's schools were desegregated following independence in 1980. Since that time a number of dramatic changes have taken place throughout the school system:

- Some blacks moved out of the townships into white neighborhoods and registered their children in previously white schools. Private and city schools increasingly attracted children of wealthy blacks. In integrated city schools, the proportion of black and white students is similar to that of Zimbabwean society at large, the great majority of students being black. However, three-quarters of the black children still live in township and rural areas and go to school there. Most of these schools have only black children. The majority of children have not experienced integration, and township and rural schools remain uniracial and inferior.

- In integrated urban schools, there has been an increase in class consciousness and a decrease in racial discrimination. Black and white students from city areas get along well with each other, but blacks from the townships are not accepted by either whites or blacks from the suburban areas. Discrimination is based not on race but on class. Township blacks are stereotyped as dirty, diseased, rowdy, trouble-making, poor and as children of cooks and garden boys. Furthermore, township students who attend city schools are discriminated against by township students unable to attend city schools.

- As the number of black students in urban schools increased, white and Indian children began leaving city schools, sometimes into other schools where there were black and "colored" children, not because of the black students in the city, but because it appears that standards in those schools were decreasing as a result of increases in class sizes. In addition, white teachers began leaving city schools because they do not like interacting with black township children.

- The teacher shortage has led to the use of unqualified teachers and a reduction in the quality of schooling. Black teaching and administrative staff began getting jobs in the formerly white schools (Frederikse 1992).

Female Education

In Zimbabwe, it is harder for girls to succeed at school than it is for boys. When girls go home, they are given domestic and farm work to do rather than reading and study. Some people say that it is the African custom for girls to work around the house. Also, both male and female teachers tend to neglect female students in favor of male students. Boys receive more attention and are often given priority in the distribution of scarce materials (Frederikse 1992; Graham-Brown 1991). Some people are concerned that higher education of females could lead to conflict in marriages in which a husband's authority is challenged (Graham-Brown 1991). In addition, female students are often pulled from school to look after younger children, especially in urban areas, since there is no child care for many children under school age. Another problem is the pressure on young women to marry and have children by the age of 18-20, sometimes motivated by family economic pressures (Graham-Brown 1991).

Female literacy has increased in Botswana, Lesotho, Swaziland and Zimbabwe. Adult literacy rates are now 60-70%; with over 50% female literacy. Lesotho has a female literacy rate of 84% (SAE 1992).

Language of instruction

In multi-lingual African countries, choosing a language of instruction is a very difficult task. Selecting one language over another may be strongly resisted by various linguistic groups. Some of the languages are less suitable than others for technical, academic and scientific instruction. For some languages, little or no instructional material is available and the cost of developing materials is prohibitive. To recognize the diversity of languages in schools would require engaging impossible amounts of time, resources and expertise (Jansen 1989).

In Botswana, Zimbabwe, Zambia, Namibia and South Africa, students' mother tongue is used as the medium of instruction during the first three or four years of education, then English becomes the medium of instruction while the mother tongue is retained as a school subject. In practice, however, some teachers continue teaching in the mother tongue when they should be using English. There are several reasons for this practice: some teachers lack confidence in the use of English, and often students have not mastered English and therefore have difficulty learning from English instruction.

In Zimbabwe, in integrated, formerly white, city schools none of the African languages are taught; African children learn to read and write English or Afrikaans but not their mother tongue. In fact, many African students in these schools are ashamed to be heard speaking African languages (Frederikse 1992).

In South Africa, blacks have to learn three languages, their mother tongue, English and Afrikaans, and have to shift from one language to another in primary school. Unfortunately, South African blacks not only face the challenge of learning three languages, they also have to study and write their exams in what is technically a foreign language. Thus, they are at a substantial disadvantage when attempting to compete with white students (Hartshorne 1992).

As the black, South African students demonstrated in the student uprisings beginning in 1976, they were against the use of Afrikaans as a medium of instruction. Most blacks also prefer English over mother tongue, as the latter has been associated with the language of Bantu Education, and is perceived as an inferior language of instruction intended for black South Africans.

In South Africa, all blacks in rural areas, urban areas and independent national states have opted for the use of English as the medium of instruction in senior primary and secondary schools. For the initial four years of schooling, the mother tongue is used as the medium of instruction (Mphahlele 1991).

The future

As was mentioned in the beginning of the paper, enormous improvements have been achieved in African education since independence, in spite of almost overwhelming limitations of economic, human, technological and material resources. African education continues to evolve. In many areas massive changes are currently underway. For example, South Africa, recently freed from the shackles of apartheid, will soon undergo many changes in various aspects of its educational programs. The following suggestions, derived from the literature, and from the experiences of many developing countries, are designed to assist the evolution of education in Southern Africa.

The over-riding recommendation is that all aspects of education should be research-based. Given that a) curricular, instructional and assessment methods used successfully in one context are often not successful when moved to a different context; that b) methods that appear beneficial in theory may not be successful in practice; and that c) well-documented difficulties have been frequently associated with attempts to introduce educational innovation in developing countries, it is imperative that all educational programs should be based on indigenous research and continuous evaluation to insure that the programs are as effective as possible in their own contexts and with their own students.

Curricula

The following recommendations relate to the design of curricula.

- Curricula should be ecologically valid. That is, curricula should teach the knowledge and skills required to function effectively in the political, cultural, economic and geographical contexts in which students live and in which they are likely to participate in future. Baine (1991) has described, in detail, an anthropological approach for developing ecological inventories.

- The knowledge and skills taught in curricula should be based on an analysis of local, regional, national, continental and international trends in technology, industry and population migration, in addition to other types of changes that may influence future conditions.

- Given the high drop-out rates in schools, especially in the early years, primary level training should not prepare students merely for successive levels of academic training, which many of the students will never achieve, but for fulfillment of common, daily tasks which the students are or will be required to perform in the environments in which they live, now and in the future.

  Basic education should involve a careful blending of academic and practical skill training so that students acquire the knowledge and skills necessary to perform effectively in their daily lives. In addition, basic education should provide students with the highest level of academic education of which they are capable so as to facilitate their progress along the continuum of academic development.

  Basic education should integrate academic knowledge and skill training, where contextually appropriate, in subjects such as: communication, computation, political institutions (structure, operation and advocacy); domestic science (economics; nutrition; water, food and waste management; family and community problem-solving); consumer science (purchasing, credit and banking); agricultural science (the environment; use of fertilizers, herbicides and pesticides; land management); health (disease prevention and treatment), etc.

- Academic subjects such as history, social studies and geography should initially be related to the context within which students live so as to make the teaching more relevant to them. However, to avoid a narrow perspective, as early as possible, and to the extent possible, the curriculum should expand to a broader, comparative perspective, recognizing regional, national, continental and international contexts.

  The curriculum should teach the relationship between development of the individual, the family, the community and the nation. Students must be made aware of the reciprocal rights and responsibilities that exist between them and their communities, in many spheres of activity, social, environmental, economic, and political, so as to promote complementary development of both the individual and the community.

  Comparative analyses of other cultures should be based upon analyses of the problems and procedures of growth and development achieved in other cultures so as to lead to the adoption and/or adaptation of methods that have been effective, and to avoid the use of techniques that have resulted in failure.

  Curricula should include comparative analyses of indigenous and exogenous values. That is, the curriculum should incorporate indigenous religious, political and other types of knowledge, methods, beliefs and values. In addition, to promote growth and development of the world community, comparative analyses should be undertaken to insure knowledge, methods and values continue to evolve so as to benefit all people.

- The curricula should promote reflective education that goes beyond rote learning, while teaching students to critically evaluate the acquisition and use of knowledge and skills. A reflective education should be related to personal and cultural development. Students should be taught methods of problem-solving, application, analysis, synthesis and evaluation of knowledge. Instruction should involve active participation and involvement of students in the learning process. This process should involve hands-on experience in the laboratory, the workshop, the library and in various parts of the community.

  Curriculum development should be based on comprehensive, ongoing evaluation of process and outcome measures in terms of cost-effectiveness and benefits to students. There is a need to develop and conduct comparative evaluation of contextually valid, alternative curricula and methods of instruction.

Vocational-Technical Education

In the past, there has been a disproportionate emphasis on academic education. A false distinction has been made between intellectual and manual work. A stronger link must be created between theory and practice, between knowledge and skills and their application, and between attitudes and behaviors (Hartshorne 1992). There must be a wider range of career oriented education.

For many 15-16 year olds, the school is neither the best nor the most attractive environment for further learning experiences. A combination of work and further education and training provide a better option. Business and industry will have to take new responsibilities for providing work on a part-time basis, and funding further education and training alongside work experience (Hartshorne 1992; Urevbu 1988).

Instructional Delivery

Research evidence on the use of interactive radio in developing countries indicates that it is an effective method for:

- providing well-designed instructional programs;
- increasing student knowledge and skill acquisition;
- compensating for teacher shortages and lack of sufficient teacher knowledge and skill in specialized areas of the curriculum, such as mathematics and foreign languages;
- reaching remote, rural areas; and
- equalizing the quality of instruction in impoverished and more affluent areas (Lockheed and Verspoor 1991; Rakubutu 1992).

Interactive radio may be used in conjunction with classroom workbooks and materials. Student involvement in interactive radio may take several forms such as a "dialogue" between broadcaster and students; during mathematics instruction, students may be required to estimate, to count objects, to use materials, and to solve problems. Interactive radio has been successfully used in Lesotho (Lockheed and Verspoor 1991). In Soweto, a project called Open Learning System Education is experimenting with the use of radios in instruction.

Another promising method of instruction is cross-age tutoring, which has been extensively researched in the United States (see, e.g., Baine 1991; Jenkins and Jenkins 1982). The success of the approach to both the tutee and tutor, in a variety of subject areas, warrants trial of the method in developing countries.

Textbooks

Textbooks deliver the curriculum, with the aid of workbooks and teacher guides. The latter are particularly effective when they describe clearly what to teach, and how to teach it, and when they provide diagnostic tests that help teachers monitor student learning and guide appropriate modification of daily lessons. Every effort should be made to provide classrooms with an adequate number and type of culturally appropriate instructional materials, since when textbooks are available, instructional time is not wasted while teachers and students copy text to and from the chalkboard. Research studies in developing countries indicate that provision of a sufficient number of textbooks has a substantial effect on learning (Lockheed and Verspoor 1991).

Shortages of Schools and Classrooms

Mud-walled and thatch-roofed schools are often described as inadequate. However, the evidence indicates that elaborate school facilities are no more effective. Sapere and Mills (1992) described methods for blending traditional and modern architecture for constructing rural schools from inexpensive local materials. The approach uses indigenous, low-cost building materials that are - well-tried and appropriate to environmental, social and economic conditions. These structures may be readily constructed by local trades people.

Examinations

A number of recommendations can be made about examinations and more generally about assessment.

- Examinations should be content valid. That is, the examinations should test the knowledge and skills taught in the curriculum. If a curriculum goes beyond rote learning and teaches comprehension and application of knowledge and skills, problem-solving and critical thinking, then the examination must test the same knowledge and skills.

- Assessment must go beyond periodic annual testing and become an integral part of the teaching process, testing what was taught and teaching what was tested. In this manner, both the teacher and the student receive prompt feedback regarding their respective successes and failures, and appropriate collective changes can be made to enhance effective teaching and learning.

- Unfortunately, when feedback is delayed, students who are most in need of quality instruction receive the most practice performing tasks inappropriately. These students also experience frequent failure and frustration and are likely to be motivated to withdraw from instruction. Making students successful learners of functional skills is one of the most effective ways to keep students in school.

  Effective assessment should be based not simply on examinations but upon performance of homework and classroom assignments, hands-on skills demonstrations, and job site and laboratory work.

- Rather than using norm-referenced tests in which students are compared to national averages, or using tests in which students are assigned a global score or percentage reflecting their total score on the test, criterion-referenced tests may be more informative, describing the specific skills that a student can and cannot perform. Competency-based tests, designed to assess student performance on particular curricula, have the most instructional relevance. Ongoing classroom assessments and the related instructional adaptations do result in enhanced student learning. For example, the time spent monitoring and evaluating students in a program in Swaziland was related to improvements in mathematics achievement (Verspoor and Lockheed 1991).

Instructional Personnel

Hartshorne (1992) observed that South Africa has reached a point at which it simply cannot afford to continue present approaches to the education and training of black teachers. Demographic trends together with backlogs in the provision of education to black children demand that increasing numbers of black teachers be trained. The present system is marked on the one hand by growing numbers of colleges for black teachers struggling to cope with the increasing demand, and on the other hand by unused and under-utilized facilities in the white sector. The only realistic step is to educate and train the nation's teachers together in common programs.

In-service training must be provided in the form of short-term residency programs, continuous on-site training and distance-education courses (correspondence courses, educational television or radio). Of least benefit is the one-shot, no follow-up approach. Ongoing programs that monitor and evaluate teachers regularly show much promise for improving teaching in developing countries. The primary advantage of distance education is its cost-effectiveness: teachers-in-training do not need to stop teaching; no substitute teachers are required; there are no transportation or lodging costs, and no additional instructional personnel are required (Hartshorne 1992). Baine (1985) has described a competency-based, pyramid approach to teacher training that may be useful in some circumstances. To be effective, all methods of in-service training should provide teachers with an incentive - such as bonuses for enhancing student learning. Improvements in teacher salaries and working conditions would also enhance morale and increase motivation to acquire more skills and improve the instructional process.

Lengthy teacher training programs in which teachers acquire comprehensive skills in content areas, and in instructional, classroom management and assessment methods may not be necessary for all instructional personnel. An effective precedent is the use of paraprofessionals in the field of medicine, "barefoot doctors" in China, and village health workers in various developing countries. Paraprofessionals or teaching assistants could be given relatively short-term courses in the use of specific instructional materials and/or methods. Several instructional assistants could work under the direct supervision of a fully trained and experienced teacher.

If competency-based instruction was used in the training of instructional aides, they would have to demonstrate specified competencies before being given a certificate to teach particular skills. A certificate could be issued for each set of competencies demonstrated, and salaries could be related to the number and type of certificates an assistant had earned. Over a period of time assistants could earn enough certificates to gain full teacher certification.

Time for Learning and Double-Shifts

Research has shown that the amount of time available for teaching and learning academic subjects, and how well that time is used by students, particularly poorly functioning students in the early grades, is consistently related to how much children learn while they attend school.

When instructional time is reduced by double-shifting, the remaining instructional time becomes focused on language and mathematics, and the number of hours devoted to practical agriculture and home economics is correspondingly decreased (Lockheed and Verspoor 1991). Lockheed and Verspoor (1991) recommended that the school year should be lengthened if it is shorter than the international standard of 880 hours.

Bishop (1989) has suggested that teaching time may be increased by offering year-round schooling with staggered staff and student holidays. In this manner, more students could be served for longer periods of time, without extra capital expenditure and only minor increases in recurrent costs, particularly if staff holidays were reduced to one month per year, as Bishop suggests.

Class size

According to research reported by Lockheed and Verspoor (1991), it is probably worthwhile to reduce class sizes to no more than 40 to 50 students. However, further reductions in the number of students would generally have no significant benefit until class sizes reached approximately 20 students. In developing countries, reducing class size to this number is prohibitively expensive, would require more teachers (who are already in short supply), and in many cases, would lead to double shifting, thereby reducing the number of hours of instruction and the amount learned.

Language of Instruction

Hartshorne (1992) has recommended that in the new South Africa, the mother tongue should be used as the language of instruction in the early grades. He claimed that there is strong support for the use of mother tongue in the early years for establishing early cognitive development, reading and writing. Thereafter, English should become the major language of instruction. Transfer to English medium should take place no later than the end of the sixth year, although it could take place much earlier; what is important, is that the transfer from mother tongue to English should be gradual. English should be seen not as a subject area but as a working tool across all subject areas in the curriculum. As Hartshorne pointed out, however, use of English as a common linking language is not without its problems. At present probably more than half of all South Africans are not able to use English at a level of functional literacy; English has tended to be a possession of an elite who have benefitted from higher secondary and tertiary education. There needs to be more effective teaching of English within the school system, and provision of effective English programmes at literacy and higher levels outside the system.

In addition, Hartshorne has recommended that African languages need to be developed and actively promoted among all sectors of South African society so they are not considered as being of less importance than English. The number of languages primary pupils should be required to learn should be limited to two; a third language should not be introduced before Standard 5.

Economics

Many educators, according to Cosser (1991), believe that the proportion of state funding allotted to education has reached its limit. Cosser suggested alternative funding methods such as: levies from industry, payment in kind by parents doing volunteer work for schools, an education tax with cross-subsidization between wealthy and poor areas, lotteries and private schools subsidized by state funding. Graham-Brown (1991) added the suggestion of mobilizing community and private resources to create schools.

As previously mentioned, the cost-effectiveness of all "improvements" to schools must be examined. In developing countries, not all improvements are affordable or effective in proportion to the investments required. Two examples, cited by Lockheed and Verspoor (1991), are that although it may be desirable to improve the physical structure of schools, the evidence indicates that elaborate schools are not more effective in producing learning than are modest facilities. Also, as mentioned, even though it may be desirable to decrease class sizes, if size reduction results in double shifting and increasing numbers of teachers, the costs and the benefits to students are not warranted.

These are exciting times in the field of education in Southern Africa. Countries in the region have placed high priority on education as a key to individual and national development (Mwamwenda & Mwamwenda 1992). Many dramatic developments are currently underway, and the future shows considerable promise.

References

Adams, M.N. and Kruppcnbach, S.E. 1987. Gender and Access in the African schools. *International Review of Education* 33: 437-454.

Baine, D. 1985. Training Instructional Staff for Special Education in Developing Countries. *The Association for Persons with Severe Disabilities, Newsletter* 11: 7-8.

Baine, D. 1991. *Handicapped Children in Developing Countries. Assessment, Curriculum and Instruction.* Edmonton, Alberta: Educational Psychology, University of Alberta.

Bergmann, H. 1985. Agriculture as a Subject in Primary School. *International Review of Education* 3: 155-174.

Bishop, G. 1989. *Alternative Strategies for Education.* London: Macmillan.

Chikombah, C.E. 1991. Zimbabwe. In: W. Wickremasinghe, ed., *Handbook of World Education.* Houston TX: American Collegiate Service.

Cosser, E. ed., 1991. Education for Life: The Challenge of Schooling for All. Johannesburg, SAM: Christian Research, Education, and Information for Democracy.

Frederikse, J. 1992. *All Schools for All Children: Lessons for South Africa from Zimbabwe's Open Schools*. Cape Town, SA: Oxford University Press.

Graham-Brown, S. 1991. *Education in the Developing World.* New York: Longman.

Hartshorne, 1992. *Crisis and challenge: Black Education: 1910-1990.* Cape Town, SA: Oxford University Press.

Heyneman, S.P. 1990. Economic Crisis and the Quality of Education. *International Journal of Educational Development* 10: 115-129.

Husen, T. 1978. *Teacher Training and Student Achievement in less Developed Countries*. Washington: World Bank.

Jansen, J. 1989. Curriculum Reconstruction in Post-Colonial Africa: A Review of the Literature. *International Journal of Educational Development* 9(3): 219-231.

Jenkins, J.R. and Jenkins, L.M. 1982. *Cross-age and Peer Tutoring.* Reston, VA: Council for Exceptional Children.

Kaluba, L.H. 1986. Education in Zambia: The Problem of Access to Schooling and the Paradox of the Private School Solution. *Comparative Education*. 22: 159-170.

Kassam, Y. 1983. Nyerere's Philosophy and the Educational Experiment in Tanzania. *Interchange* 14(1): 56-68.

Lockheed, M.E. and Verspoor, A.M. 1991. *Improving primary education in developing countries*. Washington, DC: World Bank.

Matoti, S. M. 1990. *The State of Education in Transkei—1990*. Umtata, Transkei: Faculty of Education, University of Transkei.

Matsela, Z.A. 1991. Lesotho. In: W. Wickremasinghe, ed., *Handbook of World Education*. Houston TX: American Collegiate Service.

Mackenzie, C.G. 1988. Zimbabwe's Educational Miracle and the Problems it has Created. *International Review of Education* 34: 337-353.

Mphahlele, M.C. 1991. South Africa. In: W. Wickremasinghe, ed., *Handbook of World Education*. Houston TX: American Collegiate Service.

Mungazi, D. 1986. Educational Innovation in Zimbabwe: Possibilities and Problems. *Journal of Negro Education* 54(2).

Mwamwenda, T.S. and Mwamwenda, B.B. 1987. School Facilities and Pupils' Academic Achievement. *Comparative Education* 23: 225-235.

Mwamwenda, T.S. and Mwamwenda, B.B. 1989. Teacher Characteristics and Pupils' Academic Achievement in Botswana Primary Education. *International Journal of Educational Development* 9: 31-42.

Mwamwenda, T.S. and Mwamwenda, B.B. 1992. Quest for Quality Education in Botswana. *South Africa Journal of Education* 12(1): 45-49.

Peil, M. 1990. Intergenerational Mobility through Education: Nigeria, Sierra Leone and Zimbabwe. *International Journal of Educational Development* 10: 311-325.

Psacharopoulos, G. 1985. Curriculum Diversification in Colombia and Tanzania: An Evaluation. *Comparative Educational Review* 29: 507-526.

Psacharopoulos, G. 1987. To Vocationalize or not to Vocationalize? is the Curriculum Question. *International Review of Education* 33: 187-211.

Rakubutu, M. 1992. Interactive Radio: Affordable Village Technology. *Matlhasedi* 11: 64-65.

SAE 1992a. Education for All. *Southern African Economist* 5(1): 5-7.

Sapere, D. and Mills, G. 1992. Blending traditional and modern architecture: Rural School Buildings. *Matlhasedi* 11: 40-44.

Sargent, R.A. 1991. Swaziland. In: W. Wickremasinghe, ed., *Handbook of World Education*. Houston TX: American Collegiate Service.

Selvaratnam, V. 1988. Limits to Vocationally-Oriented Education in the Third World. *International Journal of Educational Development* 8: 129-144.

Tlou, J.S. and Mautle, G. 1991. Botswana. In: W. Wickremasinghe, ed., *Handbook Of World Education*. Houston TX: American Collegiate Service.

Uchendu, V., ed., 1979. *Education and Politics in Tropical Africa*. New York: Conch.

Urevbu, A.O. 1988. Vocationalizing the Secondary School Curriculum: The African Experience. *International Review of Education* 34: 258-269.

World Bank. 1989. World Bank Report on Education in Sub-Saharan Africa. *Comparative Education Review* 33: 93-103.

— 11 —
UNIVERSALIZING ACCESS AND PROMOTING EQUITY IN EDUCATION—THE BOTSWANA CASE

John C.B. Bigala and Fazlur R. Moorad

Introduction

Equality of educational opportunities is a very common slogan for politicians, educators and parents. Yet, it is both ambiguous and difficult to define. It has been a concept of educational policy for both developed and developing countries. The diversity in it's meaning is attributable to the evaluative and ideological differences that exist among different individuals and social groups in different societies and at different historic periods. Underlying the concept of equality of educational opportunity are different and often contradicting visions of the nature of society; what it means to be educated; the contribution of education to the pursuit of social justice; how society ought to be organised for the pursuit of the common good; and principles of equality and social justice. Given these contradictory ideological visions, it is inevitable that the concept of equality acquired different meanings for different societies. There are at least two different ways in which the concept of equality of educational opportunities has been used.

Universalising of access can mean expanding educational services of quality and reducing disparities, so that we reach all children in every country with an affordable package of basic education, to meet their learning needs. To reach this goal, most countries will have to develop flexible, alternative and multiple approaches in the form of both formal and non-formal school systems, with emphasis on access, efficiency, effectiveness and relevance. This is generally referred to as equality of access. Equality of conditions is closely related to equality of access, since the latter would be meaningless if nothing is done to counteract the negative effects of poverty and deprivation on school achievement. As Turner (1986:36) states "all competitions in the race should start at the same point with appropriate handicaps". To guarantee equality of conditions and ultimately of opportunity and outcome, there should be policies and programmes, which would adequately check the disadvantages and deprivations, which learners find in or bring along to the school.

The concern for equality of educational opportunity is noted in the increasing realisation on the part of educators, that the educational system perpetuates inequalities and injustices in society in so far as it discriminates against certain social groups, either by denying them access, or by transmitting a kind of cultural capital, which they could not adequately master, thus engendering high dropout rates among these groups. It is this concern with the issues of injustice, that has provided the impetus for equalising educational opportunity (Heath, 1984). However, these are not the only justifications for equality of educational opportunity. In many developing countries of Sub-Saharan Africa, e.g. Uganda, the attempt to equalise educational opportunity was based on the realisation of the fact that ethnic and class disparities with access to education—the direct outcomes of colonial educational policies—could constitute a serious threat to national integration. There is therefore, the need to widen access to education in order to contain the tension, which ethnic, tribal and class inequalities in educational provision might engender. This is important, because education in Uganda as in other developing countries of Africa, has been a major determinant of social mobility and income and has also served as one of the avenues to power and privilege.

The Universal Declaration of Human Rights in 1945 asserted among other things that: "Everyone has the right to education. This shall be free at least in the elementary and primary stages".

Elementary education should be compulsory. If these rights are to be realised, every child should be given all the necessary opportunities and assistance to achieve his/her potential as long as he or she is a member of the society. Equal educational opportunity, however, is not synonymous with equity in education, but equal educational opportunity can be achieved if there is equity in education. Equity as defined by (Bowles, 1969) is "the quality of being fair or impartial". Therefore, for equity to be realised, there should be fairness in financing education; in the curriculum development and it implementation; the provision of physical, human and material resources; and fairness in budgetary allocations to schools. True equity should also be reflected in government's policy in the distribution of welfare and social amenities to all communities. This will in turn enhance equality in education and bridge the traditional and inherent gap in educational development between the rural and urban communities.

The claims of this chapter are that the assumptions made by

supporters of universal education that educational reform could be used to redress deep rooted social problems such as injustice and inequality is fundamentally flawed in so far as the structural causes of inequality are ignored. In other words, educational reform by itself is incapable of solving the problems of injustice and inequality in society. For equality of opportunity to be meaningful and attainable, there is the need to embark upon a large scale programme of reform, which is aimed at reduction of poverty and general inequality existing in the society.

One can claim that despite the intention of the supporters, equality of educational opportunity has in practice been reduced to equality of access to educational institutions without any due consideration for the need to address issues relating to inequality of conditions and outcomes.

What does equal outcome mean? Does it mean that all children must reach the same level of attainment e.g. the same level of knowledge and skills? Does it entail a conscious policy of depressing the intellectual abilities of some (brighter) children in order to enable children of lower abilities to catch up with them? The realisation that the achievement of equal learning outcomes for all children is pedagogically and politically difficult leads on to look for other measures of equality of outcomes. These are usually non-educational and such measures of outcomes focus on the effect of schooling on income, social mobility, access to power and privilege.

> It is clear that equality of outcome envisaged here is that representation of the different social groups classified in terms of class, racial or ethnic origin, sex etc. at the various educational levels should be in proportion to the size of the group within the general population. Thus the principle of equality of results would be satisfied not if every working class child (Black or White) had equality college education, but rather when working class children were present in an Institution of higher education in numbers proportionate to the size of the working class within the total population. (Entwistle, 1977)

It is the use of non-educational outcomes that has dominated the debate on equality of educational opportunities in many African countries.

Equality of Educational Opportunity in Sub-Saharan Africa.

The optimism, enthusiasm and political commitment which African leaders had towards education at the time of independence are reflected in the ambitious programmes, which the Ministers of Education, who met in Addis Ababa in 1961 set for themselves to be achieved by 1980: Free compulsory Universal Primary Education (UPE) throughout the continent; education at the secondary level to be provided to at least 30 percent of the primary school leavers; higher education to be provided mostly in Africa to at least 20 percent of those, who complete secondary education; and the improvement of the quality of schools and universities to be a constant aim.

> 'The citizens of Africa', declared the Ministers, 'see in education a means by which their aspirations may be met. They are willing to sacrifice for their attainment of this, means for gaining economic and social development and wish to provide more people education suited to their desires.' (UNESCO, 1961)

Independent Africa had to catch up with the rest of the world. In fighting the three enemies; ignorance, poverty and disease, no time was to be wasted. Africans had to run, while others walked.

Inspite of the great enthusiasm and faith placed in education and the heavy public expenditure devoted to formal schooling, most African countries have not made any spectacular advances either in educational development itself or in the expected economic growth and public welfare or in achieving such desirable social and political goals as national unity, the unification of Africa and the promotion of human rights and respect for law and order. On the contrary, coup d'etats, upheavals, revolutions and violent power struggle have become a permanent feature of post independence Africa. Our continent has the largest and rising number of refugees in the world, estimated to be over 10 million in 1993, (Timberlake, 1985:21). Inspite of relatively abundant natural resources such as uncultivated land and lakes teeming with fish, natural forests rich in timber, and minerals, unemployment, incessant famines and object poverty remain the major features of our continent. Excessive infant mortality rates, violent deaths in all forms persist. Awesome disparities in income and social amenities still exist between the vast majority of the people, who live in rural areas, and the five percent, who dwell in cities. Universal free Primary Education (UPE) and the elimination of adult illiteracy, which were expected to have been achieved throughout Africa by 1980 are far from being attained.

With estimated population growth rates of 2.8 to 4 percent per annum between 1980-2000, and burdened with back-breaking external public debts, most sub-saharan countries, are running as fast as possible merely to remain in the same place, and in some cases to slip backwards. There are still yawning gaps between the participation rate of males and those of females, particularly in higher education (World Bank, 1989:11).

Different African economic and social "models" like Ujamah, education for self-reliance (Tanzania), move to the left humanism, authenticity (Zambia), the economic war (Uganda), all have come and gone, leaving no dent in African poverty. Marxist, Capitalist, Socialist and mixed economic models in Africa have so far suffered the same fate. The poor of Tanzania, Kenya, Uganda, Angola or of South Africa, according to Brian Walker, President of the International Institute for Environment and Development, face approximately the same bleak uncomprising future (World Bank, 1989:20). The African poverty trap, in a word, has treated competing doctrinaire idealogies with much the same contempt. Problems, such as those mentioned above, can be a source of frustration or a source of stimulation. They can serve as a launching pad for corrective action or as a terminal of disgust and disarray. By taking examples from Botswana the authors will show that attempts to equalise universal education have succeeded and failed largely because they have either addressed or not addressed the specific ways in which unequal conditions have a negative effect on both access to education and outcomes.

Equality of Educational Opportunity in Botswana

Botswana, like so many other developing countries after achieving independence simply joined the quest for achieving the U.P.E. goal set at Addis Ababa in 1962. Thus, the initial emphasis was simply qualitative expansion. The first decade saw an uncoordinated and not so properly planned educational expansion albeit the emphasis was on secondary schooling. This was due to the need to develop fairly rapidly, a skilled/educated labour force which had been hitherto totally neglected by the former colonial administration.

Quite clearly, the framework policy guidelines for the development of Education in Botswana were formulated as late as 1977, a decade after independence when the first National Commission on Education had been established and thereafter published their report entitled, "Education for Kagisano" which means "social harmonony". Enshrined at the heart of this philosophy are the overarching principles of equity and social justice.

The report together with its subsequent white paper had identified all the important areas and levels of education such as primary, secondary and tertiary education. The latter included vocational, technical and university education. Other areas also focused on, were teacher training and the curriculum. The commission examined each of these levels and sectors identified the weaknesses/gaps and came up with a list of recommendations most of which were fairly clear, feasible and relevant. This could also be planned into short and long term implementation strategies. This first commission's report had become the Blue Print for the entire education system right into the current decade, when the Botswana Government decided to establish its second commission on education in 1992.

The need for this second commission had been, accentuated by the rapid, complex, social and economic changes that had taken place since 1977. The Government had therefore identified the urgent and crucial review of the education system once again. Before one proceeds to examine the important aims, strategies of the second commission on education it would be useful to examine some of the major achievements during the period between the two important commissions i.e. 1977-1992.

This first commission clearly had a mammoth task on hand. They had to examine and analyse the entire educational system including the organisational and structural dimensions. They had to look at management and financial considerations as well. Issues of relevancy, feasibility and equality were all addressed. In short, the Education for Kagisano report had become the Blue Print for policy makers, planners, academics and researchers.

In reference to basic education, a number of relevant issues had been addressed e.g. access with a particular emphasis on the role of Communities and Government partnership venture to expand educational provision especially at the junior secondary level. This led to the establishment of the Community Junior Secondary Schools (CJSS) programme which helped the Government to speed up access for the basic education programme. The CJSS model was replicated and to a large extent, the Government was also able to provide a fairly equitable middle level school throughout the country.

The number of Primary schools increased from 316 in 1974 to 657 in 1993. The increase is attributed to state schools, which rise from 293 to 591 during that period. Private schools also increased from 13 to 53 for the same period. The enrolment more than doubled from 145, 459 to 305, 479. (See Table 5 & 6)

TABLE 5: NUMBER OF PRIMARY AND SECONDARY SCHOOLS 1970-1994

School Ownership (Primary)					School Ownership (Secondary)		
Year	Mission/ Grant Aided	Private	Local Authority (Councils)	Total	Govt. & Aided	Private	Total
1970					11		11
1971					13		13
1972					15		15
1973					14		14
1974	10	13	293	316	15	14	29
1975					15	14	29
1976					15	17	32
1977					15	17	32
1978	11	13	353	377	18	17	35
1979	11	12	371	394	20	17	36
1980	12	12	391	415	22	17	38
1981	11	9	403	423	22	17	41
1982[1]	12	17	434	463	22	17	42
1983	13	25	464	502	22	17	42
1984	13	28	471	512	23	35[2]	58

Year	Mission/ Grant Aided	Private	Local Authority (Councils)	Total	Govt. & Aided	Private	Total
1985	13	26	489	528	23	42	65
1986	13	23	501	537	23	50	73
1987	13	26	518	557	23	59	82
1988	13	21	525	559	23	68	91
1989	17	27	540	584	22	97	119
1990	12	35	555	602	23	120	143
1991	14	48	564	626	23	149	172
1992	13	51	579	643	23	150	173
1993	13	53	591	657	23	163	186
1994					27		

Source 1. Primary: Educational Stats. 1974/78/84/87/95, Human Development Data Book 1996

1. Prior to 1984, "Private Schools" include all self-help schools such as Itireleng and Ipelegeng; also included are high cost schools such as Maru-a-Pula.

2. In 1985 all self-help schools became Community Junior Secondary Schools but have been included under private schools. The figure for the private schools is an estimate. Note that study centres that have been established since 1994 are not included. There are only four private high cost schools. Maru-a-Pula, Legae, Westwood (all in Gaborone), and "John Mackenzie" in Francistown.

TABLE 6:
ENROLLMENT AT PRIMARY LEVEL BY YEAR AND GENDER

INDICATOR (SECOND LEVEL) SECONDARY SCHOOLS ENROLLMENT BY YEAR & GENDER

Year	Male	Female	Total	% Female	Male	Female	Total	% Female
1978	65,211	80,248	145,459	55.2	7,105	8,981	16,086	55.8
1979	70,457	86,207	156,664	55.0	7,387	9,329	16,716	55.8
1980	78,111	93,803	171,914	54.6	8,042	10,283	18,325	56.1
1981	81,975	96,132	178,107	54.0	8,935	11,277	20,212	55.8
1982	87,284	100,934	188,218	53.6	9,482	11,500	20,982	54.8
1983	92,593	105,735	198,328	53.3	10,411	12,392	22,803	54.3

Year	Male	Female	Total	% Female	Male	Female	Total	% Female
1984	99,055	110,767	209,772	52.8	12,653	14,724	27,377	53.8
1985	106,423	117,185	223,608	52.4	14,997	17,175	32,172	53.4
1986	113,693	122,248	235,941	51.8	17,066	18,900	35,966	52.5
1987	120,196	128,627	148,823	51.7	19,022	20,353	39,375	51.7
1988	126,327	135,025	261,352	51.7	19,833	20,524	40,357	50.9
1989	133,608	141,829	275,437	51.5	23,527	25,773	49,348	52.2
1990	137,217	146,299	283,516	51.6	26,562	30,330	56,892	53.2
1991	142,117	150,116	292,233	51.4	32,119	36,880	68,99	53.5
1992	147,414	154,068	301,482	51.1	35,146	40,727	75,873	57.7
1993	150,751	154,728	305,479	50.7	39,880	45,807	85,687	53.5

Source: Primary: Ed. Stats. 1978, 1984, 1990, 1995
Source: Educational Statistics, 1990/1992/1995

The number of secondary schools also increased from 11 in 1970 to 186 in 1994. What is of interest is the increase in the middle level community junior secondary schools mentioned earlier. This increase, to reiterate, was mainly due to the community participation in the financing and management of schools (see Moorad 1989; Swartland and Taylor 1988; Kann and Tshireletso 1987).

With specific regards to Basic Education during this period, one will note significant achievements. Botswana is one of the few African countries to attain an almost total universalization of primary education (See Table 7).

TABLE 7: UNIVERSAL PRIMARY EDUCATION

Year	Population (Age 7-13)	Total Enrollment	Enrolment (Age 7-13)	Enrolment (Age 6-13)	Ger	Ner
1981	181,069	178,107	150,591	161,908	98.4	83.2
1982	187,627	188,218	159,139	171,098	100.3	84.8
1983	194,186	198,328	170,641	177,042	102.1	87.9
1984	200,744	209,772	178,175	184,031	104.5	88.8
1985	207,303	233,608	189,750	195,360	107.9	91.5
1986	213,861	235,941	199,642	205,129	110.3	93.5
1987	224,100	248,823	209,640	214,737	11.0	93.5
1988	234,900	261,352	218,819	224,568	111.3	93.2
1989	246,100	275,437	277,984	235,037	111.9	92.6
1990	257,935	283,516	233,800	242,690	109.9	90.6

Source: Human Development Report, 1991; NDP 7, 1991

In Botswana, basic education now covers ten years of schooling i.e. seven years of primary and three years of junior secondary. The tenth year having been added on in 1995. According to the National Development Plan 7 (1991-1997):

> There was significant progress towards UPE (Universal Primary Education), but it is difficult to be certain of how many `missing children' did not enter the school system. The 1990 World Conference on Education for all called on developing countries to achieve an 80 percent enrolment target for Basic Education by the year 2000. Botswana was already exceeding this for the seven years of Primary Education, and is making rapid progress towards providing access to all to the nine years basic education cycle. (NDP 7, 1991:317)

It is fairly evident from the above statement that Botswana is making remarkable progress towards the goal of universalizing Basic Education.

It is important to note that Botswana reaffirmed its status vis a vis this goal by participating in the World Conference on Education for All held in Jomtien, Thailand in March 1990. In addition, Botswana was also party to the World Summit on Children held in New York 1990**. The result of this conference was the setting up of the Botswana National Plan of Action specifically targeting disadvantaged children by the year 2000. Furthermore, Botswana was only the fourth country by 1993 to carry out a human development initiative which was an attempt to evaluate its entire development strategies from a human development perspective. The result of this, was a report entitled, "Planning for People (1993)" which also focused inter alia on disadvantaged groups namely the Remote Area Dwellers (RADS); the street children, cattle herders and children with disabilities. (See Tables 8.1, 8.2 and 10.00)

However, despite tremendous progress in making education more accessible, available evidence suggests that not all social groups have equal access to education. There are still products of primary school age children outside the school system as evidenced by research findings. Mbere (1992) among other things, describes the various programmes for children with special emphasis on the disadvantaged groups, including the disabled; AIDS and HIV infected children; street children, remote areas dwellers and abandoned and abused children.

She makes specific suggestions as to areas of future focus. These include Remote Area Dwellers Children in Urban areas and Children in specially difficult circumstances. The themes covered, are community participation/involvement; parental involvement; reintegration of the father/man; training of trainers, institutional building and coordination.

** The title of this summit was: World Declaration on the Survival, Protection and Development of Children and Plan of Action for Implementation in the 1990's.

TABLE 8.1: POPULATION AGED 12 YEARS WHO NEVER ATTENDED FORMAL SCHOOL, BY AGE GROUP AND GENDER (1993)

		NEVER ATTENDED SCHOOL			
		AGE SPECIFIC GROUP		PERCENT	
Age Group	Population 12 Years +	Total	Rate (%)	Male	Female
12-24	120,801	1,594	2.1	59.0	41.0
15-19	162,443	6,857	4.2	66.7	33.3
20-24	117,582	9,224	7.8	56.8	43.2
25-29	96,078	13,530	14.1	50.3	49.7
30-34	83,023	19,244	23.2	40.7	59.3
35-39	65,618	17,151	26.1	39.3	60.7
40-44	51,225	15,453	30.2	46.6	53.4
45-49	41,761	14,360	34.4	44.1	55.9
50-54	32.489	13,751	42.3	45.5	54.5
55-59	25,126	11,504	45.8	45.3	54.7
60-64	21,490	10,271	47.8	45.8	54.2
65+	78,594	53,132	67.6	39.3	60.7
Unknown	13,285	6,591	49.6	36.9	64.1
TOTAL	909,515	193,662	21.3	45.2	54.8

Source: Majelantle *et al.* (1995) Census Dissemination Seminar Paper. Human Development Data Book 1996

TABLE 8.2: MAJOR REASON FOR NEVER ATTENDING FORMAL SCHOOL, BY GENDER (1993)

Reason	Male	Female	TOTAL	%
Looking after cattle	71.3	28.7	78,303	40.4
Parents unwilling	28.6	71.4	42,177	21.8
Helping at Home	6.0	94.0	24,181	12.5
Too expensive	35.8	64.2	14,930	7.7
No school is area	35.4	64.6	10,777	5.6
Not interested	48.6	51.4	5,936	3.1
Ill Health	33.7	66.3	3,392	1.8
Did not know benefits	28.9	71.1	3,357	1.7

Source: Majelantle *et al.* (1995) 1991 Census Dissemination Seminar Paper. HDI Data Book 1996

TABLE 9: STRATEGIES TO ACHIEAVE ACCESS AND EQUITY

Projections of Population 6-12 Years

Year	Population 6-12 years	% Increase
1991	281,741	—
1996	324,286	15, 1
2001	357,217	10, 1
2006	392,941	10, 1
2011	430,290	11, 1

Source: Central Statistics Office. Populations projections 1991-2011.

The primary school population was projected to grow from 281,741 in 1991 to 430,290 in 2011. The 1991 primary school enrolment was 285,183 representing 101% of the age group. The reason for this is, that there are children outside this age bracket in primary school. Assuming that the average class size is 45, about 3225 additional classrooms and ancillary facilities would be required with the 20 year period between 1992 and 2011. This is additional to the backlog that already exists. Assuming the present pupil-teacher ratio of 1:30, the teacher requirement at the same period would be 4,886.

Even though access to primary education is high, universal primary education remains to be achieved. Several reasons why children do not go to school can be identified;

> those, who do not live in walking distance to school; those, whose lifestyle and cultural patterns pose barriers to school attendance; those, who do not attend on account of disability; and those, who have access to school but for poverty, or other reasons for not attending school" (Kann et al, 1989).

TABLE 10: PERCENTAGE DISTRIBUTION OF DISABLED SCHOOL AGE (5-17) POPULATION BY AGE GROUP, SCHOOL ATTENDANCE, GENDER AND TYPE OF DISABILITY (1991)[***]

Table 10 (part 1)

			TYPE OF DISABILITY (CODE)							
Age	School Attendance	Sex	11	12	13	14	21	22	23	24
5-6	Never Attended	M	54.5	51.1	50.0	30.8	40.8	39.6	62.5	51.1
		F	45.5	36.2	40.0	69.2	49.0	54.5	37.5	48.9
	Still at School	M	-	3.5	6.7	-	4.1	2.2	-	-
		F	-	4.3	3.3	-	2.0	3.7	-	-

[***] Table 10 had to be divided into eight parts. Any text refererences to Table 10 in the text could refer to any of the parts 1-8.

Age	School Attendance	Sex	11	12	13	14	21	22	23	24
	Left School	M	-	-	-	-	2.0	-	-	-
		F	-	-	-	-	2.0	-	-	-
	Total	M	54.5	59.6	56.7	30.8	46.9	41.8	62.5	51.1
		F	45.5	40.4	43.4	69.2	53.1	58.2	37.5	48.9
Total			22	47	30	13	49	134	8	45

Table 10 (part 2)

			TYPE OF DISABILITY (CODE)							
Age	School Attendance	Sex	31	32	41	42	51	52	61	62
5-6	Never Attended	M	60.9	60.0	58.8	55.3	64.6	46.2	-	
		F	32.5	47.5	37.3	42.4	27.7	50.0	-	
	Still at School	M	2.6	0.8	2.0	-	3.1	-	-	
		F	3.3	1.7	2.0	1.2	1.2	4.6	3.8	
	Left School	M	-	-	-	-	-	-	-	
		F	0.7	-	-	1.2	-	-	-	
	Total	M	53.6	50.8	60.8	55.3	67.7	46.2	-	
		F	36.4	49.2	39.2	44.7	32.3	53.8	-	
Total			151	120	51	85	65	26	-	

Table 10 (part 3)

			TYPE OF DISABILITY (CODE)							
Age	School Attendance	Sex	11	12	13	14	21	22	23	24
7-12	Never Attended	M	8.39	9.8	15.8	24.0	6.1	11.8	6.7	21.5

Age	School Attendance	Sex	11	12	13	14	21	22	23	24
		F	9.9	16.1	9.6	30.0	9.4	8.2	-	25.4
	Still at School	M	33.9	38.0	42.1	6.0	43.1	36.2	53.3	26.2
		F	41.3	30.6	23.7	28.0	37.6	37.5	40.0	26.2
	Left School	M	4.1	2.4	5.3	4.0	2.2	4.9	-	-
		F	2.5	3.1	3.5	6.0	1.7	1.3	-	0.8
	Total	M	46.3	50.2	63.2	36.0	51.4	52.9	60.0	47.7
		F	53.7	49.8	36.8	64.0	48.6	47.1	40.0	52.3
Total			121	255	224	50	181	680	30	130

Table 10 (part 4)

				TYPE OF DISABILITY (CODE)						
Age	School Attendance	Sex	31	32	41	42	51	52	61	62
7-12	Never Attended	M	18.1	38.7	22.0	44.0	25.4	38.4	-	
		F	13.0	30.0	10.5	28.0	10.0	24.7	50.0	
	Still at School	M	43.0	15.7	33.5	16.1	33.3	16.4	50.0	
		F	23.5	12.7	29.0	9.8	25.9	15.1	-	
	Left School	M	1.6	2.0	3.0	0.5	4.0	5.5	-	
		F	0.9	1.0	2.0	1.6	105	-	-	
	Total	M	62.6	56.3	58.5	60.6	62.7	60.3	50.0	
		F	37.4	43.7	41.5	39.4	37.3	39.7	50.0	
Total			447	300	200	193	201	73	2	

Table 10 (part 5)

			TYPE OF DISABILITY (CODE)							
Age	School Attendance	Sex	11	12	13	14	21	22	23	24
13-17	Never Attended	M	12.1	7.0	10.7	24.6	3.3	7.9	12.9	24.5
		F	8.4	9.9	7.4	28.1	4.6	5.6	-	20.2
	Still at School	M	36.4	25.3	41.0	22.8	36.2	35.4	16.1	26.6
		F	24.3	42.1	26.2	15.8	33.6	31.7	58.1	21.3
	Left School	M	12.1	5.9	10.7	7.0	7.9	13.0	6.5	3.2
		F	6.5	9.9	4.1	1.8	14.5	6.5	6.5	4.3
	Total	M	60.7	38.1	62.3	54.4	47.4	56.3	35.5	54.3
		F	39.3	61.9	37.7	45.6	52.6	43.8	64.5	45.7
Total			107	273	122	57	152	432	31	94

Table 10 (part 6)

			TYPE OF DISABILITY (CODE)							
Age	School Attendance	Sex	31	32	41	42	51	52	61	62
13-17	Never Attended	M	11.9	28.9	7.8	23.2	113.3	16.7	-	
		F	6.7	27.7	6.3	24.1	7.7	30.6	-	
	Still at School	M	43.9	18.7	31.3	16.1	31.5	19.4	20.0	
		F	22.0	13.3	30.2	17.0	22.4	13.9	-	
	Left School	M	7.9	7.8	13.0	15.2	15.4	13.9	20.0	
		F	7.6	3.6	22.5	4.5	9.8	5.6	60.0	
	Total	M	63.7	55.4	52.1	54.5	60.1	50.0	40.0	
		F	36.3	44.6	47.9	45.5	39.9	50.0	60.0	

Age	School Attendance	Sex	31	32	41	42	51	52	61	62
Total			328	166	192	112	143	36	5	

Table10 (part 7)

			TYPE OF DISABILITY (CODE)							
Age	School Attendance	Sex	11	12	13	14	21	22	23	24
15-17	Never Attended	M	14.0	11.8	17.3	25.0	9.4	13.4	15.9	27.5
		F	12.4	14.8	12.0	33.3	12.6	12.3	4.3	27.5
	Still at School	M	32.0	29.6	37.6	14.2	35.3	32.3	30.4	21.9
		F	30.4	33.9	22.6	19.2	31.4	31.9	43.5	20.1
	Left School	M	7.2	3.8	7.1	5.0	4.5	7.1	2.9	1.1
		F	4.0	6.1	3.4	3.3	6.8	3.0	2.9	1.9
	Total	M	53.2	45.2	62.0	44.2	49.2	52.9	49.3	50.6
		F	46.8	54.8	38.0	55.8	50.8	47.1	50.7	49.4
Total										

Table 10 (part 8)

			TYPE OF DISABILITY (CODE)							
Age	School Attendance	Sex	31	32	41	42	51	52	61	62
15-17	Never Attended	M	22.9	38.2	20.1	40.5	27.4	34.1	-	
		F	13.9	32.9	11.7	30.0	12.0	31.1	14.3	
	Still at School	M	36.7	13.5	28.9	12.6	27.9	14.1	28.6	
		F	19.7	10.6	26.4	10.0	21.3	12.6	-	
	Left School	M	3.6	3.2	7.0	4.6	7.3	6.7	14.3	

Age	School Attendance	Sex	31	32	41	42	51	52	61	62
		F	3.2	1.5	5.9	2.3	4.2	1.5	42.9	
	Total	M	63.2	54.9	56.0	57.7	62.6	54.8	42.9	
		F	36.8	45.1	44.0	42.3	37.4	45.2	57.1	

DISABILITY CODE	11	12	13	14	21	22	23	24	
GRAND TOTALS	250	575	266	120	382	246	69	269	

DISABILITY CODE	31	32	41	42	51	52	61	62	
GRAND TOTALS	926	586	443	120	390	409	135	7	

Source: Majelantle *et al.* (1995) 1991 Census Dissemination Paper

DISABILITTY CODES DEFINITION:

11 Defect of Seeing on One Eye
12 Defect of Seeing in Two Eyes
13 Blindness in One Eye
14 Blindness in Two Eyes
21 Defect O Hearing on One Ear
22 Defect of Hearing in Two Ears
23 Deafness in One Ear
24 Deafness in Two Hears
31 Defect of Speech
32 Inability to Speak
41 Inability to Use One Leg
42 Inability to Use Two Legs
51 Inability to Use One Arm
52 Inability to Use Two Arms
61 Moderate Retardation
62 Severe Retardation

In order to achieve universal access to primary education the recent National Commission on Education (1993) addressed itself to the problems faced by the children and recommended that:

> *Immediate steps be taken to establish one or two teacher schools, where these are needed to solve the problem of small settlements. There are no reliable statistics on disabled in Botswana. However, it is estimated that in developing countries they usually constitute a significant group of children. Thus, more special schools should be built for the disabled. Problems of some communities go beyond distance to school. They include social cultural factors cited earlier such as language, family ties and inability to speak Setswana. It is necessary therefore to sensitise teachers to cultural differences. Bursary or destitute allowances to cover costs of school attendance for the poor should be provided. It is also relatively easy to absorb this category of children upto primary school by instituting social welfare programmes that provide for the needs of poor children and by sensitising parents to the need to send their children to school.*

The question of children with disabilities has been coming up under the spotlight and already the Government has a policy in place. Simply it calls for the mainstreaming of children with disabilities. Quite obviously this is based on the assumption that Botswana has those "special" requirements like teachers and other needed resources to bring such children at that level. This is therefore one of the challenges ahead. Already steps are being taken in terms of providing special education programmes for teachers.

Inspite of rapid growth in enrolment, the provision of classroom facilities has lagged behind.

TABLE 11: SHORTAGE OF CLASSROOMS, 1992

	NUMBER OF CLASSROOMS	NUMBER OF STREAMS	SHORTAGE OF CLASSROOMS	% AGE OF SHORTAGE
NORTHEAST	336	447	111	24,8
CENTRAL N	486	752	111	35,4
CENTRAL C	1091	1629	266	33,0
CENTRAL S	454	695	538	34,7
KGATLENG	316	424	241	25,5
KWENENG	793	1152	108	31,2
SOUTHERN	767	1183	359	35,2
SOUTH EAST	237	262	416	9,2
KGALAGADI	190	277	25	31,4
GHANZI	146	172	87	15,1
NORTH WEST	476	62	26	37,5
GABORONE	399	541	286	26,2
FRANCISTOWN	288	316	28142	8,9
LOBATSE	121	152	31	20,4
SELEBI PHIKWE	159	217	58	26,7
JWANENG	67	76	9	11,8
TOTAL	6326	9057	2731	30,2

SOURCE: Central Statistics Office, Education Statistics, 1991

From the table showing shortage of classrooms by District in 1991, for the total of 9,057 streams, there were only 6,326 classrooms. This means that 30.2% of all classes did not have any classrooms. The NDP7, 1991-1997 target is to construct 250 classrooms each year. This would work out to a total of 1,500 for the whole plan period.

TABLE 12: TRAINED AND UNTRAINED TEACHERS BY DISTRICT, 1991

DISTRICT/ URBAN COUNCILS	TRAINED TEACHERS	UNTRAINED TEACHERS	TOTAL NUMBER OF TEACHERS	% UNTRAINED
NORTH EAST	430	50	480	11,6
CENTRAL N	654	176	830	21,2
CENTRAL C	1568	187	1755	10,7
CENTRAL S	649	125	774	16.1
KGATLENG	402	56	458	12,2
KWENENG	1065	196	1261	15,5
SOURHERN	1129	111	1240	9,0
SOUTH EAST	267	17	284	6,0
KGALAGADI	255	59	314	18,8
GHANZI	165	24	189	12,7
NORTH WEST	644	166	810	20,5
GABORONE	554	63	617	10,2
FRANCISTOWN	310	30	340	8,8
LOBATSE	154	12	166	7,2
SELEBI PHIKWE	203	29	232	12,5
JWANENG	80	3	83	3,6
TOTAL	8529	1304	9833	13,3

SOURCE: Central Statistics Office. Education Statistics, 1991

In 1991, more than 86% of primary school teachers were trained. This is a remarkable improvement over 1979 when only 64% were trained. The table shows the distribution of trained and untrained teachers by District. About 14% of the Primary School teachers were untrained having dropped from 26% in 1985 and this is expected to drop gradually to about 3% by 1996. With such a high proportion of trained teachers at this level, it could be expected that there would be significant improvements in the performance of primary school children. However, this does not appear to be the case as indicated by the apparent low quality of primary school leavers entering junior secondary education.

(Mautle et al. 1993) indicate that learning achievement at primary level is low given that this is the foundation of formal schooling. Such low achievement adversely affects the upper levels (Mautle et al. 1993). Qualitative improvement to primary education is therefore a priority.

It appears that the quantitative achievements in terms of trained teachers for primary education have not been matched with the desired qualitative education.

The present requirements into primary teacher training were initially at three levels; Junior Certificate fail or Standard 7 with at least two years teaching experience; a Junior Certificate pass and one year teaching experience; or Cambridge Oversees School Certificate (COSC) or GCE. Due to the increase in COSC school leavers this entry qualification is now becoming the requirement. In addition to the above qualifications, candidates without a COSC have to pass an entrance examination including an oral interview.

The need to improve the quality of teaching and learning at the primary level is of paramount importance. The Primary Teacher Training Colleges are now implementing a 3 year Diploma programme which is intended to be an improvement on the previous 2 year Certificate.

One of the major instruments for improving the quality in primary education is the curriculum. This can cover broad areas such as making the curriculum more practical; using it to inculcate cultural and moral values in children; and increasing emphasis on Science and Mathematics in the curriculum. The Government is encouraging science related programmes as a career option by providing free scholarships.

Conclusion

The persistence of inequality of educational opportunity is largely due to the failure of African Governments to not only deal with the problem of inequality of access but also of conditions which, as mentioned earlier, inevitably engenders inequality of outcomes. As one sees it, the problem of inequality of condition has much to do with both social problems such as mass poverty and cultural deprivation; and learning conditions, which encompass issues such as the availability of teachers, facilities, teaching/learning materials, the nature of the curriculum and its relevance to the different needs of various social groups. Even if access to education is increased through qualitative expansion of schools, the problem of inequality of conditions will persist, and since conditions determine the quality of education received, it is an important factor in determining learning outcomes.

In many parts of Sub Saharan Africa, the massive expansion of education at all levels has been accompanied by deterioration of the quality of the physical conditions under, which learning takes place. Scarcity of teaching and learning materials; inadequate facilities; insufficient number of teachers; the deplorable conditions under, which pupils live and learn, are common problems.

The experiences in these countries suggest that quantitative expansion of schooling alone is not sufficient to guarantee equality of education opportunity. There must be a conscious attempt to address issues relating to equality of outcomes. Britain and the United States are examples of countries, whose attempts to equalise opportunity failed, because the root causes of educational disadvantages were left untouched while most of the efforts were directed at equalising access to schooling.

In this Chapter an attempt has been made to show that the goal of universal education is unlikely to be achieved by educational policy alone. Education liberation, like all other movements in the extension of freedom, can only follow a broader struggle for economic, social, and political liberation. Most achievements of the ambitious educational expansion in most Sub-Saharan African countries were quantitative.

However, quantity and quality are difficult to reconcile. It is accepted that universal educational balance cannot be achieved without some quantitative expansion. But in the short run it may still not be achieved because of the quantitative expansion, which as we have noted involves some deterioration of quality.

Botswana's case study shows a remarkable growth from going beyond universalizing primary education to include 3 more years of junior secondary schooling for all. However, various gaps have been identified such as children with disabilities, Remote Area Dwellers, street children, and cattle herders, which have to be properly addressed in order to achieve the goal of equity.

References

Bernard Van Leer Foundation (1991) *Child Development in Africa: Building on Peoples Strengths*. The Hague: Bernard Van Leer Foundation.

Bigala, J.C.B, Seboni, N.M. and Monau, R.M. (1993) *The Learning Needs of the Botswana Children in Standards One and Two*. Gaborone: Botswana, UNICEF.

Entwistle, H. (1979) *Class, Culture and Education*. London: Metheun. Government of Botswana. *Education Statistics*, 1970-1995. Gaborone:Central Statistics Office

Government of Botswana, UNICEF, UNDP (1993) *Planning for the People. A Strategy for Accelerating Human Development in Botswana*. Gaborone: Sygma Publishing (Pty) Ltd.

Government of Botswana, (1993) *Report of the National Commission on Education*. Gaborone: Government Printer.

Heath, A, (1984) *Class and Meritocracy in British Education Seven Oaks*, Kent: The Open University.

Kann, U. and Tshireletso, L. (1987) *Village Community Schools and Rural Development*. Report for the Botswana National Commission for UNESCO, Gaborone.

Kann, U, Malepolelo, D. and Nleya, P. (1989) *The Missing Children Achieving Universal Basic Education in Botswana*. Gaborone: University of Botswana.

Majelantle et al (1995) *The 1991 Population Census Seminar*. Central Statistics Office Gaborone. Government Printer.

Mautle, G. Konespillai, K. and Lungu E. (1993) *The Quality of Primary School Completers and it's Implications for Form 1 Organisation and Teaching*. Gaborone: Botswana Educational Research Association.

Mbere, N. (1992) Botswana: *A Country Report on Early Childhood Care and Education Programmes*. The Hague: Bernard Van Leer Foundation.

Moorad, I.R. (1989) *An Evaluation of the Community Junior Secondary Schools with particular emphasis in Decentralization and Community Participation*. Ph.D Thesis, University of London.

Myers, R. (1992) *The Twelve Who Survive*. London: Routledge.

Nyati-Ramahobo, L. (1992) *The Girl-Child in Botswana: Educational Constraints and Prospects*. Gaborone: Botswana, UNICEF.

Republic of Botswana. *The National Development Plan 7 (1991- 1997) Ministry of Finance and Development Planning*. Gaborone: Government Printer.

Sharp, R. (1980) *Knowledge, Ideology and the Politics of Schooling*. London: RKP.

Silver, H. (1980) *Education and the Social Condition.* London: Metheun.

Swartland, J.R. and Taylor, D.C. (1988) *Community financing of schools in Botswana*, in Bray, M. & Lillis, K. (eds) Community Financing of Education: Issues and Policy Implications in Less Developed Countries. Oxford: Pergamon Press.

Timberlake, L. (1985) *Africa in Crisis*. London: Earthscan

Turner, B. (1986) *Equality*. London: Tavistock.

World Bank (1989) *From Crisis to Sustained Growth.* Washington D.C.

— 12—
SOUTH AFRICA: EDUCATION IN TRANSITION

Eleanor M. Lemmer

Introduction

The first democratic elections in South Africa held in 1994 signalled the end of the notorious apartheid period and ushered in the post-apartheid era. Major initiatives in all areas of national life have since been launched to create a democratic society and redress past inequalities. Education, which was the arena for both the implementation of major apartheid policies as well as powerful resistance to them, clearly forms an integral part of national reconstruction.

Comprehensive policy initiatives aimed at creating a non-discriminatory, unitary system of education and training acceptable to all South Africans, which will meet local and national needs have rapidly appeared. This has dispelled any doubts that it would take years to establish a new educational dispensation. Bolstered by a strong research infrastructure established during the apartheid era by non-official structures for policy development, the framework for a new education system is being speedily developed by fully consultative processes of decision-making, including concerned government departments, education and training providers and major national stakeholders in education and training. Policy already passed as legislation include the South African Qualifications Act (September 1995) and the South African School Bill (October 1996).

In the light of these changes, this chapter gives an overview of current educational developments in South Africa in the new democratic era (1994-). This is done against the background of a brief history of education and the educational legacies of the apartheid era.

Historical Development of Education

The nature and structure of South African society has been determined by a policy of racial separatism since its founding. From 1949 onwards, separatism or apartheid was entrenched by the Nationalist government. According to the Population Registration Act of 1948 (scrapped in June 1991), the South African population was divided into four categories, namely Africans, Asians, coloured (mixed race) and whites. Nationalist policy was to establish self-governing states (the so-called homelands) within the borders of South Africa for Africans. The homelands policy was aimed at satisfying the political aspirations of Africans by granting them independence in ethnic enclaves (Claassen 1995:454).

Before and during the nineteenth century education for coloureds and Africans was provided mainly by missionary societies and the churches. In 1910 the Union of South Africa, a British dominion in the Commonwealth, was formed out of the four political units of the past. The franchise was mainly restricted to whites. After 1910, education for white and coloured people came under the administration of the four provinces, while the responsibility for African education gradually came under increasing state control, culminating in the Bantu Education Act of 1953. This was based on the assumption that African children required a schooling different from that of white children. The Bantu Education Act of 1953 centralised African education under a single education department. With political and economic power firmly vested in the hands of a white minority, education was strictly segregated by the unequal provision of separate educational facilities for the four main population groups. Thus education reflected the segmentation and inequality of larger society.

The first direct challenge to segregated education was the Soweto school riots of 1976-77 which constituted a rejection of apartheid eduction as unequal and illegitimate. In response the state initiated a reform process yet within the framework of political reformism and separation. This process was characterised by incremental reforms in schooling for Africans and the quantitative increase of educational opportunities for Africans. For example, endeavours were made to upgrade the qualifications of African teachers, establish parity in teachers' salaries and improve per capita funding to African education.

Furthermore, a national enquiry conducted by the Human Sciences Research Council (HSRC) into educational provision in 1981 resulted in the *HSRC Report on Education Provision in the Republic of South Africa* (HSRC 1981). This was the first thorough national inquiry into education to have been held in South Africa. However, only a piecemeal selection of the assumptions, intentions and outcomes of the Report were consolidated in subsequent legislation. Most significantly, fundamental issues of segregated education were not addressed by these reform measures (Hartshorne 1990). Consequently, the latter half of the 80s saw African schooling continue in crisis as education became firmly enmeshed in the broader liberation struggle. This led to the virtual breakdown in teaching and learning in schools in many areas. During this period various alternative movements around education were mobilised. The most important was the National Education Crisis Committee (NECC) movement officially launched in 1985 as the education component of the anti-apartheid Mass Democratic Movement and comprising community and political leaders, trade unions, parents, teachers and students (Wolpe 1990).

The reform initiatives received new momentum in February 1992 when the African National Congress (ANC) and many other organisations were unbanned and the first steps taken to dismantle apartheid legislation. In March 1990 permission was granted for opening white state schools for the first time, albeit subject to parent referendums and ministerial approval. In May 1990 the Committee of Education Heads (co-ordinating body of heads of education departments) initiated an investigation with a view to comprehensive education reform and a proposed strategy, the *Educational Renewal Strategy* (ERS) was produced in 1991. However, this still reflected the Nationalist governments spirit of reformism rather than radical transformation. In 1993, NECC published its own comprehensive policy document framework for a new educational dispensation in post-apartheid South Africa (NEPI 1993). In January, 1994 the ANC produced its first national policy framework for education and training. Finally, with the first democratic elections held in April 1994, a government of National Unity led by the ANC was established. Consequently, a non-racial, unitary education system based on equality, was instituted. The long struggle against apartheid education was over, at least in theory.

Educational Legacy of Apartheid Era

At the dawn of the democratic era, education in South Africa is marked by the paradoxes and ambiguities of the educational legacy of apartheid (White Paper No. 1 1995). On the one hand, South Africa has the most developed and well-resourced system of education and training on the African continent with the highest participation rates at all levels of the system. In the best-resourced, well staffed, highly motivated elite sector of the school system virtually all students succeed in the school leaving examinations and impressive numbers qualify for higher education. Yet, on the other hand, the majority of South African children attend school in poorly resourced schools where there is a high attrition rate and the majority fail school leaving examinations (White Paper no 1 1995:18). Some of the most pressing problems inherited by the government of National Unity are briefly described in the ensuing paragraphs.

Administration and Control

Administration and control of education at the end of the apartheid period was characterised by fragmentation and bureaucratic duplication. A number of racially segregated education subsystems provided education for a specific population category and for the African in the ten homelands. In addition to the Department of National Education, the overarching body which had determined national education policy and budgetary allocations on behalf of the central government, there were 18 executive education departments which functioned as separate entities isolated from each other. This meant the existence of separate educational institutions, each with its own configuration of models of school ownership, governance and funding (White Paper No. 1, 1995:18). A major challenge is the absorption of the multitude of education bodies which administered education and training during the apartheid era into a single non-racial system.

Language in Education Policy

Previously only two languages, English and Afrikaans, were recognised as official languages. Either English or Afrikaans was the medium of instruction for all students. In African schools the mother tongue was commonly the medium of instruction up to the end of the fourth year of schooling after which English was the popular choice as medium of instruction. None of the indigenous African languages enjoyed the status of official language. The African languages had an inferior status and their development was not considered a priority. Thus, language in education policy during the apartheid era privileged those whose home language was either English or Afrikaans and disadvantaged speakers of the African languages. The revision of language in education policy is a priority issue in the democratic era.

Schooling

Schooling at the close of the apartheid era was compulsory only for whites and to a lesser extent for Asians and coloureds. Compulsory education did not exist for Africans. Different types of schools with different funding structures and unequal provision of education characterised this period. Figures for 1992/3 describing the situation in the different types of schools follow (White Paper No. 1, 1995:72):

- Community schools: In the former homelands, community schools accounted for 87% of all schools and all enrolments. These schools were built and maintained by communities and were partly subsidised by the state.

- State-aided schools: State-aided schools for Africans (including farm schools) accounted for 70% of all schools but 19% of all enrolments. In addition, state schools were owned and financed by the state. Farm schools on private farms catered for the children of African farm workers and were partly subsidised. State-aided schools which were racially segregated for Asians and coloureds also existed.

- Model C schools: This was a type of state aided school introduced at the end of the apartheid period. It comprised the predominant school type for whites. The state paid staff salaries according to a fixed teacher/student ratio. Models C schools were governed by a governing body elected by parents of the school.

- Private schools: Private schools were established by a variety of secular and religious sponsors and account about l% of all schools in the country. These schools range from well-funded school to poorly resourced inner city schools and received partial state subsidy.

- Special schools: Provision for learners with special education needs was also racially fragmented and unequally provided, partially in special schools. Mainstreaming of many African children took place mainly by default due to inadequate facilities (Steyn 1997).

Curriculum

In all school types, schooling generally follows a junior primary (first three years of formal schooling,); senior primary phase (fourth to sixth year of schooling); junior secondary phase (seventh to ninth school year of schooling) and the senior secondary phase (tenth to twelfth year of schooling). The final year of schooling is concluded with the matriculation certificate examination. School curricula are academically oriented and Eurocentric, based on a Western ideal of liberal education which was of questionable relevance to a country with both first and third world characteristics (Smit 1990). Teaching has tended to be characterised by passive, rote learning, single textbook examination oriented approaches. An excessive emphasis on academically oriented education at the expense of technical and career oriented education and a prejudice towards technical and career oriented education led to a failure to equip the young with the necessary work and entrepreneurship skills needed to meet requirements especially in the engineering and technical fields. Only 9% of white matriculants and 1% of African matriculants followed a technical course in 1992 (Claassen 1995:477).

Higher Education

South Africa's system of higher education is the most developed and well-resourced in Africa (NCHE 1996). Higher education includes universities, technikons, technical colleges and teachers' training colleges. South Africa has 21 universities, including two distance education universities. A feature of the system of higher education at the end of the apartheid era is the existence of historically white universities and historically African universities. A major deficiency in the system of higher education is the unequal distribution of access and opportunity for students and staff along categories of race, gender, class and geographic distribution. This calls for a programme of large—scale redress for disadvantaged institutions and individuals. Moreover, the system is marked by a long history of organisational and administrative fragmentation and weak accountability (NCHE 1996:1). It also lacks clearly articulated national goals and has been unable to respond meaningfully to the economic and social needs of the majority of South Africans.

New Aims and Guiding Principles for Education

Since the democratic elections of 1994, the reconstruction of South African society has been guided by the *1993 Interim Constitution* (the final Constitution is yet to be ratified by the Constitutional Court) and the *Reconstruction and Development Programme (RDP)* of the African National Congress. The first steps to the development of a new education system were outlined in the *White Paper No. 1: Education and training* (1995). These three documents together provide a vision, aims and principles for education and training policy which are underpinned by the five core values of democracy, liberty, equality, justice and peace.

A vision for education and training is based on the country's new *Charter of Fundamental Rights* and Article 32 of the 1993 Interim Constitution. Here it is stated that every person shall have the right:

(a) to basic education and to equal access to educational institutions;

(b) to instruction in the language of his or her choice where this is reasonable and practicable; and

(c) to establish, where practicable, educational institutions based on a common culture, language or religion, provided that there shall be no discrimination on the ground of race.

The *Reconstruction and Development Plan* (RDP) expressly states that education and training is a fundamental priority of its strategic plan for national transformation. Furthermore, the White Paper No. 1 (1995:21-22) expounds the following values and principles for the construction of an integrated system of education and training:

- Education and training are basic human rights and the state has the obligation to protect and advance these rights irrespective of colour, race, class, belief or sex.

- The education of children is the primary responsibility of parents or guardians and they have the right to be consulted by the state with regards to the form of education. Parents have an inalienable right to choose the form of education best for their children.

- The state has an obligation to provide advice and counselling on education services and render appropriate care and educational services for parents and young children in the community.

- The over-arching goal of policy should be to enable all individuals to value, have access to and succeed in lifelong education and training of good quality.

- Open access to education and training opportunities of good quality for all children, youth and adults must be promoted and means provided for learners to move easily from one learning context to another.

- Special emphasis should be placed on redress of educational inequalities among the disadvantaged.

- Resources should be deployed according to the principle of equity to ensure that all citizens receive the same quality of learning opportunities.

- Quality of education and training must be improved and quality mechanisms introduced through a national qualifications framework.

- The rehabilitation of educational institutions disrupted by the political struggle must be linked to the restoration of ownership of these institutions to their communities by the establishment and empowerment of governance bodies.

- Democratic governance should be reflected in every level of the system and should take place by means of consultation and appropriate forms of decision-making.

- To establish a culture of teaching, learning and management, a culture of accountability and responsibility should be created in educational institutions. This should be based on the values of democracy, liberty, equality, justice and peace and mutual respect for diversity. Moreover, the culture of violence should be countered by promoting democratic values and human rights.

- Independent and critical thought should be encouraged through the curriculum, teaching methods and textbooks at all levels and all programmes of education and training.

- To equip youth and adults with the education and skills required by the economy, curriculum choice must be diversified, especially in the post-compulsory phase. Appropriate mathematics, science and technology education is essential. Environmental education should permeate all programmes.

- Two operational principles of productivity and sustainability should be upheld.

Administration and Governance of Education

The restructuring of the country's boundaries and the incorporation of the former self-governing homelands into South Africa has led to replacement of the four provinces with nine relatively autonomous provinces. Subsequently, the 1993 constitution provides for a national administration and nine provincial administrations for education. The staff and functions of the previous 18 education departments (par 3.1) have been rationalised into a new national Department of Education and Training and nine education departments within a single public service, each headed by a minister. These are now responsible for the development and implementation of all aspects of education and training policy.

The new national Department of Education and Training is organised in three branches: Education and Training Systems and Resources, Education and Training Programmes and Education and Training Support (White Paper No. 1, 1995). Therefore the administration and governance of the education system has been changed from a racially differentiated system to a geographically differentiated one. Centralised control is exercised by the national department and decentralised control by provincial departments (Claassen 1995:470).

Language in Education Policy

The Interim Constitution of South Africa (1993) makes provision for the recognition of English, Afrikaans and nine African languages as official languages of South Africa. This is a step to empower all South African languages and to promote multilingualism. Similarly, a new language policy for education is in the process of development. A Language Policy in Education Committee has been appointed by the Deputy Director-General of Education in response to the request of the Minister of Education with the task of informing the Ministry of Education about the language policy and its implementation in schools. A discussion document appeared on 15 November 1995 for public debate and consultation. Comments were collected from stakeholders by February 1996.

This document emphasises the discriminatory aspects of previous language in education policy and makes recommendations to remove language discrimination. For example, schools are encouraged to provide at least two languages of instruction from the reception phase of which at least one is a home language of a considerable number of pupils. Strong emphasis is placed on a multilingual approach in teaching and learning. The South African Schools Bill (1996) already makes provision for the right of learners to be taught in the official language or languages of their choice in a public school where practicable. No racial discrimination may take place in the implementation of the school's language policy which is to be determined by the governing body of each public school. A practical challenge to the implementation of a more multilingual approach in schooling lies, however, in popular attitudes which favour an English only approach in schooling, particularly among African communities. Many African parents associate upward mobility with proficiency in English and demand a straight for English approach. This is an obstacle to the implementation of the educationally sound principle of home language as language of instruction for the first years of schooling.

School Reform

Much needed school reform was initiated by the Minister of Education in March 1995 when he appointed a Review Committee to investigate the question of school organisation, control, governance and financing. The committee's report entitled *Report of the Committee to Review the*

Organisation, Governance and Funding of Schools was published on 31 August 1995. It formed the basis for the White Paper No. 2: *The Organisation, Governance and Funding of Schools* (February 1996). After wide consultation with stakeholders and intense debate, the *South African Schools Bill*, which incorporates the main recommendations and amendments to the White Paper No 2 was passed by the South African parliament on 16 October 1996. This historic legislation redresses the imbalances in state schooling brought about during decades of apartheid education.

South African Schools Bill (1996)

The South African Schools Bill provides for only two categories of schools: public schools and independent (private) schools. The public schools category comprises all schools previously known as community schools, farm schools, state schools and state-aided schools (including Model C schools). Collectively these schools comprise over 98% of the country's schools and 99% of all enrolments. As the public school category is so broad, room is made for variety within it. All state and state-aided schools for learners with special education needs would become public special schools. Some schools which are owned by religious organisations or industries could be taken into the public school system subject to certain conditions on the basis of partnership agreements negotiated between the owners and the provincial education departments concerned. The independent schools category comprises all schools currently known as private or independent schools.

Public Schools

By bringing all present public sector schools into one single 15 category of public schools, a process of orderly change has been set in motion. The aim is the maintenance of the positive characteristics of all existing school models and the nurturing of a spirit of partnership between the provincial education authorities and local communities (White Paper no 2 1996).

Public schools will share the following characteristics (White Paper 1996:14):

(1) Each public school will represent a partnership between the provincial education department and the local community;

(2) Public schools will be funded totally or largely from public resources, that is, provincial education department budgets and their property will be owned by the state;

(3) Admission policies will support the national and provincial governments' responsibilities for the provision of education. No school can exclude children through an admission policy;

(4) The mission, policy and the ethos of each public school will be determined within the national and provincial frameworks by a governing body comprising elected representatives of the main stakeholders of the school. The Ministry of Education proposes the empowerment of governing bodies to assume their responsibility within the national and provincial policy frameworks.

(5) The salaries of teachers in each public school will be paid by the provincial educational department according to a staff provision scale, and these teachers will be appointed in each public school by the provincial education department on the recommendation of the school's governing body.

Independent Schools

Independent schools should be registered by law with the provincial department and comply with the conditions of registration laid down by the province. Home schools are a specific case of independent schools (White Paper No. 2, 1996). Home schooling might be a reasonable option in various cases. The Department of Education is examining the relevant laws of other countries to determine the most suitable framework for the recognition of home schooling (White Paper No. 2, 1996).

School Governance

A major change in schooling in the democratic era is the governance of schools by the key stakeholders, parents, students and teachers, through their inclusion in the governing bodies of schools. All public schools will have governing bodies with significant responsibilities. Some would take on wider responsibilities from the province than others, especially financial responsibilities, depending on their capacities and inclinations. Core values of democracy form the basis of governance policy for public schools (White Paper No. 2, 1996). Farm schools, schools on tribally-owned land, schools for learners with special education needs, and technical schools will be governed in basically the same way as the other public schools, but the distinctive needs of such schools would be accommodated. The public school governing bodies will consist of the following elected representatives (White Paper No. 2, 1996):

(1) Parents or guardians of learners currently enrolled at the school. Parents must comprise the majority of members with voting rights on the governing body.

(2) Teachers at the school.

(3) Students (in the eighth grade or higher).

(4) Non-teaching staff.

(5) The principal.

(6) Members of the community may be co-opted by the governing body but will not have a right to vote.

According to the Bill (1995:15), governing bodies can:

- administer, maintain and improve the property, buildings and grounds of the school.
- determine the admission policy of the school.
- determine the language policy of the school.
- determine school times.
- determine the policy with regard to the practice of religion in the school.
- determine the out-of-school curriculum of the school and the choice of subject choices within the provincial curriculum policy.

- recommend the appointment of teachers.
- appoint non-teaching staff.
- determine and collect school fees paid by parents of learners.
- purchase textbooks and educational material for the school.
- pay for services done for the school.
- join voluntary associations which represent governing bodies of public schools.
- allow the reasonable use of the facilities of the school for community, social and school fundraising functions.

These new powers make the training of members of governing bodies imperative. Therefore, the Schools Bill makes provision for the capacity building of new members of governing bodies by schools.

Compulsory Education

The South African Schools Bill (1996:50) makes provision for compulsory education for all learners from the age of seven until the age of fifteen or the completion of the ninth grade (ninth year of formal schooling). No learner may be refused admission to a public school on the grounds that the parent has neglected to pay school fees.

Discipline

The South African Schools Bill (1996) makes provision for the discipline of learners. The governing body of a public school should compile a code of conduct of learners in consultation with learners, parents and teachers. Expulsion from a school may only take place on the grounds of serious misconduct and the learner or parent has the right to appeal against this decision. All forms of corporal punishment are banned.

Funding of Schools

The South African Schools Bill (1996) makes provision for the state to fund public schools on a reasonable basis. The Minister, in consultation with the Council of Education Ministers and the Minister of Finance, will determine norms and standards for the funding of both public schools and private schools. The governing body of a public school should establish a school fund and can determine school fees under certain conditions. A parent is accountable for the payment of school fees unless he or she is excused from payment. The governing body can enforce the payment of school fees by means of legal procedures.

National Qualifications Framework (NQF)

South African education has traditionally separated education and training both in its organisation and in the way they are regarded by society. As has been mentioned in paragraph 3.4, academic study has generally been perceived to be more valuable than training. The White Paper No. 1 (1995) called for an integrated system of education and training which will accommodate people who are in conventional schools, colleges and training programmes as well as those South Africans who have not enjoyed formal education and training due to the inequalities of the apartheid era.

To achieve this end, the White Paper No. 1 (1995) introduced the concept of a *National Qualifications Framework* (NQF). The NQF is a major initiative which seeks to provide a single, coherent and unified approach to education and training. The NQF is a framework for providing access to lifelong learning by means of nationally recognised levels on which all learning standards and qualifications will be registered. It is based on a system of credits for learning outcomes achieved. Qualifications might be achieved full time, part time, by distance learning, work-based learning or by a combination of these together with the assessment of prior learning and experience (HSRC 1995:7).

This integrated approach will recognise both education and training as legitimate sites, where learning of skills, knowledge and the generic abilities such as communications, problem solving and working with people, can be acquired. It will take into account and give value to the kind of learning that people have already achieved in their lives, whether at school, on the job or on the street. This recognition of what people already know is called Recognition of Prior Learning. People should be able to enter or access the education and training system at a point that depends on their prior learning. Moreover, according to this approach, learners can keep progressing up levels by gaining credits for successfully completing units. They can also move across different fields which mean that their credits are portable or transferable (HSRC 1995:7).

South African Qualifications Act (1995)

The development and implementation of the National Qualifications Framework has been established by the *South African Qualifications Act* (1995). The Act provides for a coordinating structure, the *South African Qualifications Authority* (SAQUA). This national body will put the National Qualifications Framework into operation. Inter alia, this body will define levels, formats for unit standards and requirements for the registration of qualifications. Other structural elements outlined in the Act are:

- National Standards Bodies registered by SAQUA will set standards in particular areas of learning;
- Education and Training Qualification Authorities (ETQAs) accredited by SAQUA will ensure that the standards set are delivered (HSRC 1995:9).

The Organisation of Learning According to the NQF

The National Qualifications Framework aims to unify qualifications in education and training based on set standards and assessment procedures that are nationally applicable. The National Qualifications Framework organises learning according to three different bands consisting of eight levels as follows:

Band 1: General Education and Training Certificate (GETC) Level 1
Band 2: Further Education and Training Certificate (FETC) Levels 2-4
Band 3: Higher Education and Training (HET) Levels 5-8

TABLE 13: THE NATIONAL QUALIFICATIONS FRAMEWORK (HSRC 1995:20)

Band: Higher Education and Training					
NQF Level	TYPES OF QUALIFICATIONS AND CERTIFICATES		LOCATION OF LEARNING FOR UNITS AND QUALIFICATIONS		
8	Doctorates Further Research Degrees		Tertiary/Research/Professional Institutions		
7	Higher Degrees Professional Qualifications		Tertiary/Research/Professional Institutions		
6	First Degrees Higher Diplomas		Universities/Technikons/Colleges/ Private/Professional institutions		
5	Diplomas, Occupationsl Certificates		Universities/Technikons/Colleges/Private/ Professional institutions/ Workplace/etc.		
FURTHER EDUCATION AND TRAINING CERTIFICATE					
Band: Further Education and Training					
4 3 2	School/College/Trade Certificates: Mix of units from all School/College/Trade Certificates: Mix of units from all School/College/Trade Certificates: Mix of units from all		Fomal high schools/ Private/ State schools	Technical/ Community/ Police/ Nursing/ Private colleges	RDP and Labour Mar-ket schemes, Industy Training Boards, union, work-place, etc.
GENERAL EDUCATION AND TRAINING CERTIFICATE					
Band: General Education and Training					
1	Std 7/Grd 9 (10 years) Std 5/Grd 7 (8 years) Std 3/Grd 7 (6 years) Std 1/Grd 3 (4 years) 1 year Receptpion	ABET Level 4 ABET Level 3 ABET Level 2 ABET Level 1	Fomal Schools (Urban/ Rural/ Farm/ Special)	Occupation/ Work-based training/ RDP/ Labour Market schemes/ Upliftment programs/ Community programes	NGO/ Churches Night schools/ ABWET programes/ Private providers/ Industry training boards/ Unions/ Work-place, etc.

The General education and training band is divided into the following phases: Early childhood and development phase and Foundation Phase, Intermediate Phase and Senior Phase. It includes Adult Basic Education and Training (ABET) levels 1-4 which are not specifically equated to different school grades/standards.

The Further Education and Training band, Levels 2-4 include a variety of school, college and trade certificates. The Higher Education and Training band, Levels 5-8 include occupational certificates and diplomas, degrees, higher degrees and professional qualifications.

Curriculum Reform

The integration of education and training and the establishment of the National Qualifications Framework impacts the school curriculum. The proposed structure of the NQF necessitates an overhaul of the learning programmes in the nation's schools and colleges (White Paper No. 1, 1995). To address this need, 41 National Curriculum Committees on which the national and provincial Departments of Education and other representative stakeholders serve, have been established. These committees are coordinated by a representative Coordinating Committee for the School Curriculum.

Curriculum design is to be guided by certain principles (Curriculum Framework for General and Further Education and Training 1995):

(1) *Human resource development*. It is the role of education and training to prepare learners with a strong foundation of general education and with a desirability to continue to learn, to apply and to develop knowledge.

(2) *Learner-centredness*. Curriculum development should put learners first by recognising their skills, experiences, abilities and responding to their individual needs.

(3) *Relevance*. Learning programmes should be relevant to meet both the current and anticipated needs of the person and the country.

(4) *Integration*. An integrated approach to education and training

removes the rigid division between academic and applied knowledge.

(5) *Differentiation, redress and learner support.* The learning programme should create opportunities for all learners, including those with disabilities or those who were disadvantaged in the previous dispensation. Provision should be made for learners with special needs or other disabilities in mainstream education.

(6) *Nation-building and non-discrimination.* Education and training promote the development of national unity and national identity. The curriculum should also protect human rights.

(7) *Critical and creative thinking.* The learning programmes should enhance learners' ability to think critically and creatively.

(8) *Flexibility.* Learning programmes should provide an increasing range of learning possibilities by offering learners choices of what, where, when, how and at what pace they want to learn.

(9) *Progression.* It should be possible for learners to move ahead on the basis of achieving particular learning outcomes and not through age or course cohorts.

(10) *Credibility.* Education and training must have comparable standards to those in the rest of the world. It means that learning programmes should have both internal and international credibility.

(11) *Quality assurance.* The South African Qualifications Authority (SAQA) through criteria it applies in the appointment of National Standards Bodies, registered unit standards and qualifications and accredited Educational and Training Assurers will assure the quality of education and training.

The identification and definition of knowledge areas is an important element of curriculum development, including outcomes based curriculum development (Curriculum Framework for General and Further Education and Training 1995). As mentioned in paragraph 3.4, curricula were previously largely academically oriented and content-based. The shift to an outcomes-based education and training system has the advantage of mobility from one learning context to another; integrating education and training; opening access to learning; and recognising prior learning.

The focus of outcomes-based education and training is on what learners know and can do at the end of a course of learning and teaching (Curriculum Framework for General and Further Education and Training 1995). Outcomes-based curriculum development processes will have as their point of departure the intended results (outputs) of learning and teaching rather than the selection of prescribed input (knowledge areas or content). This does not imply that learning outcomes should replace knowledge areas, but that learning outcomes should be the first step in the curriculum development process (Curriculum Framework for General and Further Education and Training 1995). The Curriculum Framework includes a number of Areas of Learning appropriate to the South African context. The term Areas of Learning rather than subjects or fields is chosen because of the tentative boundaries of each of the knowledge areas. The following Areas of Learning are proposed for the General and Further Education and Training Bands 1 and 2 (Curriculum Framework for General and Further Education and Training 1995):

- Communication, Literacy and Languages;
- Numeracy and Mathematics;
- Human and Social Studies;
- Physical and Natural Sciences;
- Physical Education and Health;
- Culture Arts and Artistic Crafts;
- Technology Education and Training;
- Occupational Learning/Learning for life;
- Economic Science; and
- Spiritual Development.

National Commission on Higher Education

In spite of its flaws derived from its apartheid history, the system of higher education in South Africa has considerable capacity in terms of research, teaching and community service. Because of the pivotal role that higher education can play in the reconstruction and development of the country, the new government regards the transformation of the system as a priority. Therefore, the Minister of Education appointed the National Commission on Higher Education (White Paper No. 1, 1995) to carry out an audit of all aspects of higher education and develop a new policy framework for higher education transformation. This comprehensive national enquiry into higher education is the first of its kind ever undertaken in the country. Through a process of consultation involving all higher education stakeholders, the NCHE produced its report, *A framework for Transformation* which was released in 1996.

The policy document reflects the ideals of the Constitution, the goals of the RDP and the aims and guiding principles of White Papers No. 1 and 2. The proposed system is underpinned by the key principles of equity, democratisation, development, quality academic freedom, institutional autonomy, effectiveness and efficiency. The document recommends three central features of the new framework. The first is the increased participation through the expansion of student enrolments from a greater distribution of social groups and classes. Such expansion implies the transition from an elite to a mass system of higher education (massification). The second feature of the new framework is greater responsiveness within higher education to social interests and needs. This has implications for the content, form and delivery of the curriculum which should respond to client demand. Thirdly, the new framework should increase cooperation and partnerships between institutions of higher learning and structures with an interest in higher education, such as commercial enterprises, research bodies and non-governmental organisations (NCHE 1996).

Furthermore, the NCHE makes a number of proposals for transformation and suggests a framework for implementation. The three prioritised proposals follow. A single co-ordinated system of higher education is proposed encompassing universities, technikons, colleges (including teaching training colleges) and private providers. This should enable South Africa to increase its higher education participation rate to approximately 30% (as a percentage of the 20-24 year old cohort) over the next decade. The second proposal is for a new model of co-operative governance of higher education. In order to realise this the formation of two statutory bodies are suggested. A Higher Education Form (HEF) with representation by organised constituencies will deliberate policies. A Higher Education Council (HEC) will have a coordinating function and carry out planning within the principles set by the HEF. The third proposal comprises recommendations for goal-oriented funding of higher education.

The funding proposals include block grants according to a funding formula for institutions as well as earmarked funding for institutions with programmes which are in accordance with highly specified policy objectives (NCHE 1996). At present the proposals of the NCHE are under debate with a view to future legislation.

Teacher Education

Teacher education in South Africa has primarily been provided by teachers' training colleges or colleges of education which fell under the administration of the former four provinces. In addition to teachers' training colleges, faculties or schools of education at universities, which fall under the national ministry of education, have also trained teachers. The number of teacher training colleges proliferated dramatically during the 80s in an attempt to address the educational crisis of the apartheid era. The vast majority of colleges catered for African students and were often inefficient and cost-ineffective (Claassen 1995:481).

At present the system of teacher education is under review. In this regard the White Paper No. 2 (1996) and the NCHE (1996) recommend that teacher education should be seen as a unified field which belongs in a system of higher education. This recommendation has led to the closing of several teacher training colleges and the planned incorporation of colleges into the system of university governance.

Norms and Standards for Teacher Education

In order to develop an integrated national policy on teacher education, the Committee on Teacher Education Policy (COTEP) was established. COTEP has produced a document entitled *Norms and Standards for Teacher Education (1995)* which has already replaced the policy document which was used for decades to determine teacher training standards. COTEP calls for the adaption of courses for teacher education over a period of four years to the new norms and standards for teacher education. COTEP also makes important recommendations regarding the governance of teacher education to the NCHE and has conducted a situation analysis of all teacher education in order to develop a data base for future planning.

National Teacher Audit

A major step to reform teacher education has been the conducting of the first national teacher audit. The National Teacher Audit of teacher education in South Africa which transcended racial, regional, departmental provincial and institutional divisions was completed in December 1995. The most important findings of the audit were as follows (Hofneyr and Hall 1996):

- Teacher education (including PRESET and INSET) is the largest sector of higher education, involving at least 281 institutions and over 480,000 registrations in 1995. However, there is no coherent vision for teacher education.

- Over a third of all teachers are un- or underqualified.

- Teacher education is very fragmented and diverse. Non governmental organisations (NG0s) and distance education institutions play a considerable role in provision.

- In most provinces there is an over-supply of teachers. This finding has been determined by a teacher:pupil ration of 40:1. (This ratio is often not realised with vast disparities between schools and geographical areas). The primary-secondary output ratio indicates, however, a need for secondary school teachers to meet national needs after 2000.

- The scale of INSET is enormous, in terms of teachers studying for higher qualifications and programmes aimed at improving classroom competence.

- The quality of teacher education is not defined, developed or controlled. In general, the quality of PRESET and INSET programmes are poor. Quality is often mistakenly associated with qualifications which are rewarded with an automatic salary increase. Moreover, huge disparities across institutions as a result of apartheid and the rural/urban divide. The present system is inefficient as a result of high failure rates and cost-ineffective institutions.

- Distance education as a mode of delivery for teacher education is growing rapidly. However, distance education is primarily a print-based correspondence system with little contact support, use of other media or use of communication technologies. There is little conscious support for student learning in texts, contact tutorials or counselling.

- The professional mission of teacher education institutions is partially subverted by the large numbers of students who use teacher education as an affordable route to higher education without the intention to teach.

Proposed National Policy on Teacher Supply, Utilisation and Development

The National Teacher Audit has provided a data base upon which policy planning in teacher education can now occur. A discussion document: *National Policy on Teacher Supply, Utilisation and Development* (Department of education 1996) was released in August 1996 for public debate and comment by stakeholders. An International Conference for stakeholders was also held in October 1996 with the view to generating recommendations by key stakeholders.

This document outlines a broad vision for teacher education. It suggests that the primary purpose for teacher education is to improve the quality of professional practice and thereby the quality of learning for all South Africans. Teacher supply policies should ensure an adequate cost effect supply of competent teachers for all subjects, levels and parts of the country. Moreover, teachers, as the most expensive resource in the education system, should be efficiently and equitably utilised. Teacher education should be based on the five basic principles underlying education according to the Interim Constitution; global and national relevance; learner centredness, professionalism; cooperation and collegiality; and innovation. Furthermore, the document identifies five priority areas for immediate action with regard to teacher supply, utilisation and development. There should be an integrated approach to the policies for teacher supply, utilisation and development which will require close co-operation between those engaged in teacher education and those engaged in conditions of service. The curriculum for both PRESET and

INSET should be congruent with COTEP and the NQF and should include training for Early Childhood education, Adult Basic Education and Training, vocational education and Education for Learners with Special Needs. The colleges of education should be transferred into the governance system of higher education. Subsequently, a coherent funding strategy should be devised for teacher education. Mechanisms should be established to define quality and put into place quality assurance procedures. Finally, capacity building, that is the development of the necessary knowledge, attitudes and skills, is required by staff in the system of teacher education at provincial and national levels.

Conclusion

The demise of apartheid and the new democratic era in South Africa is considered a modern day miracle. The country now has a unique opportunity to redress the inequality of the past and to build a better and fairer society which will benefit all. In this endeavour particularly high expectations are cherished of education. However, a new political dispensation does not automatically ensure improved education. In terms of policy initiatives considerable progress towards a new system has been made as is illustrated in this chapter. The implementation of this policy, the evaluation of innovative strategies and its continuous improvement are the challenge of the immediate future.

Bibliography

ANC (African National Congress) January 1994. A policy *Framework for Education and Training.*

ANC (African National Congress) March 1994. *Reconstruction and development Programme.*

Behr, AL 1988. *Education in South Africa. Origins, Issues and Trends: 1652-1988.* Pretoria: Academica.

Claassen, JC 1995. *The Education System of South Africa* in Dekker E & Lemmer EM (eds) 1995. *Modern Education Systems.* 1995. Second edition. Durban: Butterworths.

COTEP (Committee on Teacher Education Policy) 1995. *Norms and Standards for Teacher Education.*

Curriculum Framework for General and Further Education and Training.

December 1995. Discussion document developed by the Consultative Forum on Curriculum. Pretoria: National Department of Education.

Department of National Education. 1992. *Educational Renewal Strategy*. Pretoria.

Department of Education, 1994. *Interim Core Syllabi.*

Department of Education, 31 August 1995. *Report of the Committee to Review the Organisation, Governance and Funding of Schools.* Pretoria: Department of Education.

Department of Education 1996. Discussion document: *National Policy on Teacher Supply, Utilisation and Development.*

Hartshorne, K. 1992. *Crisis and Challenge: Black Education 1910-1990.* Cape Town: Oxford University Press.

Hofmeyr, J. & Hall, G. 1996. *The National Teacher Education Audit: Synthesis Report.*

HSRC (Human Sciences Research Council) 1981. *Education Provision in the RSA*. Pretoria: Human Sciences Research Council.

HSRC (Human Sciences Research Council). October 1995. *Ways of Seeing the National Qualifications Framework.*Pretoria: Human Sciences Research Council.

Lifelong Learning through a National Qualifications Framework. Report of the Ministerial Committee for the Development Work on the NQF. February 1996. Pretoria: Department of Education.

NCHE (National Commission of Higher Education) 1996. *A Framework for Transformation.*

NEPI (National Educational Policy Investigation)1993. *The Framework Report*. CapeTown: Oxford University Press.

RSA (Republic of South Africa) 1993. Constitution of the Republic of South Africa Act 200 of 1993.

Smit, A. 1990 A race between education and disaster. *MiningSurvey* (2): 3-12.

South African Qualifications Authority Act, No. 58 of 1995. October 1996. *Government Gazette* 364(16725).CapeTown.

South African Schools Bill. 1996. *Government Gazette*. Cape Town.

White Paper no 1. 15 March 1995. Education and Training in a Democratic South Africa. *Government Gazette* 357(16312) Notice 196 of 1995. Capetown:Department of Education.

White Paper No. 2. 14 February 1996. The Organisation, Governance and Funding of Schools. *Government Gazette* 368 (16987) Notice 1130

of 1996. Pretoria: Department of Education.
Wolpe, H. 1990. *Three Theses on People's Education.* Colchester: RESA.

Part IV
Education and the State

— 13 —
EDUCATION AND NATION BUILDING

Mark Bray, Peter Clarke and David Stephens

The boundaries of most African countries were determined by European colonial powers in the last century. In most cases, the Europeans paid little attention to ethnic territories or the boundaries of African kingdoms, and countries were formed from arbitrary amalgamations of people. In other cases, peoples were deliberately split in a policy of `divide and rule'. To give just two examples, the Yoruba live in present-day Benin Republic and Nigeria; and the Wolof are divided between The Gambia and Senegal. The arbitrary nature of many African boundaries can be seen just by glancing at a map: a high percentage of them are straight lines as if drawn with a ruler.

Although these arbitrary boundaries were not necessarily appropriate to the needs of independent countries, one of the first pronouncements of the Organization of African Unity, in 1964, was that international colonial boundaries should remain intact.[1] That decision was made to reduce claims by neighbouring territories to each others' land and to avoid the breaking up of African countries. In the period just before independence, many nationalist leaders found that one major factor binding peoples together was opposition to colonial rule. With the achievement of independence, that common goal no longer existed, and in many countries the threat of internal divisions increased.

Because of these factors, the fostering of a national identity has become one of the most important tasks of African governments, and education is seen as a major instrument for doing this. Both the formal school system and adult education campaigns are often explicitly geared to this end, while informal education plays at least as significant a part. Before discussing the ways education can promote unity, however, we should note some important theories about the organization of society.

Theories of Social Organization

Many different types and levels of social organization exist, and many different sociological theories have been developed to explain them. It is useful, first, to notice a distinction made by Emile Durkheim, a French sociologist, at the end of the last century.[2] Durkheim distinguished between societies of the `mechanical' and the `organic' type. Those of the first type, he suggested, are simple and undifferentiated, and their members have similar attitudes, skills and lifestyles. A small nomadic group of hunters with very little specialization of labour is an example of this type of society; each person masters the same basic skills of hunting, and the society survives because no single member is indispensable.

Organic societies are much more complex, and are organized on the basis of difference rather than similarity. This type of society is increasingly dominant in Africa, and is the one which concerns us at the national level. There is considerable specialization and division of labour, and most individuals and groups have specific attitudes, skills and lifestyles that are not common to the whole. In these societies, there is considerable interdependence, for specialization usually means that individuals gain skills in one task at the expense of skills in others. If one group breaks away or dies, the whole society is liable to collapse because it is unable to replace their knowledge and expertise. Education plays a role in maintaining this type of society not only by providing individuals with skills but also by providing them, particularly during childhood, with attitudes which permit the whole society to function. Laws are made to regulate the way each individual behaves for the benefit of all. Sometimes individuals threaten society by breaking these laws. In these cases society controls them by sending them to prison or regulating their behaviour in some other way.

In this description of an organic society, it will be noticed that society itself has an identity independent of the identities of its individual members. This idea has been further developed by Talcott Parsons and the `functionalists', who compared society to a living organism. An organism has its own identity, but is composed of such mutually dependent parts as the head, eyes, legs and so on, each of which performs a separate function. Organic societies, these theorists suggest, are similarly composed. Just as a body can die, so can a society; and just as a body can do without a few of its parts, so can a society.[3]

The functionalist approach to sociology is often identified with `consensus theory'. This theory assumes that each part of society shares common values, and that there is consensus, or agreement, between the, parts. The approach may be contrasted with `conflict theory', which examines society from a different angle. Consensus and conflict theorists both view society as a system of interrelated parts, but the point at issue is the extent to which members of society benefit, equally or unequally. The conflict theorists are chiefly inspired by the work of Karl Marx. They feel that Parsons paid too much attention to the beneficial aspects of social organization, neglecting the extent to which established social arrangements operate to the disadvantage of some groups. Again, education plays a role in this process. As we shall see in Chapter 4, education is an agent of social stratification—assigning social roles to different groups and by distributing greater rewards to some groups than to others.

The Marxist model provides a theory to explain the changing nature of society: economic changes, it suggests, are the basis of social ones, and they themselves arise from conflicts between social groups and alterations in power structures. Thus, whereas the consensus theorists imply that all parts are mutually and more or less equally interdependent, the conflict theorists suggest that some parts are more important and more powerful than others. In political terms, the consensus theorists have come to be viewed as basically right-wing and capitalist, while the conflict theorists are basically left-wing and socialist. Socialists also generally seek change whereas consensus theorists generally support the status quo.

While these theories are introduced at the beginning of this chapter on national development, they are also applicable to the discussions in other chapters. Thus, at the international level, a functionalist interdependence may be identified, though we have pointed out that the benefits of interdependence are not evenly distributed. For example, it was pointed out in Chapter 1 that most African countries receive low prices for their agricultural exports but have to pay high prices for manufactured imports. Similarly, a form of functionalism exists in a school, where the head master, the teachers, the prefects and the other pupils all have assigned roles and are part of a common body. A knowledge of these theories is useful because it enables us to understand how individuals and groups relate to each other in a wider context.

The Goals of Nation Building and the Role of Education

The principal goal of nation building in Africa is to promote the evolution from simpler and more localized forms of social organization to wider and more-complex ones. Mechanical societies of the hunting type are being threatened by a wider process of economic development and social change, and ultimately will be displaced by organic societies. Similarly, in some parts of Africa organic societies headed by kings, emirs or chiefs and involving considerable specialization of labour but usually with fairly local allegiances, are being replaced by wider organic societies with a national focus.

It is useful at this point to distinguish between two types of integration. Horizontal integration describes the unification of ethnic, racial, religious and linguistic groups, many of which inhabit distinct geographical areas. Vertical integration describes the relationship between rulers and ruled in a common network of communication, so that ideas and demands can flow `upward' and `downward'.

Education can promote horizontal integration in four main ways. The first concerns the curriculum, in which the importance of language must be emphasized. Nations composed of many ethnic groups have a corresponding multiplicity of languages. Formal education usually promotes a common language, which permits communication between members of different ethnic groups. Most African countries have chosen to use a European language for official purposes. This is because internal rivalries prevent use of an indigenous language, and French, English, Portuguese and Spanish are considered `neutral'. In sub-Saharan Africa, only in Tanzania and Somalia has a local language been sufficiently widespread for it to become the principal official one. Many governments encourage schools to teach several widely spoken local languages, in order to promote communication. However, they usually place stronger emphasis on the international, former colonial language. Governments also seek to promote unity through other aspects of school curricula and through adult education programmes. For example, in geography lessons pupils learn about different parts of their country, and in social studies or civics they learn about such national symbols as the flag and the national anthem and about official government policies in an international context. The material of adult literacy classes and of general public enlightenment is also frequently directed towards national issues, and informs the public about the policies of the head of state and other members of government.

Secondly, some countries have educational institutions in which pupils are selected by equal quota from different parts of the country. This policy is based on the idea that if pupils grow up together, they will become acquainted on a personal basis with people from other ethnic, racial, religious and linguistic groups, and the fears and ignorance which underlie much discrimination will be avoided. This is the principle on which Nigeria's Federal Government Colleges are based, for example.

Thirdly, several African countries, including Ghana, Nigeria, Zambia, Guinea, Chad, Tanzania, Kenya, Botswana, Malawi and Sierra Leone, operate national service schemes for school leavers. These schemes may be either voluntary or compulsory, but strong emphasis is always placed on national identification. Participants usually perform some community service, often outside their home areas. These schemes have a strong educational function, even though they are not always organized by the Ministry of Education. The Zambian and Tanzanian schemes, for example, operate under the Ministry of Defence, while the Kenyan one comes under the Ministry of Labour.

Finally, educational projects often attempt to reduce regional imbalances, which frequently correspond to imbalances between ethnic and religious groups. This policy is often manifested in universal primary education schemes, for it is argued that 100 per cent enrolments by definition eliminate numerical imbalances, at least at the bottom level. All individuals from all regions, it is suggested, are then able to compete for employment on a more equal basis. Botswana, Cameroon, Congo and Gabon have almost reached universal primary education, and major campaigns were launched in Nigeria in 1976 and in Tanzania in 1977.

Turning to vertical integration, it is worth noting two main ways in which education can promote unity. Firstly, extension of literacy makes it possible for more citizens to read newspapers, books and reports. This may mean that the population becomes better informed about local and national issues. Governments may inform the governed about the intentions of their policies, and individuals and groups have a medium through which they can make their feelings known.

Secondly, as education becomes more widespread, the basis on which individuals can compete for employment becomes more equal. Where education reaches only a small group, it may encourage élitism. But as it is expanded so that more or all groups receive some education, then a greater proportion of the population can be brought into the cash economy, and all groups can be placed on a more equal footing. In this instance the functionalist role of education in creating a unified society is evident.

Constraints on the Extent to Which Education Promotes Nation Building

Although the mechanisms that we have just mentioned may promote horizontal and vertical integration, it cannot be assumed that they necessarily will do so. A large number of other factors, usually beyond the control of the Ministry of Education and sometimes beyond the control of the government, must be considered. They include political rivalries between individuals and groups, trends in employment, and the general level of economic prosperity.

Taking first the impact of schools on the attitudes of their pupils, it must be stressed that there is no such thing as a `politically neutral' education system. All systems transmit and foster values, though in some cases the process is more obvious than in others. Some observers express considerable concern about what they describe as the indoctrination existing in some educational systems, particularly in socialist countries. But in every society the school system transmits values. In so far as this is not made explicit in some countries, or is unrecognized, it could be considered even more dangerous than in cases where it is more open.

Policies which deliberately set out to shape pupils' attitudes will only be wholly successful if the message communicated is clear, consistent and emphatic. We must distinguish between the formal and informal aspects of education, for they do not necessarily complement each other. Although the official curriculum may emphasize a national orientation rather than local or ethnic ones, this is not always similarly stressed by the *actions* of teachers, pupils and others taking part in the education process. There is a substantial difference between teaching or learning a subject such as civics for examination purposes and actually employing the principles in one's life outside the classroom. Pupils often enter what they see as a different world with different rules when they move into the school compound, and when they return home. When they leave school they often do not or cannot apply the `theories' they have learned in the classroom.

Because of its importance, many studies have been made of the political outlook of school children. Fischer's Ghanaian work indicated a clear relationship between national identification and amount of schooling. He pointed out that some of the changed perceptions were due to age rather than schooling, and that many older primary pupils still had no clear attachment to the nation or its relevant symbols.[4] Nevertheless, the importance of education itself was evident, and has been supported by other researchers.[5]

At higher educational levels, however, the national orientations of students are less clear. Sawyer's work in Liberia, which is likely to be typical of African countries in this respect, suggested that while the national outlook of pupils tended to increase until secondary school level, it decreased again at the university level.[6] This, he indicated, arose partly from the students' greater interest in politics and partly from the specific political situation. Many politicians have found that the best way to compete in the national arena is to secure a strong regional or ethnic base, and they try to gain the support of students as much as others. In some cases the power of an individual derives from his ability to threaten national unity.

Aside from the purposes of education, the school system is itself often the focus of regional and ethnic disputes. Because formal education is a major route to wealth, status and economic security, individual and regional competition for schools is frequently intense. Politicians are therefore usually sure of gaining support from the regions and groups which benefit from allocation of educational institutions. Kenya's Harambee Institutes of Technology are one example of establishments opened more for political reasons, arising out of inter-ethnic rivalry, than for economic or educational ones. Twelve institutes were opened during the 1970s, chiefly because politicians demanded establishments for their own areas and refused to cooperate in common organizations. There were serious doubts about whether some institutes were economically appropriate, and it has been argued that they caused misallocation of national resources as well as being a focus for ethnic discord.[7]

One way in which governments seek to reduce ethnic, racial and religious educational imbalances is through the use of quotas. These also tend to become a focus for discord, however, for positive discrimination in favour of less educated groups can only be provided at the expense of more educated ones. The latter, usually backing their arguments with a desire to avoid declining academic standards, generally oppose the quotas. To the advantaged groups, the concept of equality implies that all individuals should compete within the existing education system without external intervention to assist some groups. But the quotas are based on the idea that the system itself is unequal—that it favours some groups at the expense of others, and that unless the disadvantaged groups are assisted, educational imbalances will be perpetuated. The two different sets of assumptions lead to conflict, for attempts to change the nature of the system inevitably threaten the position of those who benefited from the old arrangement.

Another way in which governments attempt to remove regional development imbalances, and therefore to avoid inter-ethnic tension, is by launching universal primary education campaigns. However, this strategy works only in the long term, for even if universal primary education is achieved, imbalances usually persist at post-primary levels. Different areas are also likely to experience qualitative variations, which partially negate the value of quantitative advances. Indeed, because schools in the disadvantaged areas have to expand most to achieve universal enrolments, they tend to experience the greatest qualitative problems. Also as enrolments expand, students of a different type are increasingly brought into the system.

When the school system is small, strongly motivated students comprise a greater proportion than when it is larger; particularly if they are also paying fees, these pupils tend to be more receptive to the values imparted by the authorities. Thus, even if the education system has had a strong impact on pupils' attitudes in the past, it does not necessarily follow that an expanded system will have the same impact on every child. Finally, development imbalances involve much more than education, and universalization policies must be complemented by other economic and political measures if they are effectively to promote equality. Even when qualitative imbalances have been reduced or eliminated, access to jobs often remains strongly influenced by non-academic criteria, and some groups still experience discrimination because of their ethnic identity. Turning to the matter of vertical integration, we must note first that although the use of a common national language may permit members of different ethnic groups to communicate, if the language chosen for official business is not an indigenous one, it is likely to extend the gap between rulers and ruled. The rulers usually conduct their business in a European language and because only rarely are proceedings translated into vernaculars, most of the ruled cannot understand them. When education systems reach only a minority they can be instruments for division, not for bonding.

Secondly, Western education has brought a new set of values which has destroyed, rather than reinforced, much of the old societies. Kofi Busia, who was Prime Minister of Ghana from 1969 until 1972, has strikingly related the impact of schooling on his own outlook.

> At the end of my first year at the secondary school I went home to Wenchi for the Christmas vacation. I had not been home for four years, and on that visit, I became painfully aware of my isolation. I understood our community far less than boys of my own age who had never been to school. I felt I did not belong to it as much as they did. It was a traumatic experience.[8]

In this quotation, the divisive effects of Western education are made very clear. The divisions go further than this, however, for there is often a gulf within the educated group. B.S. Kwakwa, building on Busia's point, has gone further to suggest that:

> ...the effect of the western type of education has been to produce...three nations in the country, each unable to communicate effectively with the other. Many of those who have passed through the formal education system do not understand the ways of the `educated'. In many circumstances the two do not understand each other. Then there is even a third group, the `half educated', who understand neither the ways of their own indigenous society nor those of the `highly educated'.[9]

In some ways, this is not an educational but an economic problem. African societies are experiencing a transition from `traditional' economies based on self-employment in the rural areas to `modern' ones based on wage employment in the towns. Each type of economy has its own requirements and set of values, and education is merely the bridge over which individuals cross from one economy and society to the other. Schooling is frequently seen as a passport to escape from the village. In their desire to reach the other side of the bridge, individuals sometimes consciously reject the values of the society they hope to leave behind.[10]

Social dislocation is often particularly acute when individuals have not succeeded in completely crossing the bridge from one society to the other, and when they are unemployed. The last two decades have witnessed increasing unemployment in Africa, and corresponding disillusion among school leavers. Problems have been particularly acute when the unemployed have received many years of education and have had high expectations, as has increasingly been the case. In many countries widespread unemployment leads to political instability and threatens the cohesion of the nation. Major political crises were exacerbated by the educated unemployed in Congo in 1964 and Tanzania in 1966, to cite just two examples.[11]

However, although unemployment causes strong disillusionment and is a destructive experience for the individual, it must not be assumed that it always results in political instability. Gutkind has pointed out that the unemployed are frequently poorly organized, and that their leadership is often `bought off' by governments in times of disturbance.[12]Moreover, schooling often trains the individual to feel that if he fails, it is his own fault rather than that of the system.[13]Countries such as Kenya and Zambia have in the past experienced quite high levels of unemployment without being threatened by political instability.

The education system may thus be compared to a vehicle which carries people from one place to another. The people reach their destination more rapidly than they would if they were walking or bicycling, but the vehicle is not independent, and the direction in which it moves is mainly controlled by the people inside it. The driver is the person with the greatest control, but he is unlikely to choose a road without consulting at least some of his passengers. The passengers who will have the greatest influence on the driver are those nearest to him, those able to shout loudly, and those who can promise the greatest rewards if the vehicle goes where they want it to (or threaten the greatest problems if it does not). But even if the driver ignores all his passengers and chooses his own destination, he is still restricted by the capacity of his vehicle, the skill of those who maintain it and the availability of roads, and he may still find it impossible to reach his goal.

In the same way, education should not be considered an independent or even a flexible force for change. The direction in which the educational vehicle takes society depends firstly on the intentions of the government and other members of society, and secondly on the resources available. Even then, policy makers are restricted by the nature of the vehicle and, if resources are abundant, by the time it takes to adapt the vehicle or build new roads.

Thus, knowledge of a common language, for example, may be promoted through the education system, and may permit members of different ethnic groups to communicate with each other. But it does not necessarily follow that they will communicate, or that what they communicate will lead to unity rather than division. Similarly, literacy may promote vertical integration by providing a means for communication between governors and governed. But, while literacy provides them with another vehicle, it should not be assumed that illiterate people are always unable to make their feelings known, and therefore that education will necessarily make possible something that was previously impossible. Also, it should not be assumed that extension of literacy will ensure that the governors and governed will communicate. Newspapers and books are often not available in rural areas, and if they are, only a minority of people buy them. Much literature is written in complicated language, and many books especially official reports—are boring. Finally, for information to flow both from governors to governed and vice versa, each side must be willing to listen as well as to talk. People in authority often do not wish to listen to the opinions of those they govern, and are only concerned with implementing their own ideas.

Case Study: Education and Nation Building in Nigeria

To build a single nation out of the multitude of cultures and interests encompassed within Nigerian boundaries is no small objective. In the pre-colonial period, a number of cohesive units, such as the Sokoto Caliphate, the Benin and Songhai Empires and the Kingdom of Oyo, operated independently, albeit with some economic, religious and cultural links. But the existence of these units had little influence on colonial boundary determination, and kingdoms were grouped together or divided entirely arbitrarily. Today, with over 90 million citizens, Nigeria is by far the most populous country in Africa. Within her boundaries are over 250 ethnic groups, and though no precise figure is known (which is itself indicative of Nigeria's problems), nearly 400 languages are spoken.[14]In addition, most of the sects of Christianity are represented, as are the major Islamic brotherhoods and a wide diversity of indigenous religions.

During the last three decades, Nigerian politics have been characterized more by division than by unity. The political parties of the 1950s developed along ethnic and religious lines, and, as recognized even in an official publication, `the only common factor that united them was the struggle for independence'.[15]Once independence had been achieved in

1960, this common objective no longer existed. During the years that followed, regional and ethnic disputes became increasingly serious, and in 1967 the country was plunged into civil war following the secession of the self styled Republic of Biafra. The war was won by the federal forces, and the military continued to form the government until 1979. Some observers have suggested that the political parties which came to power that year were little different in their membership and outlook from those of the 1950s and 1960s. In 1983 the civilian regime was overthrown again.

The memory of the civil war has caused the Nigerian authorities to be highly conscious of the need for horizontal integration, and they have placed considerable faith in the ability of education to promote it. The *National policy on education*, for example, identified unification as one of the five basic objectives of the education system.[16]School curricula strongly emphasize the role of national institutions, and children learn about the flag, the national anthem and the geography of other parts of the country. Each day, children are required to recite:

> I pledge to Nigeria, my country To be faithful, loyal and honest,
> To serve Nigeria with all my strength, To defend her unity And
> uphold her honour and glory; So help me God.

The widespread knowledge of a common language, which is taught in schools, is also considered a major factor in horizontal integration. Although Hausa, Igbo and Yoruba are each spoken by over 10 million people, it has proved impossible to choose any one of them as the official national language because such a selection would encounter strong opposition from speakers of the other two languages. Consequently English, which is considered politically `neutral', has been made the main official language.

Programmes for vertical integration in the last two decades have been weaker than those for horizontal integration. A major adult education campaign was launched in the north during the 1950s, but since that time adult education has been neglected, and in 1980 only 30 per cent of adults were estimated to be literate. Official emphasis on communication between the governors and governed, particularly during the period of military rule between 1966 and 1979, was one-sided. The government has been more concerned to inform the people about its programmes than to listen to their opinions. The late 1970s saw increased emphasis on local government participation, however, and a major adult literacy campaign was launched in 1982.

The Nigerian authorities have been very conscious that much strife has been caused by unbalanced development, of which wide variations in school enrolment have been both a cause and a symptom. Because of this, they have launched a number of educational projects which seek to reduce imbalances. The most obvious of these was the Universal Primary Education (UPE) scheme initiated in 1976.

Although the UPE scheme has encountered major difficulties, there were indications in the late 1970s that quantitative regional gaps at the primary level were being reduced.[17] Qualitative regional gaps were more difficult to close, however, and because they remained at least as great as before, the UPE scheme did not make so great a contribution to unity as had been hoped. Moreover, quantitative imbalances remained at the post-primary level, and the south had many more secondary schools than the north, despite having approximately the same population. At the university level, the federal government has established institutions in every state. Its calculation has taken no account of the fact that some states have many more people than others, and has clearly been motivated more by political than by economic or educational considerations. However, even at a quantitative level, imbalances have remained, for states have been permitted to open their own universities. Oyo State in the south already had two, Anambra State opened its own in 1980. Further, although admissions are supposed to reflect Nigeria's federal character and embrace students from all states, some universities manage this better than others. There are very few northern students in the south, whereas there are many southerners in the north.

The education system of any country reflects society as well as shapes it, and despite the strong official emphasis on horizontal integration, the Nigerian experience exemplifies the limitations of educational strategies when they are not supported by other economic and political forces. One case in which this was apparent during the 1960s concerned Ibadan University. This institution, as Eleazu has remarked, was at one time a place where Nigerians met as Nigerians. They came in from parochial secondary schools such as Igbo Anglican, Igbo Roman Catholic, Yoruba Methodist, Yoruba Aladura, Hausa Muslim, Tiv, Sudan Interior Mission and so on, but they re-emerged as Nigerian. In the early years, however, this nationalizing process was mainly the result of events outside the walls of the university and the desire for independence. During the 1960s, regional conflicts became more marked. The opinions of the student body at Ibadan also polarized, presenting the same picture as the outside political scene.[18]

By contrast, the experience of a different body, the National Youth Service Corps (NYSC), has been more encouraging. The NYSC was initiated in 1973, and involves one year's obligatory service for all university graduates. The majority of graduates who do not have another specific skill become teachers, and all have to perform some kind of community service such as road construction. Corpers are required to serve in a state other than that of their origin. The majority of participants acquire more positive attitudes towards fellow Nigerians, and the NYSC has reduced educational imbalances by permitting the less developed northern states to benefit from the greater number of southern graduates.[19]

Questions and Project Work

1. What is meant by `horizontal integration'? Discuss the extent to which the education system of your country has promoted horizontal integration, and the obstacles to the achievement of further integration.
2. Do you consider your own home area to be educationally advanced or educationally backward? Outline the historical reasons for this situation, and support your answer with current educational statistics.
3. Discuss the view that education is one of the least important factors in national building. Find copies of the recommended primary and secondary school social studies and history textbooks in your home area. Examine the ways in which they discuss matters of national and ethnic identity. Comment on the impact you think these books have on the way pupils perceive issues and on the attitude of teachers towards these subjects.

Notes

1. Cervenka, Zdenek *The Organisation of African Unity and its Charter*. C. Hurst, London 1969, p. 94.
2. Durkheim, Emile *The Division of Labor in Society*. Free Press, New York 1964 (first published in French in 1925).

3. Parsons, Talcott *The Structure of Social Action.* Free Press, New York 1949 (first published in 1937). A useful summary of this and other theory is contained in Worsley, Peter *et al. Introducing Sociology*. Penguin, Harmondsworth 1980, Chapter 9.
4. Fischer, Lynn F. `Student Orientations toward Nation-Building in Ghana' in Paden, John N. (ed.) *Values, Identities and National Integration: Empirical Research in Africa.* Northwestern University Press, Evanston 1980, p. 276.
5. Klineberg, O. and Zavalloni, M. *Nationalism and Tribalism among African Students: A Study of Social Identity*. Mouton, The Hague 1969; See also other papers in Paden, ibid.
6. Sawyer, Amos `Social Stratification and National Orientation: Students and Nonstudents in Liberia' in Paden, ibid., p. 297.
7. Godfrey E.M. and Mutiso, G. `The Political Economy of Self-Help: Kenya's Harambee Institutes of Technology' in Court, David and Ghai, Dharam (eds.) *Education, Society and Development: New Perspectives from Kenya.* Oxford University Press, Nairobi 1974, p. 254 ff.
8. Busia, K.A. *Purposeful Education for Africa*, quoted in Kwakwa, B.S. `Formal Education and Conflict in Ghanaian Society'. *Legon Observer* 23/7/73, p. 125.
9. Kwakwa, ibid.
10. Many novels in the Heinemann African Writers Series (HAWS) deal with this theme. See e.g. Conton, W. *The African*, HAWS No. 12; and Dadie, B. *Climbié* HAWS No. 87.
11. Hanf, Theodor *et al.* `Education: An Obstacle to Development? Some Remarks about the Political Functions of Education in Asia and Africa'. *Comparative Education Review*, Vol. 19, No. 1, 1975, p. 84; Morrison, op. cit., p. 195 ff.
12. Gutkind, P.C.W. `The Unemployed and Poor in Urban Africa' in Jolly, Richard *et al.* (eds.) *Third World Employment.* Penguin, Harmondsworth 1973, p. 131 ff.
13. See Carnoy, Martin *Education as Cultural Imperialism.* David McKay, New York 1974, pp. 12-13, 344-5.
14. Federal Republic of Nigeria *Nigeria: A Guide to Understanding.* Federal Ministry of Education, Lagos, n.d., p. 6; Hansford Keir *et al.* `A Provisional Language Map of Nigeria'. *Savanna*, Vol. 5, No. 2, 1976.

15. Federal Republic of Nigeria *The Struggle for One Nigeria*, Nigerian National Press, Apapa 1967, pp. 2-3.
16. Federal Republic of Nigeria *National Policy on Education*. Federal Ministry of Information, Lagos 1981, p. 4. This document was originally published, in slightly different form, in 1977.
17. Bray, Mark *Universal Primary Education in Nigeria: A Study of Kano State*. Routledge and Kegan Paul, London 1981, pp. 82-4.
18. Eleazu, Uma O. *Federalism and Nation Building: The Nigerian Experience*. Arthur H. Stockwell, Ilfracombe 1977, pp. 124-5. See also van den Berghe, Pierre L. *Power and Privilege at an African University*. Routledge and Kegan Paul, London 1973, p. 222 ff.; and Beckett, Paul and O'Connell, James, *Education and Power in Nigeria*. Hodder and Stoughton, London 1977.
19. Marenin, Otwin `National Service and National Consciousness in Nigeria'. *Journal of Modern African Studies*, Vol. 17, No. 4, 1979, p. 653 and *passim*.

— 14 —
Education, the State and Civil Society in Malawi

J. R. Minnis

Abstract

By assuming that civil society as a sphere of activity is separate from both the state and the economy, the article examines how a vibrant system of education can emerge in Malawi if the relationship between state and civil society is fundamentally altered. Against the backdrop of the change from a single to a multi-party system, it is argued that education needs to be re-cast in the form of a contested terrain stressing diversity and pluralism in terms of provision and power sharing between state and non-state interests. The article outlines six areas of contestation which can contribute to revitalizing education in an atmosphere of democratic change.

Education, the State and Civil Society in Malawi

The premise of this article is that the present decline and uncertainty in education in Malawi is reflective of a larger socio-political malaise, namely, the unequal and oppressive relationship between state and civil society. As one of the last sub-Saharan countries to embrace multi-party politics, the national election held on May 17, 1994 promises to end thirty years of repression and human rights abuses under the dictatorship of Hastings Kamuzu Banda. As a country in transition from one-party rule to a multi-party system, the sustainability of democracy, and by extension, the emergence of a responsive and vibrant education system, is dependent on a number of factors. Foremost among these is the emergence of vital civil associations and the development of free markets. The former is essential to democratic institution-building; the latter will stimulate the entrepreneurial spirit and productive energies that the state has repressed or mismanaged. The future development of education is therefore caught up in the midst of many political and economic tensions that confront the society. For Malawians, the decline of state capability to provide meaningful and relevant education has been one of the major disappointments of the eighties. The uncertainty created by escalating public demand for education in the midst of a declining economy and high unemployment has left many confused as to education's long-term stability and relevance. This has led to a certain loss of legitimacy of the state, its ruling élites and the bureaucrats charged with managing the education system. The recent analysis by Moyo (1992) leaves no doubt that education growth and quality of provision has become problematic in the nineties compared to the sense of purpose evident in the policies and achievements of the sixties and seventies.

The recent experience of other sub-Saharan African countries suggests that grassroots, rural and cultural organizations cannot develop without the cooperation of the state (Buchert, 1992). Only by strengthening civil society through collective self-empowerment can citizens effectively tackle problems on their own and generate in the state the political will and mobilized support to attack the interrelated facets of the Malawian crisis.

For its part, the state must, at minimum, allow people to help themselves. Empowerment, by enhancing the accountability, responsiveness and capability of the state, builds the basis for meaningful collaboration between it and civil society. The future shape and direction of education, like so many other aspects of Malawian society, is thus caught up in this swirling vortex of the state-civil society dynamic.

Purpose of the Paper

The demise of one-party rule in Malawi offers educators and others interested in improving education an opportunity to influence the future shape, ethos and policy direction of the state vis-a-vis civil society. The paper speculates on how this can be achieved and is divided into four sections. First, a working definition of civil society is provided and secondly, a brief analysis of state-civil society relations in Malawi is presented. Third, the present relationship between education and the state is discussed with emphasis on key conflicts that require resolution if education is to become a vibrant force in the society. And finally, an attempt is made to re-cast education in the form of a "contested terrain". This will entail some application of free market principles to education, such as more competition, etc. but the more important aim is try and influence the way in which formal education is conceived. Education does not have to be equated solely with the state—it can also be thought of as part and parcel of civil society.

Civil Society Defined

There has been a revival of scholarly interest in civil society since the demise of the Cold War. Some sense of the historical and contemporary nature of the debate can be found in Keane (1993), Gellner (1991), Rockman (1990) and Poggi (1990). Atkinson (1992:10-11) provides a useful summary of current interpretations: 1. civil society is identified with the economy to encompass the realm where private property, labour, class divisions and market relations are located; 2. the economy is only one aspect of civil society, but civil society should not be equated completely with the economy; 3. civil society is a sphere separate from both state and the economy—it is the voluntary, non-profit sector; 4. the fourth view differentiates between civil society, the public sphere, the economy and the state.

In Africa, civil society is most often portrayed as either the third or fourth type or some combination of the two. It is an entity separate from the state sphere, highly controlled by single parties and high profile rulers who simultaneously extol the virtues of "nationhood" and "unity" and obscure the reality of tribal, ethnic and regional differences and economic problems. In effect, the state denies legitimacy to the political objectives and aspirations of civil associations in order to maintain its hegemony. This results in an all-powerful state and a weak and repressed civil society. Commenting on how this process has come about in Zimbabwe, Moyo (1993) writes that the virtual eradication of civil society has been, "...achieved by fusing the political, ideological and productive hierarchies into one single unified organizational structure" (p.2).

Moyo goes on to argue that despite the weakness of civil society, it lies nascent, ready to be revitalized under the proper conditions. Such is the case today in Malawi where, with the advent of multi-party politics, there is evidence of a growth in public-spiritedness and a determination on the part of the population to fully exploit new-found freedoms. To further guide the present discussion, civil society refers to the full panoply of cultural activities ranging from religion, education and labour practices to intellectual thought, natural science and folklore. In this sense, civil society is treated as a sphere separate conceptually from both the state and the economy.

This is essentially the view of Gramsci who puts emphasis on the need for individual empowerment and the establishment of human rights and democratic institution-building (Bobbio, 1993). Whereas Marx used the expression of civil society to refer to the totality of economic relationships, Gramsci used it to refer to the cultural and social superstructure separate from the economy (see Atkinson, 1992:18). While it is essential to have a vibrant, fully functioning multi-party political system and a healthy economy, it is not enough to sustain democracy. A fully functioning civil society is also needed. This is particularly so in Malawi which is divided into potentially antagonistic linguistic, ethnic and regional cleavages (Pryor, 1987). The danger exists that in the absence of intermediary institutions that link civil society to the state, hegemonic political parties will draw civic associations, trade unions, and cultural organizations into their shadow thus undermining their potential to act as a counterbalance (Atkinson, 1992). Sandbrook (1993) makes the point that unlike the case of liberal democracies where established political parties, interest groups and the mass media transmit demands and information between the civil and state spheres, these institutions in Africa either remain undeveloped or have typically served to secure a compliant rather than a vigilant civil society.

The diversity and pluralism inherent in Malawian society must therefore be allowed free rein rather than kept harnessed or shackled by a hegemonic "state" or "party". Even though Malawian civil society has been severely weakened over the years, it can be regenerated through the restoration of a public spirit in national politics beyond the state sphere. The challenge is to create new preconditions for something wholly new to emerge in political terms. Strengthening and democratizing civil associations will, admittedly, take years. Nonetheless, as Sandbrook (1993) suggests, the future struggle for freedom and equality in Africa will be waged both within the arenas of civil society and the state.

State-Civil Society Relations in Retrospect

The Malawian state has been called many things but there is general agreement that it was both "Leviathan" and "Predatory" (Meier, 1991; Hirschmann, 1991). It was Leviathan in the sense of being strong, highly authoritarian and very often oppressive. Administrative authority was distributed by a top-down flow of policies, decrees and directives. In this regard, the ministerial and parliamentary structures were essentially nominal reduced to rubber-stamping and rationalizing handed down policies. The state was predatory in the sense that the majority of the populace was exploited in both the realm of production (through the exploitation of artificially cheapened labour) and the realm of circulation (through the extraction of surplus by state-owned marketing boards). This predatory behaviour was made possible by a mutually reinforcing political and economic system in which the dominant political élites and their servants in the bureaucracy systematically exploited the economy for thirty years.

Since its post-colonial formation in 1964 the state sphere has been deliberately "separated" from the rest of society. In essence it consists of the ruling élites, their circle of kith and kin, a few powerful families, the state-dependent bureaucracy, and the accumulators of capital backed by patronage-based, state assistance. Counterpoised to, and in a subordinate position, is the sphere of civil society, made up of a multitude of powerless, voiceless people. The vast majority have not only been excluded from state patronage, but have been repressed and prevented from developing alternative ideas and consciousness. They have been de-mobilized and subjugated by means of both the modern instruments of coercion and other mechanisms of patrimonial domination (Mhone, 1992).

In such circumstances, the openings for political discourse and debate were extremely limited. One of the consequences was that thousands of Malawians chose to leave the country rather than live under such repression. In the name of "national unity", state power was used against rival élites and the rest of society. As well, the state took steps to suppress non-state infrastructures preventing the rise of an alternate societal-based state-society system, namely, a more liberal and democratic system of rule (Mhone, 1992).

Despite the iron grip the state had on civil society, in the years preceding and immediately after the election of this year, there is evidence of an increase in new sectarian movements, most of which have fundamentalist leanings. According to Chipeta (1992:47) right wing sects have been on the increase and conversion to Islam is rising. These sectarian movements, in the Weberian sense, transcend narrow class interests and draw their membership from a variety of social strata. Also, "new" organizations, such as savings and credit unions, the burial or funeral societies in urban areas which are more professionally oriented and confined to the middle classes, such as the Law Society of Malawi and the Institute of Engineers, are beginning to cut a niche of political space for themselves.

The argument for a vibrant civil society in Malawi is therefore an argument for people to discover a new kind of control over their own lives. With reference to Malawi, Chipeta (1992) suggests that the political space claimed by a plurality of emerging collective actors, each struggling within their own sphere, is becoming increasingly characteristic of daily life, especially in the way each of these groups, actors and movements, articulate a position for itself and with other movements. Over time, it is desirable that these groups develop the organizational capacity not only to coordinate their own activities but also to determine or inflect the sequence and development of state policy.

Education and the State: Re-drawing the Boundaries

In the present scheme of things, the state dominates policymaking in education and has complete control over the allocation of resources. Resources are subject to patronage politics which makes it difficult for non-state interests and/or organizations to enter into genuine dialogue with the state on how they might involve themselves in policy formation and the organization of education. Clearly, the status assigned to the state will not disappear or diminish quickly just because a new party is in power, although there are signs that the educational bureaucracy is more receptive to competing and innovative ideas. What is needed is a change in how bureaucrats conduct their business. Technocratic criteria must come to replace patrimonial criteria as the basis for recruitment and policy implementation. Top bureaucrats must be free to exercise judgement independent of interference or influence from ruling élites or popular politicians. Clientelism will not disappear, but it must be made secondary to merit and technocratic competence when it comes to recruitment and resource allocation.

There are four problem areas all of which are implicated in the dense system of state patronage. The goal is to manage patronage in such a way that top bureaucrats do not feel threatened to openly discuss policies and their even-handed implementation. The first challenge is to raise the status of teachers enabling them to play an active role in policy-making. Historically, teachers have been placed in a subordinate position vis-a-vis the bureaucrats in the Ministry of Education. Not only are they rigidly subordinated, but their actions in the classroom have also been highly constrained by a pre-determined curricula and the overriding threat of dismissal should they not comply with state dictates.

In the primary sector especially, where the student teacher ratio is officially stated as 60: 1 (but is in fact much greater in many areas of the country), teachers are obliged to carry out a myriad of administrative-technical tasks which often precludes substantive teaching from taking place. Thus it is not surprising that primary education takes on the appearance of a production process, an industry, driven essentially by burgeoning enrolments and a state-driven examination system (Hyde, 1994).

The current proportion of the education budget allocated for primary education is inadequate to maintain the sector at its present level of operation let alone cope with expansion. There is considerably less pressure coming from the secondary sector with a gross enrolment ratio of four percent—compared to eighty percent for the primary sector. Nonetheless, in a climate of diminishing resources, and because it makes promises to teachers by way of salary increases that it cannot possibly keep, the state has lost considerable credibility in the eyes of teachers and raised public concerns. The resulting dilemma for the African state is aptly described by Ki-Zerbo (1990:78):

> ...the state struggles under an overload of responsibilities derived from its control over the highest, most sensitive reaches of the educational pyramid. There is only one way out of this trap: the state has to share some of its responsibilities with grassroots organizations and with other inter-African agencies.

A second characteristic of state-education relations is the tendency for educational resources to be monopolized by privileged minorities and/or regions led by skilled politicians and community leaders. At the heart of the problem once again is the patronage system. The democratic solution to this problem of course is to arrive at a more equitable distribution through political and parliamentary debate. But before this can happen in Malawi a major shift in thinking on the part of those in power would have to occur. That is, there would have to be a move away from patronage toward merit on the one hand, and on the other, no special dispensation given to "region" as a basis for employment. In Malawi, one's region of origin, i.e. north, central or south, and one's position vis-a-vis the ruling élite, which in effect defines one's position in the patronage pecking order, are given first priority when it comes to jobs, consultancies, overseas postings, scholarships and government contracts.

The dilemma for education is that if patronage is allowed to dictate policy-making and the distribution of resources, no real progress can be made to revitalize the system. Without competent, highly skilled, and intrinsically motivated individuals in sensitive posts, there can be no effective long-term planning or problem-solving applied to the sector's problems.

A third characteristic is the unequal distribution of educational resources between rural and urban areas. The two major cities, Lilongwe and Blantyre, tend to attract the most highly qualified teachers and receive the lion's share of educational resources (Moyo, 1992). Urban schools tend to fare better financially than rural schools due to the presence of government workers and employees of NGOs (international non-governmental organizations) and foreign companies who send their children to these schools. Paradoxically, the children of peasant farmers (who make up approximately eighty percent of the population), and who are responsible for generating a significant share of the country's wealth, receive little if any education. The result is an illiteracy rate of fifty percent for those aged fifteen and older (Kishindo, 1993:393). Between 1966 and 1980, an average of 95,000 new illiterates were added to the population each year because primary children did not enrol or those who did dropped out before Standard 5 (age eleven or twelve) when a Malawian child is supposed to acquire basic literacy.

A fourth characteristic of state-education relations derives from the state tendency to over-invest in formal education, particularly higher education, to the exclusion of vocational technical training and non-formal adult education. The result is educational inflation. The state's incapacity to absorb into the labour force large numbers of out-of-school youth is largely responsible for the alarming growth of unemployment (Msiska, 1994). The scramble for status and job security has fuelled competition among the élites for advanced training and credentials to which it can lead, out of all proportion to the country's ability to provide commensurate employment.

Education as Contested Terrain: Toward a Market Model

In the years ahead, it may be conducive to the development of civil society if organized interests demand a voice in terms of the management and control of education. If education is viewed as a "contested terrain" based on free market principles of consumer choice, competitive pricing and quality control, it could encourage private sector expansion in education. These new institutions will belong to civil society, or link civil society to the state. The application of free market principles to education will help to shift the distribution of power more directly toward the market while the state would be assigned a residual role (i.e. regulatory). While a strict version of the model is, admittedly, unworkable in Malawi at the present time, a modified model allowing more choice and diversity for those who can afford to pay, could act to sensitize the customer and the provider as to the quality of services rendered. State-controlled education would then be forced to compete with private provision, and in order to "stay in business", the state would either have to improve the quality of its services or get out of the business of education altogether.

1. A first step would be to develop an overall policy framework that stipulates the rights and obligations for central and local government institutions, and to stimulate the growth of private and non-government educational entities. This entails a genuine decentralization effort which changes the traditional top-down approach of the Ministry of Education. Such a pluralistic framework should encourage entrepreneurs, religious and private organizations, local communities and international organizations to participate in education. Ideally, this contestation will centre on establishing a sound legal and policy framework regarding the distribution of available resources, policy formulation, quality control and management.

2. The contributions of non-governmental organizations (NGOs) in the re-configuration of educational institutions will be required. The state should encourage and facilitate their integration, assist with setting up linkages with local governments and communities, and monitor their activities. As long as public resources are limited and the public demand for education escalates, the need for outside human and

financial assistance cannot be denied.

3. If a free market environment is nurtured, it will allow considerable scope for competition in regard to students, resources and state accreditation. These competing interests will quickly learn to manoeuvre for research and policy information to strengthen their bargaining positions vis-a-vis the state thus improving their competitive edge in the educational market. The adult non-formal training sector in Malawi is a potential growth area in this regard as is higher education. In terms of the former, Malawi's two major cities possess backstreet colleges and private vocational centres run for profit and oriented toward modern sector employment. These institutions have the potential to provide the kind of vocational training so urgently needed.

   Thoughtful analyses of the problems facing out-of-school youth and the illiterate, under-skilled adult population are provided respectively by Msiska (1994) and Kishindo (1993).

4. There is a need to strengthen independent associations to represent the interests of the various groups in the educational system, such as teachers, students, parents, university academic staff and students. Ideally, the goal is to establish and consolidate the interests of these groups enabling them to not only advance their interests, but to act as intermediaries between the state and the community at large. In this way, grassroots participation and diverse views and innovative approaches in the formulation and implementation of policies can filter upward to influence decision-making at higher levels. The formation of alliances which transcend regions would act to diffuse inter-region rivalry and inter-ethnic hostility.

5. Parent associations will need to be increased in number and strengthened relative to their active participation in school management, supervision and implementation of the school curriculum. Parents need to become more vigilant about what is taught in schools and more concerned about the performance of teachers and administrators. The new climate of change is conducive to promoting amongst parents a new role in overseeing the general quality and relevance of schooling. In this regard, teacher

associations could align themselves with parents in a common front to balance and debate state decision-making.

6. Higher education may well be the future site of conflict over academic freedom, institutional autonomy, and issues of governance and accountability. The University of Malawi is seriously marginalized in terms of the production of research knowledge and data that influences state development policies. Because of recent cutbacks in donor assistance, the university will have to learn to do without external funding earmarked for expatriate teaching staff and post-graduate training for Malawians overseas. Contrary to local opinion, the decline of donor aid may have positive consequences in so far as it may force the university's four constituent colleges to look inward and seek self-determined remedies for their problems—and look outward for new sources of funding, linkages and ideas. This may stimulate a much needed country-wide debate on the future role and expansion of higher education.

Concluding Remarks

For thirty years under the Banda regime, civil society lay dormant and unorganized to the point of paralysis. There emerged a state-society model that met with general approval of the West due to its pro-capitalist, anti-communist stance. Within the context of the Cold War, this brought Malawi great benefits in terms of financial assistance, military hardware, and other forms of material support. In this paradigm, the state was legitimized as the centre of progress and modernity and civil society was assigned the role of backward periphery in which were located its primitive and disruptive forces.

With the move toward multi-party democracy, there is need for a new configuration wherein the state pragmatically operates as a buffer, or, an intermediary, protecting its legitimate interests as well as adjudicating conflicting claims and conflicts between and among various social and political groups in the civil society. If the move toward democracy is to be something more than cosmetic, then a significant measure of political initiative must be given over to organizations and associations of civil society. While this in itself will not automatically guarantee individual liberties and greater social equality in the society, it will give people a greater sense of personal and collective control over their own lives. Education can expand, prosper and indeed contribute to this new paradigm. To be sure, Malawian education is presently in need of an urgent transfusion of energy, new ideas and organization—but no genuine change can occur until a new relationship is forged between the state and civil society.

References

Atkinson, D. (1992). State and society in flux. *Theoria*, ay:1-28.

Buchert, L. (Ed.). *Education and training in the third world: The local dimension.* The Hague: Centre for he Study of Education in Developing Countries.

Bobbio, N. (1993). Gramsci and the concept of civil society. In J. Keane (Ed.) *Civil society and the State* (pp.73-100), London: Verso.

Chipeta, M. (1992). Political process, civil society and the state. In G.C.Z. Mhone (Ed.) *Malawi at the crossroads: The Post-colonial Political economy* (pp.34-49), Harare: SAPES.

Gellner, E. (1991). Civil society in historical context *International Social Science Journal*, CXXIX, 495-510.

Hirschmann, D. (1991). Women and political participation inAfrica: Broadening the scope of research. *World Development,* 19, (12): 1679-1694.

Hyde, K.A.L. (1994). *Barriers to equality of opportunity in mixed-sex secondary schools in Malawi.* Unpublished report. Centre for Social Research, University of Malawi.

Kishindo, P. (1993). The case for nonformal vocational education for out-of-school youth in rural Malawi. *Development Southern Africa*, 10, (3), (August): 393-400.

Ki-Zerbo, J. (1990). *Educate or perish: Africa's impasse and prospects*. Dakar: UNESCO-UNICEF.

Meier, G. (1991). *Politics and policy-making in developing countries*. San Francisco: International Centre for Economic Growth.

Mhone, G.C.Z. (1992). The political economy of Malawi: An overview. In G.C.Z. Mhone (Ed.). *Malawi at the crossroads: The post-colonial political economy* (pp.l-33), Harare: SAPES.

Moyo, C. (1992). Formal education policy and strategy in Malawi, 1964-1990. In G.C.Z. Mhone (Ed.) *Malawi at the crossroads: The post-colonial political economy* (pp.265-297), Harare: SAPES.

Moyo, J. N. (1993). Civil society in Zimbabwe. *Zambesia*, XX,(1), 1-13.

Msiska, F.G.W. (1994). Some practical limits of curriculum vocationalization as a remedy of school leavers unemployment: focus on Malawi. *International Review of Education*. 40, (2), 135-148.

Poggi, G. (1990). *The state: Its nature, development and prospects*. London: Polity Press.

Pryor, F.L. (1987). *The Political economics of poverty, equity and growth: Malawi and Madagascar*. Oxford: Oxford University Press.

Rockman, B.A. (1990). Minding the state—or a state of mind?*Comparative Political Studies*, 23, (1), 36-52.

Sandbrook, R. (1993). *The politics of Africa's economic recovery*. Cambridge: Cambridge University Press.

— 15 —

Education and Rural Development in Malawi: The Exaggerated Causality?

Fred G.W. Msiska

As far as Africa, South of the Sahara, is concerned, the process of modernization can be traced to as far back as the 16th Century when she first came into contact with Arab and European traders. This process of modernization has led to the creation of a dual society consisting of traditional (rural) society on the one hand and modern (urban) society on the other. Each of these sectors has its own distinct mode of production and existence. For example, in the traditional sector people, for a combination of reasons, produce goods and services mainly for their Subsistence needs. Rarely are surpluses produced for sale so that money realised could help people avail themselves of other basic needs necessary for improvement of their lives. Implicitly, traditional/rural areas have remained economically stagnant, poor and backward. Their social and political activities have equally lagged behind.

In contrast, modern (urban) sectors have enjoyed an acceptable modicum of commerce and industrialization. Here goods and services are produced mainly for sale, giving the sector a commercial outlook. Such mode of production and existence ensures adequate flow and circulation of money which enable people to buy other basic human needs. Consequently, their living standards tend to be higher and better than those of their counterparts in traditional (rural) areas.

The paradox is that more than 75% of the populations in most developing countries live in rural traditional areas. In the case of Malawi, for example, the 1987 Population and Housing Census revealed that 87% of the population lives in the rural areas with peasant farming as their predominant economic mode of existence. The disparity in development between the two areas implies that the majority of the people live a less attractive life. Aware of this, scholars, policy makers and development planners have since the 1940s looked for ways to achieve more balanced development between rural and urban areas (see Thompson 1981). However, the controversy has been on the perception and meaning of rural development, and the role of formal school in such a process.

Meaning of Rural Development

To appreciate the causal relationship between formal school (education) and rural development we need to clarify what we mean by rural development. For most people writing and commenting on the concept in the first half of the 20th Century, rural development was more about improving agriculture (the backbone of agrarian societies), encouraging the steady evolution of rural communities towards more satisfying ways of life, and enabling rural people to maintain their social and cultural integrity whilst mobilising their innate capacity to contribute to their own development (Thompson, 1981:105). Apart from specifying the need to develop agriculture in the rural areas, the definition tended to be vague. Such vagueness/made it even more difficult to begin to see the specific role of education in the development process.

In an attempt to clarify the concept, Lea and Chaudhri (1983:12-13) argue that integrated rural development endeavours:

i) to improve the living standards or well-being of the mass of the people by ensuring that they have security and that basic needs such as food, shelter, clothing and employment are met;
ii) to make rural areas more productive and less vulnerable to natural hazards, poverty and exploitation and give them a mutually beneficial relationship with other parts of the regional, national and international economy;
iii) to ensure that any development is self-sustaining and involves the mass of the people (this involves among other things encouraging self-reliance and public participation in planning);
iv) and to ensure as much local autonomy and as little disruption to traditional customs as possible. The former usually means promoting administrative decentralization and political self-government.

Msiska (1986) reiterates the point when arguing that rural development is in part about economic growth which in turn enhances the whole process of improving living standards of the mass of the low-income population residing in rural areas and making the process of their development self-sustaining.

Both Lea and Chaudhri (1983) and Msiska (1986) seem to be saying that economic growth is essential for achieving other material and non-material needs of the people. It is common knowledge that most rural people hardly meet their basic needs. As such, it seems imperative to conceive and perceive of rural development as essentially the process of enabling people to satisfy their basic human needs. Unless peoples' basic needs are satisfied to a considerable degree, all other aspects of their lives become peripheral, to say the least. Basic human needs can be grouped into two categories. The biophysical needs which include food, water energy, shelter, clothes and health; and psychological needs which include education, security, recreation and communication (Fagerlind and Saha, 1983:113). Also see Maslow, (1970) for a detailed discussion of basic human needs.

Central to the concern of this article is understanding how basic human needs are or could be met, and what the role of education is or could be. I should hasten to say that the basic needs approach to rural development has been heavily criticised by Jarvis (1986:90-91). All the same, I find Jarvis' criticisms too idealistic in their focus and too individualistic in their expectations. If one accepts Jarvis' (1986) arguments, one is lost between addressing the individual and the collectivity. This paper is about the collectivity, and what is normally accepted about a group of people sharing somewhat similar socio-economic and political characteristics.

Basically, there are two major ways in which peoples' basic needs can be met. One of them entails simply giving people all they need to live a satisfactory life. This could be referred to as the "handout" approach. The danger with this approach is that it masquerades development in that once the donor stops handing out aid, peoples' living standards stop to improve. As such, the approach pauperises rural people, a scenario which militates against self-sustenance of the development process. The boom and fall of copper and cocoa trade in Zambia and Ghana, respectively, illustrate the fragility of such development.

The other way, and in my opinion a better alternative, is where people are only helped to provide for their basic needs. This involves individual people making an effort to pull together the resources available to provide for their basic needs. The beauty with this is that it makes the whole process of rural development self-sustaining. Implicit here is the need to help rural people to acquire the relevant knowledge and skills, say for farming, tailoring, carpentry, fishing, entrepreneurship, etc. for providing for their basic needs (Mijindadi, 1978:22; Msiska, 1986:19 and Msiska,

1991:282-297). It is within this context that a realistic role of education in rural development can be identified. Otherwise, we risk over theorising and exaggerating the instrumental role of education in the process of rural development.

The Role of Education in Rural Development

All along scholars, policy makers and development planners, in developing countries in particular, have continued to view formal education as the key variable to the problems of rural development. The critical point of such a belief could be traced to as far back as 1960 when Theodre Schultz systematically articulated the Human Capital Theory of development when he made his presidential address to the American Economic Association on the theme "Investment in Human Capital". Schultz argued that education does not only improve the individual choices available to people, but that an educated population provides the type of labour force necessary for industrial development and economic growth (Fagerlind and Saha, 1983:18). While Schultz may have scored a point as far as industrial development is concerned, rural development is more concerned about enabling people to meet their basic needs and to participate in the shaping of their destiny. The two may not require the same type and amounts of education. All the same, there are serious methodological problems with Human Capital Theory when it comes to specifying the actual contribution of education in the process of economic growth and development.

Despite the methodological difficulties of measuring the actual contribution of education to improvement of labour quality, developing countries continue to believe that educating people in the rural areas will mysteriously trigger development. This has resulted into concentration of resources in the education of the rural youth and adults. Paradoxically, rural areas seem not to be making any progress. If anything, they are economically getting poorer. This could be an indication that scarce resources are going to the wrong sector.

Kreinen (1964:58-59) argues that:

> Illiteracy makes it difficult to teach new techniques, poverty prevents investment in new facilities, and land tenure system which does not establish legal land boundaries and security of tenure deprives the farmer of an asset against which to raise

loans and gives his no incentive to invest in long term improvements.

According to Kreinen (1964), apart from tackling the problem of illiteracy, education does not seem to be as centrally important as we have believed. Thompson (1981:15) argues that through primary education a cadre of enlightened leadership might be developed both in and for rural communities, a leaven of men and women who posses a more scientific understanding of the cause and effect relationship which lie at the root of improved agriculture and community living, are more aware of the possible of change and progress and have learned sufficient of variety of simple skills to be able to show the way in farming, nutrition, sanitation and so on to their less progressive neighbours. The argument is that such leaders would help to create a climate within which innovation and experiment might flourish, more receptive of whatever assistance might be afforded by specialists from outside the community.

Experience has shown that instead of staying in the rural areas and performing such instrumental roles, graduates of primary school abandon rural areas for urban centres where they think they would take up paid jobs and enjoy the gaieties of modern life. The truth is that, at least for Malawi, the majority of people living in the rural areas are those who have either done part of primary school education or have not been to school at all. The question that needs to be faced is whether or not rural development is possible without subjecting people too rigorously to much formal school.

Towards a Model of Analysis of Basic Human Needs

I have argued earlier on that at the centre of rural development is the need to enable people meet their basic needs. The rationale is that satisfying peoples' basic needs is directly related to improving their living standards, hence, development of the people and their respective areas. As such we need to analyse the instrumental role of formal schooling (education) in the process of meeting peoples' basic needs. We need to single out one or two prepotent basic human needs and analyze what is required to meet such needs, and in due course examine what could be the possible role of education. In this article food production has been used to illustrate the point.

The point is that food is very central to the survival of beings. Accordingly, our efforts to develop rural areas need to start with ensuring that people are assisted to provide for their food requirements. In this connection, there is a need to look at the problems which have continued to stand in peoples' way in their endeavours to provide adequate food for their subsistence needs. Secondly, we need to examine the could-be instrumental needs for meeting such a basic human need. And thirdly, we need to examine tools and techniques required to produce adequate food for their needs and surplus for sale (See Table 14 below). Only then can we be able to pinpoint the central role of education in rural development.

TABLE 14: MODEL OF THE MODE OF ANALYSIS OF BASIC HUMAN NEEDS

Categories of Human Basic Needs	Specific Needs	Problems	Instrumental Needs	Tools and Techniques
Sufficiency	Food	1. Poor farming techniques 2. Size of gardens 3. Inability to replenish soil fertility 4. Inadequacy of farm labour 5. Simplicity of farm tools 6. Pests and insects	1. Functional skills 2. Financial capital 3. Agricultural inputs	1. Farmer training 2. Formal schooling 3. Functional literacy 4. Farmers' club 5. Extension service 6. Roads and markets 7. Food storage techniques
Satisfaction				
Safety/ Security				
Stimulus				

Food Production Problems of Rural Farmers

Studies carried out in Khwawa and the neighbouring villages of karonga District, Ludzi and the neighbouring villages of Mchinji District, and Domasi area in Zomba District (all of malawi) in 1983, 1984 and 1994, respectively, have yielded very interesting results. An assessment (through interviews and direct observation) of the major problems of food production revealed:

i. Poor farming techniques
ii. Small size of the gardens
iii. Inability to replenish soil fertility
iv. Inadequate farm labour
v Primitive farm tools
vi. The problem of pests and insects
vii Poor and irregular rainfall.

Apart from farming techniques which could be taught either formally or informally through extension workers, the rest of the problems have nothing to do with formal schooling.

Instrumental Needs of Rural Farmers

On instrumental needs of the subsistence farmers to produce enough food, the studies found functional skills and financial capital to be central needs. Bangura (1979), Watt (1973), Harker (1973) and Coombes and Ahmed (1974), among other commentators, have emphasized the importance of functional skills as vital to the improvement of farm productivity. The point to be clarified is that we are talking of basic functional skills which every farmer already possesses by virtue of living in a farming community and participating in Agriculture. Even if they did not have such skills, experience has shown that:

> Learning the basic skills of gardening and farming in the rural community is almost certainly better done in the traditional way of participating in the farming activities than in the intermittent attempts of school farming (Lewis. 1970:101).

The point is that such skills are not all that complicated and difficult to demand establishing elaborate teaching institution as we have been made to believe, hitherto. Almost every uneducated subsistence farmer I studied appreciated planting their maize 90 centimeters apart and three plants per planting station, the need to plant with first rains (in some cases even dry planting), the necessity of weeding their gardens at least twice a season, and application of appropriate fertilizers. However, most of the farmers felt terribly deficient at acquisition of agricultural inputs such as fertilizers because of lack of financial capital. As for financial capital, as an instrumental need, the studies found that most rural peasant farmers lacked a steady and reliable source. In Malawi, the majority of people living in rural areas depend on smallholder farming for their livelihood. This means that the key to the problem of cash is the sales off the farm. Bunting (1976:34) makes the same point when arguing that:

> the rural people exchange their produce for the goods and services they need for a more productive agriculture and better life and so make their sixth contribution to development as consumers—of equipment, seeds, chemicals and other farm inputs; of consumer goods and durables; of schooling, health, transport and other services—and as tax payers.

Apart from putting agriculture at the focal point of rural development, the above quotation serves to illustrate the complementality between production of surplus and improved agriculture in the rural areas. Emphasis is and has to be on the sales off the farm because, of the many alternatives for earning cash in rural areas, it is only farming that involves everyone. Other skilled occupations such as tailoring, carpentry, bricklaying, fishing, crafting, etc are reserves of the few that have the appropriate skills. It should also be mentioned that the viability of such specialist occupations depends on adequate cash flow in the rural areas. All the same, the foregoing discussion suggests that formal school is of tangential relevance to provision of functional skills and of no direct relevance to getting financial capital for purchasing farm implements and inputs.

Tools and Techniques Available to Rural Farmers

The final stage in the application of our mode of analysis is a survey of the tools and techniques available to rural subsistence farmers in order to raise their farm productivity. The term `tools' is used to include both implements and institutions that exist to help subsistence and commercial fields within the rural areas. The major purpose of this stage of analysis is to take stock of what already is available and what needs to be added, and whether formal school is the key to provision of what is missing.

(i) Farm Tools

Every rural farmer, at least in Malawi, has the basic farm tools in the form of a hand hoe, hand axe, panga and scythe. These may be primitive tools in comparison to ploughs and tractors but they continue to be the most readily available and reliable farm implements for the majority of peasant farmers. So far they have proved to be adequate for food production. In this case, we cannot complain of lack of farm tools but of improving production technology, which is a natural process.

(ii) Farmer Training

One of the tools available to peasant farmers in Malawi to enable them to improve their productivity is farmer training in the form of field extension. Under this design, farmers are organized into `Farmers Clubs' which serve as fora for discussing farmers' problems and ways of solving them. The discussions are chaired and directed by Agriculture Field Extension Workers. The other version of extension service are group radio discussions and interviews with individual farmers on better methods of farming. This shows that there are non-formal ways of imparting vital information to peasant farmers. As such, a farmer does not have to be literate in order to benefit from such assistance.

(iii) Formal Primary School:

In Malawi Agriculture is also taught in schools as both a practical and examination subject. The thinking is that those who fail to continue with academic education can settle on the land and use the knowledge and skills acquired. The other reason for including Agriculture on the school curriculum is the belief that since extension services fail to reach every household due to shortage of staff, lack of radio sets, poor communication networks which include absence of roads in some areas and poorly maintained roads where these have been constructed, and high illiteracy rate (about 60%) among adults, the peasant farmers could be reached through their school children.

This strategy has a lot of problems. One of them is that faced with shortage of time to cover syllabuses for the impending selection examinations and lack of specialist agriculture teachers, the subject has always been treated in very general and superficial manner as if the situation was the same in every rural area. The second problem is that even if the school succeeded in imparting the required basic skills and knowledge about farming, by the end of the day one discovers that peasant farmers already know the basics and that parents may not be keen to learn from their children when they already have such knowledge. The situation is even worse in societies which respect age (see Thompson, 1981:118). The third problem is that more often than not graduates of the school have failed to practice what they learn in class because of burdensome pressure of traditional customs which compel youth to follow the practice of their elders. This is further compounded by the fact that in most cases by the time the young farmers settle on land they have forgotten most of the techniques learned at school. As such the only rational behaviour seems to be "do as the rest do" after all they have managed with the same technique for a very long period of time.

(iv) Roads and Markets

Roads and produce markets constitute genuine motivational tools available to subsistence farmers in Malawi. Roads, where they are operational offer farmers a degree of certainty to transport their produce to markets, and agricultural inputs from markets to the farms. The market network is an additional incentive and assurance to the subsistence farmers to try and produce surplus for sale since farming is the dominant and surest source of cash in most rural areas of Malawi. Markets further drive farmers to produce even more if they offer good prices to the farmer. Since the announcement of new and higher prices for agriculture produce by the Minister of Agriculture and Livestock Development in April, 1995, every Malawian is talking of how profitable farming will become and how difficult life will be for poorly paid urban workers. This seems to suggest that it is not necessarily education which motivates people to produce more for sale, but attractive prices for produce that will send people exploring ways of improving their productivity.

Formal Schooling and Agricultural Productivity

The foregoing discussion suggests that rural people, at least in Malawi, have failed to produce enough for their food requirements and surplus for sale due to six basic problems. It seems that while the school may have something to offer by way of inculcating new farming techniques, disseminating knowledge about alternative ways of improving and maintaining soil fertility, and how to deal with pests and insects, the school will never ever provide cash opportunities for the rural farmers yet this seems to be the real stumbling block for the majority of rural farmers.

Watt (1973:152) argues that the school can only help in three major ways, the inculcation of knowledge about new inputs, production techniques, and economic knowledge. Msiska (1986:73) contends that while all this remains a possibility, experience has shown that the way agriculture is taught in schools today is so theoretical and examination oriented that the school may not teach even the very basic skills (see also Msiska 1994). The problems include the subject being taught by lay teachers, lack of any meaningful practical work, and the subject is being taught to fairly young people who are not involved with food production, let alone having a desire to live in rural areas (see Msiska, 1991:156-206 on the situation in Malawi). The real problem is that you cannot effectively teach practical skills in a general and academic school curriculum.

What should be accepted is that farming in Malawi like elsewhere is increasingly becoming a business. As such every primary school needs to be orientated more towards simple skills of business. This is particularly important in the developing countries where so may children receive no further formal education once they leave school (Watt 1973: 155). All the same, this is an important skill for running and managing a business which has nothing to do with farm productivity. Even if it were directly related to farm productivity, the point still remains that faced with shortage of time to cover the examination syllabus and the desire to help as many pupils as there are possible trades, the school may generalize too much.

Some people over emphasize the role of literacy and numeracy as the instrumental skills for rural development (see Msiska 1986:75). The argument is that literacy and numeracy, among other things, enable people to decode information—know what, why, where when and how; to evaluate costs and benefits of alternative sources of economically useful information; to choose optimum combination of crops, new inputs and agricultural practices with the least number of trials; and to perform agricultural operations more effectively in the economic sense, that is to produce more from a given amount of inputs. In my opinion, these are more theoretical expectations than anything else.

Hopcraft, cited in Thompson (1981:119), found that in Kenya when it comes to applied knowledge about farming practices and husbandry techniques, there is no evidence that the farmer who has received some formal education is better off than the one who has not. My own experience in Malawi in Traditional Authority Msakambewa in Dowa District confirms Hopcraft's point. Msakambewa has a population of about 37,538 and only 35% of it is literate. Paradoxically, food production is highest in the area. Due to poor road network and lack of produce markets, surplus food rots on farmers. If formal schooling were the thing, this area would be the most starved. This anecdote and Hopcraft's systematic study in Kenya suggest that application of practices and techniques are not directly related to education of a people. Rather, it seems to be the need on one hand and appropriate assistance given which matter in farm productivity. The suggestion being that perhaps we need to carefully scrutinise investment priorities if we are going to stimulate development in the rural areas. Otherwise, investing in formal schooling for some aspects of rural development is a sheer waste of precious and scarce resources.

Possible Source of Misconception of the Role of Schooling

It seems the belief about formal schooling's role in rural development is a wholesale carbon copy of the thinking which flooded literature in the 1960 and 1970's on the relationship between schooling and economic growth and rapid industrialization. It was argued that:

> A literacy rate of about 40 per cent is necessary but not sufficient for a sustained level of economic growth.... industrialization and more rapid economic expansion cannot occur until 70 to 80 per cent of any population is literate. To this extent it seems that at least for a certain level of economic and industrial development, a fairly high level of literacy is

required (Bowman and Anderson (1973) cited in Fagerlind and Saha (1983:43).

This view is obsolete today as studies, the world over, have shown that improved economic growth is possible with or without such a literacy rate. There are ways to improve economic productivity of a society without literacy. This is particularly true of the agriculture sector where output can be increased through basic innovations and simple technology. For example, fertilizers and irrigation increased the farm productivity in Sudan, Gezira Scheme; in Malawi, Hara, Wovwe, Kaporo Rice Irrigation Settlement Schemes; In Yugoslavia, the "Kombinats" which employed modern technology together with Peasant Work Cooperatives; in South-East Asia, the Green Revolution, etc. These examples call to question the assumed magic role of formal schooling.

What is true, however, is that the contribution of schooling is relative insofar as education is not the cause of productivity increase, but only one variable in a package of factors aimed at increasing production in rural areas (see Bude 1984:211). The other point is that while it is possible to argue that raising levels of literacy would directly result in increased economic development, the correlation between the two is also very complex and requires further conceptual clarity, which has proved very difficult to most of us.

What Formal School Teaches

Formal school as it operates in Malawi and other developing countries, is concerned more with inculcation of rational thinking in the pupils than equipping them with productive skills necessary for rural development. According to Thompson (1981:122):

> The strength of the school lies essentially in what is usually termed as general education, equipping young people with the tools needed to investigate and enquire, to think, conclude and understand: it is substantially weaker in its capacity to inculcate prescribed attitudes, to train in specific production skills.

In short, the major skills general education teaches are `adeptness' and `learning to learn'. These skills are at best complementary and not that instrumental in rural development.

Most of us interested in rural development have realized that the real barrier to development of rural areas are values and beliefs people hold vis-a-vis development programmes. Unless people's values and beliefs are coterminous with development projects being initiated in the area, very little success may be achieved. The implication is that schools should change rural people's values and beliefs. Unfortunately schools are very ineffective at changing peoples values, attitudes and beliefs. The main reason for this is that schools teach alien values and beliefs, they are involved with the youths who have no authority over the elders, and are future oriented which means avoiding current and pertinent issues.

Conclusion

The basic human needs approach to understanding the role of education in rural development suggests that at best the school could be an accelerator and not the cause of development. As such, the link between formal schooling and rural development is neither myth nor practical reality. It is not just myth because formal schooling makes one adept, hence, more articulate in a dynamic context, given that everything else is provided. The second point is that in so far as schooling contributes to development and improvement of communication skills, including an awareness of the modern sector economy, it can make an important contribution to modernization of agriculture. Of course, a similar contribution can be made by the mass media and a system of agriculture extension services. It is even better if the two are mutually supportive. In this partnership formal schooling is an accelerator rather than the causative agent. It is also true that general education, particularly at primary school level, is useful in raising the consciousness and the level of receptivity to innovation in agricultural techniques and the general way of living of the people.

While all this is true of formal schooling, it is also the case that practically schooling does not initiate socio-economic development of rural areas. In fact schooling has a negative influence if stressed in a situation where one or more of the `essentials' are missing. For example, while formal schooling may inculcate knowledge and skills about farming, it may not provide cash which the rural people need to put all they have learned into action. This suggests a need to balance investment in `accelerators' and `essentials'.

It is not always true that uneducated people lack initiative. They have always had initiative as far as providing for their basic needs is concerned. Examples are numerous in which illiterate people have changed their behaviour and practices through nonformal education. More and more people in rural areas of Malawi are using condoms not because they have been to school and have developed full understanding of HIV, rather it seems the death rate has convinced them that there is need to be more careful in one's sexual behaviour. Similarly, rural people need not understand development in order to develop their areas. All they need is assistance to improve their living standards, and later appreciate living a better life.

I personally feel that we have all along over expected from formal schooling. Rural areas are still backward and possibly getting worse because we have over emphasized education at the expense of developing necessary infrastructure for developing rural areas. We need to revise this blind faith we have in education's mysterious powers to develop rural areas.

References

Bangura, J.B. (1979) The Role of Education in rural Development with Specific Reference to Sierra Leone (Unpublished M. Ed Dissertation, University of Bristol). Bude, U. (1984) "Primary Schools and Rural Development: The African Experience", in Garret, R.M. (Ed) *Education and Development*: London, Croom Helm.

Bunting, A.H. (1976) "Change in Agriculture 1968-74", in Hunter, G., Bunting, A.H. and Bottrall, A. (Eds) *Policy and Practice in Rural Development*: London, Croom Helm.

Coombs, P.H. and Ahmed, M. (1974) *Attacking Rural Poverty: How Non-Formal Educan Can Help*: Baltimore, The John Hopkins University Press.

Fagerlind, I. and Saha. L.J. (1983) *Education and National Development: A Comparative Perspective*: Oxford, Pergamon Press.

Harker, B.R. (1973) "The Contribution of Schooling to Modernization: An Empirical Analysis", in Foster, P. and Sheffield, J.R. (Eds) *The World Year Book of Education 1974: Education and Rural Development*: London, Evans Brothers.

Jarvis, P. (1986) "Notions of Development and Their Implications for Adult Education", *International Review of Education*, 32 (1), pp.

85-95.

Kreinen, I. (1964) *Israel and Africa*: New York. Praeger.

Lea, A.M. and Chaudhri. D.P. (1983) "The Nature, Problems and Approaches to Rural Development", in Lea, A.M. and Chaudhri, D.P. (Eds) *Rural Development and the State*: London, Methuen.

Lewis, L.J. (1970) "The School and Rural Environment", in Commonwealth Secretariat, *Education in Rural Areas*: London, Commonwealth Secretariat.

Maslow, A.H. (1970) *Motivation and Personality*: New York, Harper and Row.

Mijindadi, N.B. (1978) "Integrated Rural Development: Concepts and Planning Implications", *Community Development Journal*, 13 (1), pp. 21-28.

Msiska, F.G.W. (1986) Education and Rural Development: Myth or Practical Reality? (Unpublished M. Ed Dissertation, University of Bristol).

Msiska, F.G.W. (1991) A Study of the School-leaver Unemployment Problem in Malawi (Unpublished Ph.D Thesis, University of Bristol).

Msiska, F.G.W. (1994) "Some Practical Limits of Curriculum Vocationalization as a Remedy to School Leavers' Unemployment: Focus on Malawi", *International Review of Education*. 40 (2), pp. 135-148.

Thompson, A.R. (1981) *Education and Development in Africa*: London, MacMillan.

Watt, E.R. (1973) "The Educational Needs of farmers in Developing Countries", in Foster, P. and Sheffield, J.R. (Eds) *The World Year Book of Education 1974: Education and Rural Development*: London, Evans Brothers.

— 16 —
Issues in Language in Education Policy with Specific Reference to Namibia, and Zimbabwe

Eleanor M. Lemmer

Introduction

Language in education policy is interwoven with a government's espoused values and perceptions of political and economic needs (Peddie, 1991:25). Thus non-language factors as well as linguistic needs underlie all language in education policy-making at a latent and manifest level (Baker, 1993:263). Understanding of language in education policy requires that it be studied not only linguistically or pedagogically but also in its relationship to power structures and political systems in society. In particular, the choice of language of instruction and its implementation in the classroom is seldom based on educational preferences alone. In the process of implementation of a national language policy, schools are central institutions. For this reason, teachers need to be aware of how language in education policy fits into the overall language policy of the state as they are not only affected by political decisions, but they, in fact, implement those decisions in the classroom. Finally, language in education policy functions as a critical filter to the social, economic and political mobility of language minorities, since literacy in the dominant language within a society is more than merely the ability to read and write; it is also the competence to think, reason and utilise skills and concepts in a variety of situations, including civil life and democratic processes (Christie, 1991:144).

The potency of language in education policy as a filter for upward mobility and democratic participation can be illustrated by the situation in many African countries. A consequence of the prestigious position given to English in national language policy in Anglophone Africa is that this policy does not always cater in practice for the social, economic and political aspirations of the majority of the population. Since well-paid jobs in the public and private sectors as well as a political career at national level, require at least a secondary school education which is dispensed in English, it is found that children of élite groupings who have access to better equipped private or international schools are advantaged, with the result that only a minority has equal access to quality education. Thus language policy comprises a barrier to upward mobility for the masses (Swilla, 1992:512).

This chapter explores issues in language in education policy and practice in the education systems of Namibia and Zimbabwe against the background of a set of assumptions about language influencing language planners, in general and in Africa, in particular. It is based on a literature study supplemented by classroom-based observation and informal interviews with educators conducted during visits to Zimbabwe and Namibia during 1994.

Assumptions About Language

Baker (1993:247) distinguishes three basic orientations about language functioning which, he maintains, are at the root of the politics of language policy: language as a problem; language as a right; and language as a resource. These orientations reveal differences and similarities and are often present in varying degrees within the same society. They consciously or unconsciously influence policy-makers and teachers and are related to a basic philosophy or ideology held by an individual (Baker, 1993:248).

Language as a Problem

Public debate about language policy often commences with the idea of *language as a problem* which causes complications and difficulties. On an individual level, this debate may take place around cognitive problems attributed to bilingualism and social problems, such as loss of cultural identity which is associated with bilingualism. On a political level, the debate may centre on national or regional disunity and inter-group conflict caused by language diversity. According to this view, language diversity is perceived as the cause of societal conflict and this should be addressed by assimilating language minorities into the majority language. Such an argument holds that the majority language (for instance, English) unifies the diversity. Moreover, the ability of citizens to communicate with ease in English is regarded as a common leveller in society; whereas the minority language is connected with social, educational and economic disadvantage. This orientation is aptly summed up by the sentiment, `If only language minorities could speak English, then their problems would be solved.' This view absolves schools from the responsibility for the underachievement of language minority groups and attributes school failure to a minority student's own deficiencies. An obvious solution to language as a problem is the increased teaching of the majority language (e.g. English) at the expense of the mother tongue of minorities (Cummins, 1994: 297). In this context minorities are defined in terms of a deficit model and frequently referred to as limited English proficiency pupils.

Language as a Right

Another orientation to language is the notion of *language as a basic human right*. In order to realise this right, language prejudice and discrimination should be eradicated in a democratic society. Language as a human right may be derived from and underpinned by personal, legal and constitutional rights, whereas personal language rights draw on the right to personal expression. The rights of minority language groups may be expressed in policy documents, such as those which enshrine the right to preserve and be educated in the mother tongue which is protected in the courts as a constitutional right or they may be protected on a grassroots level by protest groups. However, Baker (1993:250) cautions that liberal intents regarding language rights embodied in legal documents or government reports often comprise a rhetoric of language entitlement, which is not implemented in practice. This kind of situation illustrates the danger of a "great divide between the official aim and reality" in language in education policy being realised (Skutnabb-Kangas, 1981:287).

Language as a Resource

The idea of *language as a personal and national resource* can be observed in movements which aim at increasing second language learning (e.g. learning English in Southeast Asia) or foreign language proficiency (e.g. instruction in international languages in North American schools) in order to promote a nation's foreign trade or world influence. A tendency inherent in this orientation is to value the acquisition of foreign languages, while simultaneously devaluing the speakers of those languages. For instance, the popularity of learning Spanish by Anglo-Americans has not necessarily been accompanied by increased prestige enjoyed by Hispanics. Thus, a key question to be raised when this view is articulated is *which* languages do policymakers consider a resource. Favoured languages are usually those with international economic or political clout, whereas languages of devalued minorities are neglected irrespective of the presence of large numbers of mother tongue speakers in a community (Baker 1993:252). With the exception of the advocates of bilingual education in the United States, this view is seldom linked to promoting the literacy skills of language minorities in their mother tongue (Cummins, 1994:298).

Orientations to Language in Africa

The fore-mentioned assumptions or combinations thereof provide some theoretical framework against which to interpret language policy in multilingual Africa. With the exception of Namibia, the majority of African countries have continued with their former coloniser's linguistic choice of an official language, a language of administration and a medium of instruction, particularly in secondary and postsecondary education (Swilla, 1992:509). Among the colonial languages (Portuguese, Spanish, French and English), English has proved the most widespread and convenient and has consequently obtained prominent status in Africa, both official or semi-official (Schmied, 1991:25). Although liberationist African leaders owed much of their political successes to the indigenous languages which they used to mobilise the masses, they did not replace the colonial language at independence. Even prior to independence, the expectation that English could be used to fulfil vital functions in the new state triumphed over the stigma of English as a symbol of colonial oppression. These functions and their underlying orientations are briefly outlined below.

English for Modernisation

English was regarded as a key resource by British post-war advocates of modernisation in Africa as well as by African leaders themselves. It was considered important for three main reasons: as a lingua franca; as the route to technical knowledge; and as a means of contact with world thought (Great Britain, 1953:82). Although the prestigious position of English in Africa has often been surrounded by controversy, it has survived attempts by lobbies who have tried to weaken its status by advocating the indigenous languages as a ethnic *right*. For instance, the constitutions of many African countries ensure that the position of English is shared with selected indigenous languages, but the latter are, in fact, seldom elevated to official languages or media of instruction (Swilla, 1992:510). According to Schmied (1991:20), few African countries, which are absorbed by pressing day-to-day problems, have either the funds or the time to replace English or to attempt other fundamental changes in the socio-linguistic situation.

English for Nation-Building

The *language as a problem* orientation may also be detected among policy-makers in Africa in that, for reasons of national unity, many African governments chose not to use the indigenous languages with their ethnic affiliations in a national context, in case this endangered the ethnic balance within the nation. Instead they preferred to use other symbols to demonstrate their Africanness and national unity. Thus, in linguistically complex countries, such as Nigeria with more than 400 languages spoken, English is the language of inter-ethnic communication (Olajedo, 1993:95). In addition, African nations have chosen English as a matter of economic feasibility (Schmied, 1991:31).

English for International Communication

For purposes of *international communication* as well as *pan-African cooperation* realised in forums such as that of the United Nations' Organisation or the Organisation of African Unity, English has become more, not less, important since colonial times. Moreover, its role as means of communication in political, economic or technological fields is obvious. Today even countries never colonised by the British need English because of its world-wide importance as an ecumenical language (Schmied, 1991:20).

Implications for Educational Provision

As a consequence of the role English has been expected to perform in the life of independent African countries, it has proved more durable than any other components of the colonial inheritance (Schmied, 1991:19). Its spread has not only occurred through a country's constitution, government circulars and school syllabi, but minor regulations have rooted the language in the life of African countries as the following instances illustrate. In Zimbabwe, English proficiency is required and tested as a basis for acceptance into the police force and army, while in both Malawi and Botswana, English is compulsory for participation in Parliament (Schmied, 1991:23). Similarly, in Ghana, "no constituency would elect someone...to represent them in Parliament if he could neither read not write English" (Saah, 1986:373). The result has been the creation of an educated élite who can speak English and are thus more able to partake in a country's civil and economic life.

In this situation English, not the indigenous languages, is regarded as the primary linguistic resource, in spite of rhetoric about the rights of local language communities which are embodied in the constitutions of many countries. In these contexts, education is the most important sector of public life for the implementation of national language policy. Therefore, English in schools in Africa does not only reflect the national socio-linguistic situation, but it is also an important factor in shaping that situation. In particular, the impact can be seen in the choice of medium of instruction. Ideally English as a subject should be taught for several years before a gradual switch is made to it as the medium of instruction. However, if a lack of English is blamed for general educational and social problems, then upward mobility and academic achievement are straightforwardly equated with more English (Schmied, 1991:100).

Therefore, a perceived solution to a lack of English proficiency is to introduce English as medium of instruction at a very early age. Consequently, many newly independent African countries initially adopted a `straight for English' policy, that is, English was adopted as the sole medium of instruction from the first year of schooling. Later attempts to ameliorate this position can be detected in official documents which came to recognise the essential role of mother tongue in cognitive development. Yet, in spite of these later attempts to recognise indigenous languages, the early English approach is often vigorously advocated in practice. This is the case in ethnically mixed schools where the choice of medium of instruction is clearly problematic. Furthermore, it is encountered in other situations where school authorities are pressured by parents, who regard English as a means to or a prerequisite for socio-economic advancement. This is also the case in most fee-paying private schools with an élitist ethos (Schmied, 1991:100).

Where government policy does, in fact, recommend a more gradual switch to English as medium of instruction, for instance after at least four years of schooling have been completed, private schools offering the `straight for English' approach acquire an élitist and highly sought after `edge' on those other schools, who are using the official transitional approach. Fundamental problems inherent in using English as sole medium of instruction are the management of the medium switch and the maintenance of academic standards. When and how the switch from mother tongue to English should take place as well as pupils' subsequent difficulty in mastering complicated subject matter in an unfamiliar language medium has continued to be a major problem in Anglophone Africa for the past 30 years. Furthermore, teachers continually voice concern about the standard of spoken and written English among pupils as well as their deteriorating academic performance in other school subjects. The latter is frequently attributed to the pupils' lack of competence in English (Schmied, 1991 :108).

Language in Education Policy in Namibia and Zimbabwe

Against the background of the key position of English in Africa and the concomitant problems in educational provision, the ensuing section of this article examines language in education policy in Namibia and Zimbabwe. Attention is given selectively to the following aspects: language in education policy aims, medium of instruction, teaching resources, teachers and pupils' language proficiency and classroom practice.

Namibia: Reversing the Past

Namibian language policy since 1990 has been explicitly aimed at assimilating diverse ethnic groups into a common nationhood and reversing previous social and political inequalities through an English-only education policy which attempts to reverse the historical use of Afrikaans as lingua franca.

Policy Aims

Prior to independence, Afrikaans, the dominant lingua franca in pre-independent Namibia, enjoyed official status together with English, which was seldom used. Shortly after independence on 21 March 1990, English (the mother tongue of less than 5% of the population at that time) became the sole official language with the express purpose of uniting "all Namibians, irrespective of race" (Chamberlain, Diallo & John 1981:V) into one national entity. Article 19, Culture, of *The Constitution of the Republic of Namibia* protects individual language rights provided they do not impinge on "the rights of others or the national interest". Furthermore, the document, *Provisional language policy for schools*, explicated the government's position on the 18 national (indigenous) languages stating that "they should be cherished as part of our diverse Namibian heritage" (Ministry of Education and Culture, 1991:3).

Medium of Instruction

A major obstacle to nation building through the introduction of a new official language in a situation where a de facto lingua franca has existed and continues to be a language of wide use is clearly how to spread the new official language to the population in the shortest possible time, with limited funds and resources and without destroying the indigenous languages (Cluver, 1991a:44). In this regard, schools in Namibia have been expected to make a major contribution to the spread of English, which was virtually a foreign language at the time of independence (Ministry of Education and Culture, 1990:6). Since 1970, Afrikaans had been the medium of instruction in most schools, although English was introduced as a medium of instruction with extremely limited success in the regions of the Caprivi in 1980 and Ovamboland in 1981 (Cluver, 1991b: 123; 127). The new school system introduced nine months after independence made English the national medium of instruction (to be introduced after the first four years of schooling) in all schools and tertiary institutions (USAID, 1990:5). An open-ended list of 12 national (indigenous) languages was also identified as possible media of instruction in the lower primary phase of schooling (Ministry of Education and Culture, 1991:1).

Resources

Adequate provision of appropriate teacher training and teacher development is essential to the successful introduction of a new medium of instruction. However, a large section of Namibian teachers are under-qualified and lack the English proficiency necessary for effective teaching in that medium. A *Research Note* submitted to the Ministry of Education and Culture on January 31, 1994 found that 60% of the teaching corps were unlikely to be able to teach effectively in English due to lack of English proficiency (Kotze, 1994:11). Neither teachers nor pupils have sufficient exposure to interaction with native English speakers in informal, linguistically undemanding or formal, linguistically demanding circumstances, especially in rural areas outside of Windhoek. School libraries are often absent or understocked (Chamberlain, 1993:74). In addition, the switch in medium of instruction in Nambia has been accompanied by far-reaching changes in the examination system, the curriculum and instructional materials used in schools. External school-leaving examinations previously administered by the South African Joint Matriculation Board are currently being replaced by an external national examination written at the end of Grade 10 and an external examination written at the end of Grade 12, both are administered by the University of Cambridge Syndicate of Examinations. The latter examination will be taken through medium of English by all schools in the country by 1995. This change places additional strain upon the education system and the vast inputs of aid necessary to establish effectively the new medium of instruction and examination in schools are lacking (Cluver, 1991b:110).

Classroom Practice

The effectiveness of policy implementation can be tested by the efficacy of its implementation in the school classroom. While the new language in education policy is widely accepted by Namibians, the official statements of goal bear little resemblance to what is actually happening in schools (Chamberlain, 1993:72). In many classrooms a three language medium situation is found: English, Afrikaans and mother tongue (Chamberlain, 1993:75). The present writer's observation of classroom practice in selected Windhoek schools during September 1994 showed that, while English was the official medium of instruction, Afrikaans was used as the informal classroom language by pupils, who are actually mother tongue speakers of the indigenous languages. Although a well-planned use of multilingualism in the classroom is widely recognised as a teaching resource and has been recommended as a temporary measure under "transitional conditions" by the Ministry of Education and Culture's recent language policy directive

(Ministry of Education and Culture, 1993:5), it is possible that prevailing practice in Namibian schools is one where pupils are learning through English to the detriment of their understanding of the curriculum. In order to learn effectively in a non-mother tongue medium, Macdonald (1993:70-79) points out that several language-related conditions are essential. Firstly, there should be adequate linguistic development in the mother tongue. Secondly, sufficient opportunities to develop the mother tongue outside of school in linguistically demanding, formal contexts should exist. Finally, there should be appropriate academic and community support for the learning of English, that is, both effective language teaching and the exposure to informal and authentic English contexts.

In the light of this, Afrikaans-speaking learners in Namibia who have had the opportunity to acquire and maintain their mother tongue in intellectually stimulating circumstances and in addition, learn English through the English-only approach, appear to be linguistically advantaged by the new policy. In contrast, milieu-disadvantaged pupils, who are speakers of indigenous languages, are in turn disadvantaged by the present situation. This is creating a new élite: those who speak English, in contrast to those who do not speak English (Cluver, 1993:111). During the phasing in of the new language policy (1991-1995), performance outcomes in the external national examination (at the end of Grade 10) as well as the examinations of the Cambridge Syndicate written at end of grade 12 (which have already been taken by a limited number of schools during the phasing in period) have been labelled "catastrophic". Results in several school subjects, such as mathematics, have been poorer than prior to the introduction of the new language policy (Kotze, 1994:1).

Implications of Language in Education Policy

Although the choice of English as official language has obvious benefits if spread efficiently, introducing English as a means to an end, that is, the achievement of national unity, is a major problem in Namibia. Recent poor examination outcomes suggest that this ideal could be sought at the cost of at least two generations of learners who are not proficient in English (Cluver, 1993:133). Moreover, as pupils advantage during the pre-independence phase tend to know English better, the new policy could prove to be discriminatory rather than egalitarian in the short-term (Cluver, 1993:29). Furthermore, although the new language policy is enthusiastically endorsed, it has raised unrealistic expectations about English as the gateway to social, political and economic mobility (Cluver, 1993:128). This popular sentiment is captured in the remark: "To many Namibian school children, to speak English is more important than to pass a school subject" (Van der Merwe, 1994). Finally, it can be asked whether the stated goal of promoting the national languages in Namibia will be reached, while at the same time vigorously promoting English at great financial cost.

Zimbabwe: Harnessing the Colonial Legacy

The position of English in Zimbabwe is radically different from the position of English in Namibia. Zimbabwe is less diverse linguistically with Shona and Ndebele as the major languages spoken by 80% and 15% of the population respectively (McGinley, 1987:159). Native English speakers comprise about 3.5% of the population. English was introduced as the official language and selectively used as medium of instruction following occupation by the British South Africa Company in 1890. At independence in 1980, the status of English was not changed and Shona and Ndebele were elevated to national languages. English became medium of instruction for all schools except during the junior primary phase (Beveridge & Johnson, 1991 :1). A sociolinguistic description of the status and domains of English usage shows its entrenchment in Zimbabwean society. English is used exclusively in the following domains: international and intercultural communication; national and regional official activities; education; science and technology; and almost exclusively, for government and the media (Smith, 1988:144).

Policy Aims

At independence, it was envisaged that English would contribute to socio-cultural unification and the formation of national identity; the efficient handling of government, administration and education; and national development. English was regarded as a sufficiently neutral language to function as an important nation builder (McGinley, 1987:160). The reassertion of the importance of the indigenous languages by the government was enthusiastically received, but due to socio-economic advantages associated with English, its prestigious position in the various branches of government and education has remained virtually unchallenged in Zimbabwe (Smith, 1988:142).

Medium of Instruction

English is introduced in Zimbabwean schools in the very early primary grades of school and becomes medium of instruction for school subjects by the end of the fourth year of schooling. Generally, promotion to all higher grade work entails the requirement of competent English. The major examinations are compiled and taken through the medium of English. Moreover, a pass in English in the Zimbabwe Junior Certificate (ZJC) is the minimum requirement for employment in the police force, the post office and banks. The successful completion of the Cambridge O-level examination administered by the Cambridge Examinations Syndicate with a pass in English, comprises a stringent selection mechanism in order to identify those pupils who will continue to sixth form studies, the Cambridge A-level and university. The latter opportunities are thus limited to a rigorously selected minority (Allen, 1988). Observation of daily life in Zimbabwe shows that English is also used for formal conversation, written communication and especially for matters related to education. In contrast, the indigenous languages are used for informal, intimate types of communication and are taught as school subjects. Code switching in everyday communication is common (Smith, 1988:144). Yet, to many Zimbabweans, English remains a foreign language and many pupils experience major problems with English (Frencken, 1988:66). Children are not always sufficiently proficient to use English as medium at the end of the fourth year of schooling. This is due to a lack of exposure to and use of English which is limited to the classroom, particularly in the rural areas where 80% of the population lives (Smith, 1988:150). School libraries are often stocked with old books while homes lack printed materials (Frencken, 1988:62).

Resources

The Eurocentric curriculum has been slowly replaced by domestically developed and orientated materials relevant to Zimbabwean conditions. Educated British English was the standard prior to independence and was rigorously enforced in written work by the external examination, the British Cambridge Certificate. The poor examination results of a vastly expanded school population after independence suggests a "serious mismatch between the language of the students and the exam" (Allen, 1988:160). Many schools employ a number of expatriate teachers with a "klompen-, kaugum- of lederhosenacent" for whom English is also a second language (Frencken, 1988:62). Moreover, Frencken (1988:62) maintains that a lack of English proficiency among Zimbabwean teachers and pupils contributes to the dominant classroom practice of rote learning and extensive note writing.

Classroom Practice

Zimbabwean classrooms are characterised by large classes with a pupil-teacher ratio of between 45:1-50:1. The teacher plays a frontal and central role in the classroom (Frencken, 1988:69). A wide spectrum of school systems has realised, ranging from ill-equipped rural schools on communal lands to élite independent schools in the towns. Government schools can be categorised into Group A schools (former whites only schools) situated in low density residential areas and Group B schools (former African schools) situated in high density residential areas or townships (Nhundu, 1989:247). High density schools when compared to low density schools have inferior facilities, are more crowded and often operate a platoon system with its attendant difficulties (Frederikse, 1992:33). The exodus of privileged minority white and Asian pupils as well as affluent black pupils into élitist multicultural private schools is a striking feature of Zimbabwean education (Frederickse, 1992:89).

Classroom observations of selected schools in Mutari in November 1994 made by the present writer suggested that language in education policy is implemented differently in high density and low density primary schools. The former tend to phase English in during the first four years of schooling, using both a national language (Shona) and English as media of instruction; whereas low density schools use English from the first year of schooling and are reputed to provide a better standard of English teaching, which improves the pupil's life chances. This is corroborated by the following comment made by a secondary school student attending a high density school (in Frederikse, 1992:49):

> Students in low density schools speak better English than those of us learning in high-density suburbs...nowadays there isn't any value in speaking good Shona. If you're looking for a job...it will be best for you to answer the questions in good English.

Interestingly, the more privileged pupils from low density schools are identified by an English accent considered to be closer to standard English (Frederikse, 1992:75).

Implications

Managing a smooth transition to English as medium of instruction remains a problem in Zimbabwe. Ability in English partially determines students' academic success and a pass in English is necessary for an examination certificate in any of the three major external school examinations. English is commonly regarded as the language of upward mobility and promotion to higher grade work of all kinds entails the requirement of competent English. Other key features of educational restructuring since independence in Zimbabwe has been the rapid expansion of primary and increasing expansion of secondary enrolments and a rigidly selective examination system in high school (Peil, 1990, 321); the deterioration of standards in all schools and finally, the replacement of a racial élite with a class élite, in which process language plays no mean role (Frederickse, 1992: 100). African culture and languages are neglected in many low density schools where black pupils are reluctant or even forbidden to use the indigenous languages. A mystique continues to cling to `overseas' educational standards symbolised by the Cambridge Syndicate exams, albeit now locally administered, Eurocentric content and the traditions and ethos of former white schools and expensive fee-paying private schools (Frederikse, 1992:211). According to McGinley (1987:159), the prestige which clings to English suggests that not only the language is accepted but also a broader value system.

Conclusion

The use of English in Africa as the language of world-wide communication and agent of nation-building in linguistically diverse communities appears to have been solidly entrenched. In this regard, Zimbabwe, building on its colonial past, has been established as an English second language country. Namibia, however, is endeavouring to move towards English second language status through the implementation of a radically interventionist language policy. The success with which language in education policies in these countries will succeed in redressing the inequalities of the past by extending life chances to their citizens through schooling needs some qualification. School practice in both countries is often incongruent with the intended outcomes of language in education policy. Instead of extending equal opportunities, the English-only approach often advantages the affluent, particularly those living in urban areas. Furthermore, language in education policies designed to redress former racial inequality may unintentionally create new class stratifications. Moreover, the proposed equal treatment of the indigenous African languages embodied in constitutional documents often means their decline in practice in the light of their impotency to compete with the popularity of and perceived advantages associated with English. The future of the indigenous languages may require special protection for these languages as well as programmes consciously designed to promote their use, rather than mere official status together with English.

In the light of this, Oladejo (1993:101) cautions that language in education policies in Africa are generally characterised by avoidance of key issues, vagueness, arbitrariness, fluctuations and declarations without actual implementation in schools. In order to provide effective education in linguistically diverse countries in Africa, including South Africa, it is essential that the goals of language in education policies are carefully established and the means of implementation meticulously selected. This implies that new language in education policy should be critically appraised and attempts should be made to reconcile political agendas with educational realities. To realise this aim, policy-makers, teachers and parents should be informed of the difficulties inherent in and possible outcomes of new language policies.

References

Allen, K. 1988. The Testing of English as a Second Language in Zimbabwe. In Chikombah, C. Johnston, E. Schneller, A. & Schwille, J. (eds) *Education in the New Zimbabwe*. East Lansing: Africa

Studies Centre.

Baker, C. 1993. *Foundations of Bilingual Education and Bilingualism.* Clevedon: Multilingual Matters.

Beveridge, M. C. & Johnson, D. F. 1991. A New Approach to the Assessment of Academic Literacy in a Zimbabwean Teacher College. *Lanquage and Education*, 5(1): 117.

Chamberlain, R. Diallo, A. & John, E J (eds) 1981. *Towards a New Language Policy for Namibia.* Lusaka: United Nations Institute for Namibia.

Chamberlain D. 1993. The Impact of the Language Policy for Schools in Namibia. Unpublished report for the Ministry of Education and Culture, Namibia with the support of the British Overseas Development Administration.

Christie, F. 1991. *Literacy for a Changing World.* Sydney: ACER.

Cluver, A. D. de V. 1991a. A Systems Approach to Language Planning: The Case of Namibia. *Language Problems and Language Planning*, 15(1):43-61.

Cluver, A. D. de V. 1991b. Lesse uit Namibia. In Swanepoel, P. H. & Pieterse, H. G. (eds) *Perspektiewe op taalbeplanning vir SA.* Pretoria: Unisa.

Cluver, A. D. de V. 1993. Language Planning in Namibië: The Selection of an Official Language. In Herbert, R. K. (ed) *Language and Society in Africa.* Johannesburg: Witwatersrand University Press.

Cummins J. 1994. Literacy and Relations of Power. *Literacy Across Languages and Cultures.* New York: State University of New York.

Constitution of the Republic of Namibia 1990. Windhoek: Ministry of Information and Broadcasting.

Frederikse, J. 1992. *All Schools for all Children: Lessons for South Africa from Zimbabwe's Open Schools.* Oxford: Oxford University Press.

Frencken, H. 1988. *Voor de klas in Zimbabwe.* Amsterdam: VU Uitgeverij.

Great Britain 1953. African Education, a Study of Educational Policy and Practice in British Tropical Africa. London: HMSO.

Jernudd, B. H. 1993. Planning English Language Acquisition in ESL and EFL Societies: Development and Maintenance of Languages and Cultures. *Journal of Multilingual and Multicultural Development*, 14 (1&2): 135-150.

Jones, G. Martin, P. W. & Ozog, C. K. 1993. Multilingualism and Bilingual Education in Brunei Darussalam. *Journal of Multilinqual*

and Multicultural Development, 14 (1&2): 39-58.
Kotze, C. 1994. Uitslae dui op ramp vir leerlinge in Namibië. Tempo, 13-03-1994.
Macdonald, C. A. 1993. *Towards a New Primary Curriculum in South Africa*. Pretoria: HSRC.
McGinley, K. 1987. The Future of English in Zimbabwe. *World Englishes*. 6(2):159-167.
Ministry of Education and Culture, Namibia 1991. Provisional Language Policy for Schools. Unpublished report.
Ministry of Education and Culture, Namibia 1993. *The Language Policy for Schools: 1992-1996 and Beyond*. Windhoek: Ministry of Education and Culture.
Nhundu, T. 1989. The Financing and Provision of Education in Zimbabwe: Towards Greater Equality? *Educational Review*, 41 (3):243-256.
Oladejo, J. A. 1993. How Not to Embark on a Bilingual Education Policy in a Developing Nation: The Case of Nigeria. *Journal of Multilingual and Multicultural Development*. 14 (1&2): 91-102.
Paulston, C. B. 1992. *Sociolinguistic Perspectives on Bilingual Education*. Clevedon: Multilingual Matters.
Peil, M. 1990. Intergenerational Mobility through Education. *International Journal of Educational Development*, 10(4):311-325.
Peddie, R. A. 1991. Coming—Ready or Not? Language Policy Development in New Zealand. *Language Problems and Language Planning*, 15(1): 25-39.
Saah, K. 1986. Language Use and Attitudes in Ghana. *Anthropological Linguistics*, 28: 367-77.
Schmied, J. 1991. *English in Africa*. London: Longman.
Skutnabb-Kangas, T. 1981. *Bilingualism or Not? The Education of Minorities*. Clevedon: Multilingual Matters.
Smith, I. A. 1988. Some Aspects of English Language Design and the Implications for Schools in Zimbabwe. In Chikombah, C. Johnston, E. Schneller, A. & Schwille, J. (eds) *Education in the New Zimbabwe*. East Lansing: Africa Studies Centre.
Swilla, I. N. 1992. The Relation of Local ard Foreign Languages to National Needs in Africa. *Journal of Multilingual and Multicultural Development*, 13(6):505-514.
USAID 1990. *Basic Education in Namibia*. Windhoek: Ministry of Education and Culture.

Van der Merwe, S. 1994. Interview with Director, Curriculum Development, Ministry of Education and Culture, Namibia, in Windhoek, 1994-06-05.

SELECTED BIBLIOGRAPHY

Abuchar, H. Muhamed and Patrick Moluts;. 1993. Environmental Policy in Botswana: A Critique; *Africa Today*, 40, 1.

Achola, P.P.W. 1990. *Implementing Educational Politics in Zambia.* World Bank: Washington, D.C..

Adams, M.M. and Kruppenbach, S.E. 1987. "Gender and Access in the African Schools". *International Review of Education* 33: 437-454.

Adara, O.A. 1993. Environmental Education in the Formal Sector: Problems and Prospects, in Proceedings of the First National Conference on Environmental Education, *Lagos, Nigeria*, 17-19, March 1993, Lagos, Nigerian Conservation Foundation.

Ade, Ajayi, J.F. and Oloruntimehin; B.O. 1976. "West Africa in the Anti-Slave Trade Era", in Flint, J.E. (ed.) *Cambridge History of Africa*, Vol. 5. Cambridge University Press, Cambridge.

Adimbola, Beatrice, John R.W. Alluma, Daniel Babikwa and Gabriel Obbo Katundi. June 1994: *The Status of Environmental Education in Uganda, Report to the International Development Research Centre,* Nairobi, Kenya.

Agarwal, Bina, 1991. *Engendering the Enviornment Debate Lessons from the Indian Subcontinent, CASID, Distinguished Speaker Series*, No. 8. East Lansing Michigan, Center for Advanced Study of International Development.

Ajayi, J.F.A. 1969. *Christian Missions in Nigeria 1841-1891: The Making of New Elite*. Evanston: Northwestern University Press.

Allen, K. 1988. "The Testing of English as a Second Language in Zimbabwe", in Chikombah, C, Johnston, E, Schneller, A & Schwille, J (eds.) *Education in the New Zimbabwe*, East Lansing: African Studies Centre.

Anderson, D and R. Grove. 1987. *The Scramble for Eden: Past, Present and Furture in African Conservation. P.1 in Conservation in Africa: People Policies and Practice*. O. Anderson and R. Grove (ed.s) Cambridge University Press.

ANC (African National Congress). March 1994. *Reconstruction and Development Programs.*

ANC (African National Congress). January 1994. *A Policy Framework for Education and Training.*

Ardafayio-Schandorf, Elizabeth , 1993. *Women and Forest Resources Management in the Northern Region of Ghana.* Report to

Enviornmental Liaison Center International; Nairobi, Kenya.

Atkinson, D. 1992. "State and Society in Flux". *Theoira*. May: 1-28.

Ayandele, E.A. 1982. "Africa: The Challenge of Higher Education". *Daedalus*, Vol. 111, No 2.

Baker, C. 1993. *Foundations of Bilingual Education and Bilingualism*. Clevedon: Multilingual Matters.

Bakobi, Bernard L.M. 1994. *The Status of Enviornmental Education in the SADC Region.* Summary Report to the Enviornmental Education for Youth, *Creating Awareness,* SADC-ELMS Workshop, Windhoek, Namibia.

Baine, D. 1985. Training Instructional Staff for Special Education in Developing Countries. *The Association for Person's with Severe Disability, Newsletter. 11: 7-8*

Baine, D. 1991. *Handicapped Children in Developing Countries. Assessment, Curriculum and Instruction.* Edmonton, Alberta: Educational Psychology, University of Alberta.

Bangura, J.B. 1979. *The Role of Education in Rural Development with Specific Reference to Sierra Leone* (Unpublished M. Ed Dissertation, University of Bristol).

Behr, AL. 1988. *Education in South Africa, Origins, Issues and Trends*: *1652-1988*. Pretoria: Academica.

Bergmann, H. 1985. "Agriculture as a Subject in Primary School". *International Review of Education* 3: 155-174.

Bernard van Leer Foundation. 1991. *Child Development in Africa: Building on People's Strengths*. The Hague: Bernard van Leer Foundation.

Beveridge, MC & Johnson, DF 1991. "A New Approach to the Assessment of Academic Literacy in a Zimbabwean Teacher College". *Language and Education*, 5(1): 117.

Bigala, J.C.B. Seboni, N.M. and Monau, R.M. 1993. *The Learning Needs of the Botswana Children in Standards One and Two*. Gaborone: Botswana, UNICEF.

Bishop, G. 1989. *Alternative Strategies for Education*. London: Macmillan.

Bottrall, A. (eds) *Policy and Practice in Rural Development*, London, Croom Helm.

Bowles, S. 1980. *Education, Class Conflict and Uneven Development*, in: J. Simmons (ed). *Values, Identities and National Integration:*

Empirical Research In Africa. Eranston, Northwestern University Press.

Brundtland Commission. 1987. *Our Common Future*, Oxford, Oxford University Press, 1987.

Bude, U. 1984. "Primary Schools and Rural Development, The African Experience", in Garret, R.M. (ed) *Education and Development*, London, Croom Helm.

Bunting, A.H. 1976. "Change in Agriculture . 1968-74", in: Hunter G., Bunting, A.H., *Policy and Practice in Rural Development*: London, Croom Helm.

Carnoy, 1974. *Education as Cultural Imperialism*. New York, Mckay.

Cervenka, Zdenek: 1969. *The Organization of African Unity and its Charter*. London, C.Hurst.

Chikombah, C.E. 1991. "Zimbabwe", in: W. Wickremasinghe, (ed). *Handbook of World Education*. Houston TX: American Collegiate Service.

Child, G.F.T. 1984. "Managing Wildlife for People in Zimbabwe", in J.A. McNeely and K.R. Miller (eds.) *National Parks, Conservation and Development: The Role of Protected Areas Sustaining Society*. TUCN Smithsonian Institiution Press, Washington D.C.

Chimedza, Ruvimbo, 1993. *Wildlife Resources and Household Food Security, Food Security*. Report to Enviornmental Liaison Centre International, Nairobi, Kenya.

Church Missionary Society Archives, London (CMS); 1921. *The Church Missionary Review*, Vol. LXXII, pp. 299-300.

Chung, Fay. 1987. The Situation in Zimbabwe. Paper presented at the Mount Holyoke Workshop to prepare for the Conference on the Worldwide Education of Women, Nairobi.

Claassen, J.C. 1995. "The Education System of South Africa", in Dekker E & Lemmer EM (eds). *Modern Education Systems*. Durban, Butterworths.

Clarke, P.B. 1982. *West Africa and Islam: A History of Religious Development from the 18th to the20th Century*. London, Edward Arnold.

Cole, M.et al. 1971. *The Cultural Context of Learning and Thinking: An Exploration in Experimental Anthropology*. London, Methuen.

Cochrane, Susan, H. 1981. "Education and Fertility: An Expanded Examination of the Evidence", in Kelly and Elliot, *Women's*

Education in the Third World. New York, Praeger Special Studies.

Collins, Jane L. 1991. "Women and the Environment: Social Reproduction and Sustainable Development", in Rita S. Gallin and Anne Ferguson, eds, *The Women and International Development Annual,* Volume 2, Boulder, CO., Westview Press.

Coombs, P.H. 1985. *The World Crisis in Education.* New York, Oxford University Press.

Coombs, P.H. and Ahmed, M, 1974. *Attacking Rural Poverty: How Non-Formal Education Can Help*: Baltimore, The John Hopkins University Press.

Cosser, E.. ed., 1991. Education for Life: The Challenge for Schooling for All. Johannesburg, SAM: *Christian Research, Education, and Information for Democracy.*

Coulibally, Suzanne. 1993. *Women, Migration, and the Management of Natural Resources. WEDNET Final Report*, Nairobi, ELCI.

Court, D and Kinyanjui, A. 1986. "African Education: Problems in a High-growth Sector", in: R.J. Berg and J.S. Whitaker (eds.), *Strategies for African Development*, Berkeley, Ca., University of California Press.

Curriculum Framework for General and Further Education and Training. December 1995. Discussion document developed by the Consultive Forum on Curriculum, Pretoria: National Department of Education.

Dankelman, Irene and Joan Davidson. 1988. *Women and Environment in the Third World: Alliance for the Future*, London, Earthscan.

Dasilva, Christian M., 1994. *Local or Traditional Environmental Knowledge and Environmental Education in Secondary Schools: Closing the Gap with Research.* Paper Presented at Workshop on Research Issues in Environmental Education in Eastern and Southern Africa, 29 August-2 September 1994. Nairobi, Kenya.

Department of National Education. 1992. *Educational Renewal Strategy.* Pretoria: Department of National Education.

Department of National Education, 1994. *Interim Core Syllabi.* Pretoria: Department of Education.

Department of Education, 1995. *Report of the Committe to Review the Organization, Governance and Funding of Schools.* Pretoria: Department of Education.

Department of Education. 1996. *Discussion Document: National Policy on Teacher Supply, Utilization and Development.* Pretoria:

Department of Education

Djangmah, J.S. 1994. *Educational Reforms in Ghana: The Dream and Its Implications.* A Memorandum to the Education Reform Review Committee.

Dore, R. 1980. "The Future of Education", in J. Simmons (ed.). *The Education Dilemma.* Oxford, Pergamon Press.

Dorjahn, V.R. *"The Initiation and Training of Temne Poro Members," in Ottenberg,* S. (ed.) *African Religious Groups and Beliefs.* Berkeley, California: Folklore Institute:

Drucker, P. 1961. "The Educational Revolution", in A.H. Halsy et al., *Education, Economy and Society.* New York, the Free Press.

Durkheim, Emile. 1994. *The Division of Labor in Society.* New York, Free Press, (first published in French in 1925).

Ekechi, K. Felix. 1987. "The Ordeal of an Independent African Church: The Case of the Nigerian Zion Methodist Mission , 1942-1970", in the *International Journal of African Historical Studies,* Vol 20, No. 4 pp. 691-720.

Engels, F. 1969. "Defence of Progressive Imperialism in Algeria", *in Fever* , L.S. (ed.) *Marx and Engels: Basic Writings on Politics and Philosophy.* London, Fontana Collins.

Evans,-Pritchard, E.E. 1965. *Theories of Primitive Religion*: Oxford, Oxford University Press.

Fafunwa, B and Aisiku, J.U. 1982. *Education in Africa: A Comparative Survey.* London, George Allen & Unwin.

Fafunwa, A. 1974. *Babs History of Education in Nigeria.* London, George Allen and Unwin.

Fagerlind, I., and Saha, L.J. 1983. *Education and National Development: A Comparative Perspective*: Oxford, Pergamon Press.

Filho, Walter Leal. 1994. "An Agenda for Environnment. Education Research in Africa", Paper presented to the Workshop on Research Issues in Enviornmental Education in Eastern and Southern Africa, 29th August - 2 September, Nairobi, Kenya.

Fisher, H.J. 1975. "The Modernization of Islamic Education in Sierra Leone, Gambia and Liberia: Religion and Language", in Brown, G.N. and Hiskett, M. (eds.) *Conflict and Harmony in Education in Tropical Africa.* London, George, Allen and Unwin.

Fitzgerald, Maureen. 1990. "Environmental Education in Ethiopia: The Sources of Decision-Making", in Desh Bandhu, Harjit Singh A.k.

Maitra, eds. *Environmental Education and Sustainable Development*, New Delhi, Indian Environmental Society.

Fyfe, C. 1979. *A Short History of Sierra Leone*. London, Longman.

Gbademosi, T.O. 1978. *The Growth of Islam Among the Yoruba*, London, Longman.

Graham -Brown, S. 1991. *Education in the Developing World*. New York, Longman.

Griffin, K. 1991. "Foreign Aid After the Cold War". *Development and Change*, 22:645-685,

Griffin, C. 1987. *Adult Education and Social Policy*. London: Croom Helm.

Goldschmidt, D.1987. "The Role of Universities in Development", *Development and Cooperation*, No 6.

Haile, Fekerte, 1989. "Women Fuel Wood Carriers in Addis Ababa", in Eva M. Rathgeber and Bonnie Kettel, eds., *Women and National Resource Management in Africa*, Manuscript Report, Ottawa, International Development Research Center.

Hamdun, S. and King, N. 1975. *1bn Battuta in Black Africa*, London, Rex Collings.

Hannah, Lee, 1992. *African People, African Parks: An Examination of Development Initiatives as a Means of Improving Protected Area Conservation in Africa.*Washington, D.C. United States Agency for International Development (USATD)

Harbison, F.H. 1973. *Human Resources as the Wealth of Nations*, New York, Oxford University Press.

Harker, B.R. 1973. The Contribution of Schooling to Modernization, An Empirical Analysis, in Foster, P. And Sheffield, J.R. (eds.). *The World Year Book of Education 1974: Education and Rural Development*: London, Evans Brothers.

Hawes, H and Coombe, T. 1986, *Education Priorities and Aid Response in Sub-Saharan Africa*. London, Overseas Development Administration.

Hartshorne, 1992. *Crisis and Challenge: Black Education: 1910-1990.* Cape Town, South Africa, Oxford University Press.

Heath, A. 1984. *Class and Meriticracy in British Education Seven Oaks,* Kent: The Open University.

Heyneman, S.P. 1990. "Economic Crisis and the Quality of Education". *International Journal of Educational Development 10:115-129.*

Hodgkin, T. 1972. "Scholars and the Revolutionary Tradition: Vietnam and West Africa". *Oxford Review of Education,* Vol.2, No1.

Horton, R. 1967. "African Thought and Western Science". *Africa,* Vol.37, No2.

Horton, R. 1961. "Destiny and the Unconscious". *Africa,* Vol.31, No.2, 1961.

Hummel, Charles.1977. *Education Today for the World of Tomorrow,* Paris, UNESCO.

Hunt, E.K and Sherman, H.J. 1975. *Economics: An Introduction to Traditional and Radical Views.* New York, Harper & Row.

Husen, T.1979. *The School in Question.* Oxford, Oxford University Press.

Husen, T.1978. *Teacher Training and Student Achievement in Less Developed Countries.* Washington D.C.: World Bank.

James, Valentine, 1991, *Resource Management in Developing Countries.,* Wesport, Connecticut, Bergin and Garvey.

Jansen, J.1989. "Curriculum Reconstruction in Post-Colonial Africa: A Review of the Literature", *International Journal of Educational Development* 9(3): 219-231.

Jarvis, P. 1986. "Notions of Development and their Implications for Adult Education", *International Review of Education,* 32(1), pp.85-95.

Jenkins, J.R. and Jenkins, L.M. 1982. *Cross-age and Peer Tutoring.* Reston, VA: Council for Exceptional Children.

Jenkins, D. 1988. "What is the Purpose of a University, and what Light does Christian Faith Shed on this Question"? *Studies in Higher Education,* Vol.13, No.3.

Johnson, R.W. 1975. "Educational Progress and Retrogression in Guinea" (1900-1943)", in Brown, G.N. and Hiskett, M. (eds.) *Conflict and Harmony in Education in Tropical Africa.* London, George, Allen and Unwin.

Kaluba, L.H. 1986. "Education in Zambia: The Problem of Access to Schooling and the Paradox of the Private School Solution", *Comparative Education,* 22: 159-170.

Kann, U, Malepolelo, D and Nieya, P. 1989. The Missing Children Achieving Universal Basic Education in Botswana, Gaborone: University of Botswana.

Kann, U and Tshireletso, L. 1987. *Village Community Schools and Rural Development.* Report for the Botswana National Commission for UNESCO, Gaborone.

Kann, U, Malepolelo, D and Nleya, P. 1989. *The Missing Children-Achieving Universal Basic Education in Botswana.* Gaborone: University of Botswana.

Kassam, Y. 1983. "Nyerere's Philosophy and the Educational Experiment in Tanzania". *Interchange* 14(1):56-68

Kenyatta, Jomo.1965, *Facing Mount Kenya.* New York: Vintage Books.

Kettel, Bonnie, 1993, "Gender and Environments: Lessons from WEDNET." Unpublished paper, Faculty of Environmental Studies, York University.

Khaldun, Ibn.1967. *The Muqaddimah: An Introduction to History.* Translated from the Arabic by Rosenthal, F., edited and abridged by Dawood, N.J. Routledge and Kegan Paul, London.

Ki-Zerbo, J. 1974. "Historical Aspects of Education in French-speaking Africa and the Question of Development". *Development Dialogue,* No2.

Ki-Zerbo, J. 1990. *Educate or Perish: Africa's Impasse and Prospects.* UNESCO-UNICEF.

Kreinen, I. 1964, *Israel and Africa*: New York, Praeger.

Lea, A.M. and Chaudhri, D.P. 1983. "The Nature,

Problems and Approaches to Rural Development", in Lea, A.M. and Chaudhri, D.P. (eds.) *Rural Development and the State*: London, Methuen.

Leach, Melissa, 1991. "Traps and Opportunities: Some Thoughts on Approaches to Gender, Environment and Social Forestry with Emphasis on West Africa,". Paper Presented for DSA Women in Development Study Group Meeting, Univ of Sussex, England. Institute of Development Studies.

Leader-Williams, N. and S. Albon, 1988. "Allocation of Resources for Conservation." *Nature,* V336:533.

Lee, K.H, 1988. Universal Primary Education: An African Dilemma. *World Development*, Vol 16, No. 12.

Legum, C. 1985. Africa's Search for Nationhood and Stability." *Journal of Contemporary African Studies*, October:31-42

Lewis, L.J. 1970. "The School and Rural Environment", in Commonwealth Secretariat, *Education in Rural Areas,* London, Commonwealth Secretariat.

Lindblom, C.E. 1977. *Politics and Markets*, New York: Basic Books.

Lindhe, Valdy, Miles Goldstick, Stachys N. Muturi and Paul Rimmerfors, eds, 1993. *Environmental Education: Experiences and Suggestions*, Report from a Regional Workshop, Nyeri, Kenya, 4-10 October 1992, Nairobi, SIDA. Regional Soil Conservation Unit.

Little, K.1965. "The Political Functions of the Poro

Part 1", *Africa*, Vol.35.

Little, K. 1966. "The Political Functions of the Poro: Part 2", *Africa,* Vol. 36.

Lockheed, M.E. and Verspoor, A.M. 1991. *Improving Primary Education in Developing Countries*. Washington, DC.: World Bank.

Mackenzie, Fiona, 1993. "Exploring the Connections: Structural Adjustment, Gender and the Environment": *Geoforum,* 24, 1: 71-87.

Mackenzie, C.G. 1988. "Zimbabwe's Educational Miracle and the Problems it has Created", *International Review of Education* 34: 337-353.

Mackinnon, J and Kathy Mackinnon. 1986. *Review of the Protected Areas System in the Afrotropical Realm.* Gland, Switzerland: TUCN.

Mackinnon, J and Kathy Mackinnon. 1986. *Managing Protected Areas in the Tropics*. Gland, Switzerland: TUCN.

MacKinnon, J. and Kathy MacKinnon. 1986. *Review of the Protected Areas System in the Afrotropical Realm.* Gland, Switzerland: TUCN.

Magagula, M.C.M. 1987. Education for Development. Paper Presented at the Professor's World Peace Academy Conference, Johannesburg.

Majelantle et al, 1995. *The 1991 Population Census Seminar*. Central Statistics Office. Gaborone: Government Printer.

Marks, S. 1984. *The Imperial Lion*, Boulder: Westview.

Maslow, A.H. 1970. *Motivation and Personality*; New York, Harper and Row.

Matoti, S.M. 1990. *The State of Education in Transkei-1990.* Umtata, Transkei: Faculty of Education, University of Traskei.

Matsela, Z.A. 1991. *"Lesotho", in W. Wickremasinghe, ed., Handbook of World Education.* Houston TX: American Collegiate Service.

Mautle, G. Konespillai, K and Lungu E, 1993. *The Quality of Primary School Completors and it's Implications for Form 1 Organisation and Teaching.* Gaborone: Botswana Educational Research Association.

Mazrui, A.A. 1978. *Political Values and the Educated Class in Africa.* London, Heinemann.

Mazrui, A.A. 1980. *The Africa Condition: The Reith Lectures*. London,

Heinemann.

Mbere, N, 1992. *Botswana*: A Country Report on Early Childhood Care and Education Programs. The Hague: Bernard Van Leer Foundation.

McIvor, C. 1987. "Zimbabwe Tackles Education Problem". *Development and Cooperation, No 6.*

McSweeney, Gail, Brenda and Marion Freedman, 1982, "Lack of Time as an Obstacle to Women's Education: The Case of Upper Volta", in *Women's Education in the Third World: Comparative Perspectives*, by Gail P. Kelly and Carolyn Elliot, Albany: State University of New York Press.

McWillliam, H.O.A. and M.A. Kwamena-Poh, 1975. *The Development of Education in Ghana*, New York: Longman.

Meier, G. 1991. *Politics and Policy-Making in Developing Countries*. San Francisco: International Center for Economic Growth.

Mhone, G.C.Z. 1991. "The Political Economy of Malawi: An Overview," in G.C.Z. Mhone (ed.) *Malawi at the Crossroads*: *The Post Colonial Political Economy* . Harare, SAPES.

Ministry of Education and Culture, 1986. *The Educational Reforms Program Policy Guidelines on Basic Education*, Accra, Ghana.

Morris, D.M. 1979. *Measuring the Conditions of the World's Poor: The Physical Quality of Life Index*:London, Frank Cass.

Moorad, I.R. 1989. *An Evaluation of the Community Junior Secondary Schools with Particular Emphasis on Decentralization and Community Participation,* Ph.D Thesis, University of London.

Mosha, H.J. 1986. "The Role of African Universities in National Development: A Critical Analysis". *Comparative Education*, Vol. 22, No 2.

Mphahele, M.C. 1991. *"South Africa". in* W. Wickremasinghe, ed., Handbook of World Education. Houston TX: American Collegiate Service.

Msiska, F.G.W, 1986. *Education and Rural Development: Myth or Practical Reality?* Unpublished M.Ed Dissertation. University of Bristol .

Msiska, F.G.W. 1991. A Study of the School-Leaver Unemployment Problem in Malawi. Unpublished Ph.D Thesis, University of Bristol.

Msiska, F.G.W. 1994. Some Practical Limits of Curriculum Vocationalization as a Remedy to School Leavers' Unemployment: Focus on Malawi, *International Review of Education.* 40 (2) 135-

148.

Mwamwenda, T.S. and Mwamwenda B.B. 1987. "School Facilities and Pupil's Academic Achievement". *Comparative Education,* 23: 225-235.

Mwamwenda T.S. and Mwamwenda B.B. 1989. "Teacher Characteristic and Pupils' Academic Achievement in Botswana Primary Education". *International Journal of Educational Development*, 9: 31-42.

Mwamwenda, T.S. and Mwamwenda B.B. 1992. "Quest for Quality Education in Botswana". *South Africa Journal of Education*, 12(1): 45-49.

Nyati-Ramahobo, L. 1992. *The Girl-Child in Botswana: Educational Constraints and Prospects*. Gaborone: Botswana, UNICEF.

Nyerere, J. 1974. "*Education and Liberation". Development Dialogue*. (Opening address)

Nwabara, S.N. 1978. *Iboland. A Century of Contact with Britain 1860-1960*. Atlantic Highlands, NJ: Humanities Press.

O'Connor, A.M. 1991. "Poverty in Africa: A Geographical Approach", London: Belhaven Press.

Omosa, Mary. 1992. "*Women and the Management of Domestic Energy*", in Shanyisa A. Khansiani, *Groundwork: African Women As Environmental Managers*, Nairobi, ACTS, Press.

Parrinder, G. 1969. *West African Religion*. London, Epworth Press.

Parsons, Talcott. 1949. *The Structure of Social Action*. New York, Free Press.

Peil, M. 1990. " Intergenerational Mobility Through Education: Nigeria, Sierra Leone and Zimbabwe". *International Journal of Educational Development,* 10: 311-325.

Porter, A.T. 1972. "University Development in English-speaking Africa: Problems and Opportunities". *Journal of the Royal African Society*, Vol. 71, No. 282.

Psacharopoulos, G. 1985. "Curriculum Diversification in Columbia and Tanzania: An Evaluation". *Comparative Educational Review, 29*: 507-526.

Psacharopoulos, G. 1987. "To Vocationalize or not to Vocationalize? Is the Curriculum Question". *International Review of Education*. 33: 187-211.

Psacharopoulos, G. 1990. "Why Educational Policies Can Fail: An

Overview of Selected African Experiences". Washington D.C., World Bank.

Rakubutu, M. 1992. "Interactive Radio: Affordable Village Technology". *Matlhasedi* 11: 64-65.

Ram, R. 1982. "Composite Indices of Physical Quality of Life, Basic Needs Fulfillment and Income: A Principal Component Representation". *Journal of Development Economics*, No. 11: 227-48.

Rathgeber, Eva. M. 1995. "Schooling for What? Education and Career Opportunities for Women in Science, Technology and Engineering", in U.N. *Commission for Science and Technology, Gender Working Groups*, eds., *Missing Links: Gender Equity in Science and Technology for Development*, Ottawa and New York, International Development Research Centre and UNIFEM.

Republic of Botswana, *The National Development Plan 7 (1991-1997*). Ministry of Finance and Development Planning. Gaborone: Government Printer.

Rodney, W. 1972. *How Europe Underdeveloped Africa*. Dar es Salaam: Tanzania Publishing House.

SAE. 1992. "Education For All". *Southern African Economist* 5(1): 5-7.

Sapere, D.and Mills, G. 1992. "Blending Traditional and Modern Architecture: Rural School Buildings". *Matlhasedi*: 11:40-44.

Sanneh, L. 1979. *The Jahanke*. London: International African Institute.

Sargent, R.A. 1991. "Swaziland", in W.Wickremasinghe, ed., *Handbook of World Education*. Houston TX: American Collegiate Service.

Selvaratnam, V. 1988. "Limits to Vocationally-Oriented Education in the Third World", *International Journal of Educational Development* 8: 129-144.

Schultz, T.W. 1981. *Investing in People*. Berkeley Calif., University of California Press.

Sharp, R. 1980. *Knowledge, Ideology and the Politics of Schooling*. London: RKP.

Shiva, Vandana, 1988. *Staying Alive: Women Ecology and Development*, London, Zed Books.

Sicinski, A. 1985. *Educational Objectives and Cultural Values. Reflections on the Future Development of Education.* Paris, UNESCO.

Simmons, J. (ed.) 1980. *The Educational Dilemma. Policy Issues for*

Developing Countries in the 1980's. New York, Pergamon Press.

Silver, H. 1980. *Education and the Social Condition*. London: Metheum.

Spaulding, S. 1987. "Policy and Planning in Adult Education: The International Dimension", in W.M. Rivera (ed.). *Planning Adult Learning, Issues, Practices and Directions*. London: Croom Helm.

Streeten, P. 1988. "Reflections on the Role of the University and the Developing Countries", *World Development*, Vol. 16 No. 5, 639-40.

Sunny, Grace. 1992. "Women's Role in the Supply of Fuel Wood", in Shanyisa A. Khasiani, ed. *Groundwork: African Women as Environmental Managers,* Nairobi, Acts Press.

Tata, R.J; Schultz, R.R. 1988. "World Variation in Human Welfare: A New Index of Development Status", *Annals of the Association of American Geographers*, Vol. 78, No. 4: 580-93.

Thompson, A.R. 1981. *Education and Development in Africa*. London: Macmillan.

Tibawi, A.L. 1979. *Islamic Education*. London: Luzac.

Timberlake, L. 1985. *Africa in Crisis*. London : Earthscan.

Tlou, J.S. and Mautle, G. 1991. "Botswana", in W.Wickremasinghe, ed., *Handbook of World Education,* Houston TX: American Collegiate Service.

Todaro, M. 1985. *Economic Development in the Third World*. London: Longman.

Turner, V.W. 1969. *The Ritual Process*. Harmondsworth: Penguin.

Turner, B.R. 1974. *Weber and Islam*. London: Routledge and Kegan Paul

Turner, B. 1986. *Equality*. London: Tavistock

Uchendu, V., ed. 1979. *Education and Politics in Tropical Africa*. New York: Conch.

UNESCO. 1985. *Reflections on the Future Development of Education*. Paris, UNESCO.

UNESCO-UNEP, 1992. *Environmental Education Newsletter. Changing Minds-Earthwise. A selection of Articles*, 1976-1991., Connect, Paris.

UNICEF. 1981. *Within Human Reach; and World Bank, Accelerated Development in Sub-Saharan Africa: An Agenda for Action* ,Washington D.C. World Bank.

United Nations Environment Program (UNEP). 1988. *Environmental*

Education. Srategic Resources Planning in Uganda, Vol. 8, UNEP.

United Nations Research Institute for Social Development. 1972. *Contents and Measurement of Socio-Economic Development*, New York, United Nations.

Uphoff, N.T. and Ilchman, W.F. 1972. *The Political Economy of Development: Theoretical and Empirical Contributions*. Berkeley, Calif., University of California Press.

Urevbu, A.O. 1988. "Vocationalizing the Secondary School Curriculum: The African Experience". *International Review of Education* 34: 258-269.

USAID and African Development Bank. 1991. *Proceedings of the Workshop on Education and Environment*, Abidjan, Ivory Coast.

Watson, K. 1988. "Forty Years of Education and Development: From Optimism to Uncertainty". *Educational Review*, Vol. 40, No.2.

Watt, E. 1973. "The Educational Needs of Farmers in Developing Countries", in Foster, P. and Sheffield, J.R.(eds) *The World Year Book of Education 1974. Education and Rural Development*, London, Evans Brothers.

Western, D. 1982. "The Enviornment and Ecology of Pastoralists in Arid Savannas". *Development and Change* Vol:13:183.

Wilks, I. 1968. "Islamic Learning in the Western Sudan", in Goody, J. (ed.) *Literacy in Traditional Societies*. Cambridge: Cambridge University Press.

World Bank. 1988. *Educatiion in Sub-Saharan Africa: Policies for Adjustement, Revitalization and Expansion*. Washington D.C.: World Bank.

World Bank. 1988 " World Bank Report on Education in Sub-Saharan Africa". *Comparative Education Review* 33: 93-103

World Bank. 1989. *From Crisis to Sustained Growth*. Washington D.C.: World Bank.

Yesufu, M. 1973 "The Role and Priorities of the University in Development", in T.M. Yesufu. (ed.) *Creating the African University*, Ibadan, Nigeria: Oxford University Press.

NOTES ON CONTRIBUTORS

John C.B. Bigala is professor of education at the University of Swaziland.

Mark Bray is professor in the Department of Education in Developing Countries at the University of London Institute of Education.

Peter Clarke is professor at King's College, London.

Felix Ekechi is professor of history at Kent State University, Ohio, USA.

D.K. Fobih is a senior lecturer and the Acting Head of Primary Education Department at the University of Cape Coast, Ghana.

Valentine Udo James is an associate professor of Social Science and the Director of African Studies Program at Kalamazoo College, Michigan.

A.K. Koomson is a lecturer in the Department of Educational Foundations at the University of Cape Coast, Ghana.

Eleanor Lemmer is a professor in the Department of Comparative Education and Educational Management at the University of South Africa, Pretoria.

John Minnis has taught in the Department of Educational Foundations at the University of Malawi. He is currently a professor of Educational Foundations at the University Brunei Darussalam.

Fazlur R. Moorad is a professor and head of Educational Foundations at the University of Botswana.

Fred G. W. Msiska is a senior lecturer and head of Educational Foundations at the University of Malawi.

Jonathan Nwomonoh is professor of Pan African Studies at California State University, Los Angeles.

Eva M. Rathgeber is Director of the International Development Center's Regional Office for Eastern and Southern Africa in Nairobi, Kenya.

Apollo Rwomire is a professor of Social Work at the University of Botswana.

David Stephens is professor in the Department of Education in Developing Countries at the University of London Institute of Education.

INDEX